Limited Classical Reprint Library

THE BOOK

OF

ECCLESIASTES

E X P L A I N E D.

BY

JAMES M. MACDONALD, D.D.,

PRINCETON, NEW JERSEY.

Foreword by
Dr. Cyril J. Barber

It is not the Expectation of living that makes Men infer the Reasonableness or Necessity of a Judgment, but the reasonableness and natural Expectation of Judgment which makes them infer the Necessity and Reality of a future Life.— SHERLOCK'S SERMONS, vol. i., p. 195.

Klock & Klock Christian Publishers, Inc.
2527 Girard Avenue North
Minneapolis, Minnesota 55411

Originally published by
M. W. Dodd
New York, 1856

ISBN: 0-86524-091-4

Printed by Klock & Klock in the U.S.A.
1982 Reprint

FOREWORD

When Charles Haddon Spurgeon drew up his list of recommended books for preachers and Bible students enumerating the best works extant at the time, he said concerning the exposition of Ecclesiastes by the famous Princeton pastor, Dr. James M. MacDonald (1812-1876),

Thoroughly exegetical, with excellent "scopes of argument" following each division; to be purchased if found.

Apparently James MacDonald's commentary was as much a rarity then as it is now, for having checked the most recent expositions of Koheleth's thought to be produced during the past two decades, I have failed to find a single reference to it. Spurgeon's words, therefore, still are true. This volume should be "purchased if it can be met with."

Following more than one hundred pages of introduction, Dr. MacDonald begins his exposition. The content of each expository study gives evidence of his careful exegesis. He succeeded, as far as is humanly possible, in presenting "the precise meaning of the inspired writer, rather than to have engrafted on his words the thoughts and speculations of [his] own mind" (p. vi).

Because thorough treatments of this portion of Solomonic literature are conspicuous by their absence, this work stands out as an authoritative statement of the important teaching of this book. Preachers, therefore, will welcome it for its reliability and timely insights, and lay Bible students will welcome it as a work that will introduce them to the practical truths which lie imbedded in this portion of God's Word.

Cyril J. Barber, D. Lit.
Author, *The Minister's Library*

PREFACE.

Of commentaries there are several distinct kinds. Some are designed to be mainly practical and devotional. To this class belong the excellent works of Henry and Scott, and the family Commentaries in general; for while they undertake to give the meaning of the inspired writers, and, in many instances, have done it admirably, they not unfrequently present lessons which can not always be legitimately derived from the text, but are only naturally suggested by certain phrases of our incomparable common version, which, in process of time, have come to be appropriated to express pious emotion, or to illustrate Christian experience.

Again, some commentaries are almost strictly philological and grammatical. Their authors attend principally to the derivation, sense, and construction of the original words, and thus seek to ascertain the exact meaning of the sacred writers. As they are avowedly commenting on the original, and only incidentally on translations, and for the benefit of those acquainted with, or who are studying the tongues in which the Scriptures were originally written, they do not scruple to introduce the Hebrew and Greek into their pages as freely as the vernacular words. The value of commentaries of this class, prepared by competent scholars, can not of course be easily overstated.

Then, there is another class in which the writers are equally critical, and attentive to the exact meaning, which may be described as exegetical, without being philological and grammatical; i. e., they state the results of criticism on the Hebrew, or the Greek, without giving the process by which it has been reached. By leaving it to scholars to recur to authorities, and refer to the original for themselves, they make their works useful to those who are not capable of appreciating criticisms upon the etymology of words, and the construction of sentences in these languages. This method has, perhaps, another advantage, to wit, that of a more distinct and enlarged statement of the practical teachings, and devotional bearings of the Scriptures.

To this latter class, the work which is herewith offered to the

public professes to belong. It claims to present the precise meaning of the inspired writer, rather than to have engrafted on his
words the thoughts and speculations of the author's own mind.
The author is well aware that he may have failed to accomplish
what he proposed, but it has been his aim throughout to interpret
rigidly the words, given by inspiration of the Spirit of God, in
this part of Scripture. It was not his object, even had he been
competent to the undertaking, (which he is very far from being), to
prepare a grammatical praxis for students in Hebrew. This has
been so ably and fully done by such scholars as Vander Palm, Desvœux, Rosenmüller, Gesenius, Hitzig, Herzfeld, Knobel, Burger,
Holden, and our own Professors Stuart and Noyes, that a work on
Ecclesiastes in which criticism of the original is made a prominent
feature must necessarily, to no small extent, be but a reproduction
of the labours of one or another of these critics. The author has
preferred, instead of such a reproduction, to avail himself of all
the critical helps that were accessible to him in the preparation of
this work ; but indebted as he is, he is not willing to make any
one who has preceded him responsible for the particular scheme
of interpretation presented in this volume. So far as he knows,
it has never before been set forth ; whatever, therefore, may be
its defects, he alone is responsible for them. If it shall serve to
render a difficult portion of the Scriptures more edifying, by
making its interpretation more consistent and plain, he will feel
that he is richly rewarded. Certainly, if he has succeeded in
showing that the doctrine of future retribution lies at the basis of
this book, it must in future be ranked among the most practical
and profitable portions of the word of God.

A peculiarity (perhaps it will be regarded as a novelty in a
work of this description), will be observed in the First Part, *viz.*,
the Scopes of Argument, as they are styled, which follow the
respective divisions in this Part. The writer of Ecclesiastes dis-
cusses, or philosophizes after the ancient, oriental manner, *i. e.*,
although the discussion is consecutive—logically consecutive—he
gives us no formal statement of his proposition, no signs of divisions and transitions from one topic, or from one thought to
another. It is, therefore, the object of these portions of the volume to present the subject in a form more natural to us, or more
in consonance with the habits of the modern mind trained under

rules—of dialectics and rhetoric—which were unknown among the ancient Hebrews. Although the author felt that this feature might lay his work open to the charge of being repetitious, and interfere, in appearance at least, with its professedly critical character, he was convinced that it would render it useful to a larger class of readers; and this decided the point with him not to exclude these portions of the book.

A new or revised version is printed in parallel columns with the authorized version; but the attentive reader will observe that there are very few instances in which any essential change in the translation is proposed. The changes are mainly confined to such as greater simplicity, or the idiom and laws of the English language, seemed to require. The author has risen from his work with the conviction that it would be impossible for a synod or assembly of the most learned biblical scholars of our day, to make a translation, which, as a whole, would be likely to prove as acceptable to the religious, or even learned world, as that contained in our authorized English Bibles.

It is important not to overlook the principle that to exhaust an inspired writer's own meaning, *i. e.*, the meaning of his language to himself, is not always or necessarily to reach the full meaning of the Spirit of inspiration. We are not to suppose that the writers of the different books of the Bible in all cases comprehended the full import of the language they were inspired by the Holy Spirit to employ. We are not to suppose that Daniel and John could fully and infallibly, except as they were specially inspired for this very purpose, have interpreted their own visions; nor are we to suppose that inspiration, in the case of the sacred writers in general, was the same as the gift of interpretation, or implied the possession of this latter gift. As the latter may be possessed without the former, why may not the former be possessed without the latter? Why might not an intelligent, sincere, yet wholly uninspired believer, have been as capable of understanding the Epistles of Paul, as Peter was of understanding them? He confessedly found in them "some things hard to be understood," 2 Peter, iii. 16. It follows, then, that in his case the gift of inspiration did not involve the possession of the gift of interpretation, so far as the writings of another inspired man were concerned; how then could it have insured a full comprehension of the meaning of the Spirit of inspiration, even in respect to his own writings? The books of Moses to us contain a clearer revelation than they did to David and Solomon (and may we not add to Moses himself?) for we can study their meaning in the light of a completed revelation; and in like manner the writings of David and Solomon are clearer to us than they were to Jeremiah and Isaiah, for the same reason. The doctrines of the New Testament do not supersede, but they complete, they perfect the revelations contained in the Old, and thus make them more plain. The doctrine of Christ illuminates all the shadows, types and ceremonies of the old dispensation. When he appeared he so brought life and immortality to the knowledge of men that the light was reflected back on the past, and they saw how the same blessed doctrines which fell from his lips had been taught by holy men, who spake as they were moved by the Holy Ghost. The question, then, as to what the Jewish Scriptures reveal might be answered somewhat differently, when considered as having reference to those who possess the New Testament, instead of the ancient Jews. It might be truly said that the books of Moses, and especially the book of Ecclesiastes, and the writings of the Prophets, however they may have been understood prior to the advent of Christ, clearly reveal the immortality of the soul, and a future state of retribution, to us who possess the New Testament, and acknowledge its authority. We must look at the books of the Old Testament, in the light of the Gospel. We may talk of ignoring the Gospel for the purpose of better perceiving how the Old Testament may then be understood; but this, in an important sense is impossible—as impossible as it is for a man who has once had any mystery explained to him still to regard it as it must be regarded by one to whom it remains unexplained.

While, then, in view of these considerations, the book of Ecclesiastes to us necessarily involves in its teachings the doctrine of a future life, I invite attention to the proof presented in the following pages that it was well known to the inspired author of Ecclesiastes, was propounded by him in this book, and was therefore revealed to the ancient Hebrews.

PRINCETON, May 1, 1856.

CONTENTS.

CONTENTS.

INTRODUCTION.

I. The Revelation of a Future State in the Scriptures of the Old Testament.

"There are not a few," says Archbishop Whately, in a late publication,* " who maintain, or take for granted, that the doctrine of a future life was revealed to the Jews, and was discovered by the ancient heathens; and, consequently, (for there is no avoiding that *consequence*,) that Jesus Christ did not "bring life and immortality to light," but merely gave men an additional assurance of a truth which they already knew." He then goes on with an attempt to show that while God may possibly have enlightened Moses, and other illustrious patriarchs, more fully in respect to a future state, than the great body of the people, the doctrine of a future state was not revealed by Moses; and that there are only a few faint glimpses of it in the writings of the later prophets. He further maintains, that the heathen philosophers, who taught the doctrine of the soul's immortality had not the least confidence in the truth of it themselves, but, on the ground of mere expediency, inculcated its belief on the vulgar—that is, for the sake of its restraining influence over their conduct. His chief argument in support of his opinion is, that to hold that a future life is revealed in the Scriptures of the Old Testament, or that there

* A View, etc., Concerning a Future State, Sect. I.

is any light from nature in support of this doctrine, is inconsistent with the declaration of the Apostle, that Jesus Christ
" brought life and immortality to light through the Gospel."
[2 Tim. i. 10.]

In this he follows substantially Dean Warburton, who, in a
laboured and celebrated work,* attempts to show that the Mosaic religion, in place of the restraining influence of the doctrine of a future state of rewards and punishments, represents
the theocratic people as living under an equal providence, peculiar to them as a people ; a providence which secured the
immediate reward of every observer of the law, and the punishment of every transgressor, in this life. Warburton, no
doubt, took the hint from Grotius, who says,—" Moses, in the
institution of the Jewish religion, if we consider the purport
of the law, promised nothing beyond the good things of this
life, a fruitful earth, victory over enemies, a long and prosperous life, with a good hope of an enduring posterity. For, if
there is any thing beyond, it is concealed under shadows, or
can only be made out by a skillful and difficult ratiocination."
It is Warburton's chief object to prove that the law of Moses
is of divine origin, because it maintained order and government, without inculcating the doctrine of a future state of rewards and punishments, a belief in which, among all other nations, has been found necessary to the well being of civil
society. It implied a special divine interposition, in the case
of the Jews, because that law depended for its sanctions on an
equal providence in this life, which could be secured only by
God himself. Of course it became necessary for him to prove,
if possible, that there is no trace of the doctrine of a future
life in the writings of Moses. It is not his object to show that
Moses disbelieved this doctrine, but that he omitted it with
design. Still, however, he expressly admits that the law had
a " *spiritual* meaning," and that " the mystery of the Gospel
was occasionally revealed by God to his chosen servants, the

* The Divine Legation of Moses.

leaders and fathers of the Jewish nation ; and the dawning of it was gradually opened by the prophets to the people."* He attempts to prove that the writers of the New Testament teach that the doctrine of a future state of reward and punishment did not make part of the Mosaic dispensation, and quotes the very text upon which Archbishop Whately relies,—2 Tim. i. 10,—" Jesus Christ hath abolished death, and hath brought life and immortality to light," from which he argues, that those under the law had no knowledge of life and immortality. If life and immortality were brought to light through the Gospel, " till the preaching of the Gospel," he says, " it was kept hid and out of sight. But if taught by Moses and the prophets, it was not brought to light through the Gospel ; and, therefore, the generality of those under the law had no knowledge of a future state."†

But the argument of Warburton is without strength, in one of its chief premises, viz., that the Jews were placed under an equal providence—while all other people were left under a common, or unequal providence—so that the reward of the righteous, and the punishment of the wicked were secured in this life. The proof of this is entirely wanting ; nay, there is proof to the contrary : it was the present inequality of divine providence, that is, the sufferings to which the righteous are often subjected and the signal prosperity of wicked men, of which Job complained ; and which, for a time, until they took into account a future state of recompense, staggered the faith of such men as David and Solomon. In framing an argument against skeptics for the divine mission of the lawgiver of Israel, instead of admitting their premises, that Moses had entirely ignored a future existence, it would have been better to have shown, if he could really find no direct proof of the immortality of the soul in the Pentateuch, that the Hebrews were men, having essentially the same nature as other men ; having consciences which pointed to some higher tribunal

* Div. Leg., B. v., § 5 ; B. vi., § 4.   † Div. Leg., B. v., § 6.

than can be found on earth, a soul yearning for existence beyond the grave; that they had even more direct access to the sources of primeval tradition than any of the heathen, who are presumed to have obtained their belief of immortality to some extent, at least, from tradition; nay, he might better have contended that the alleged reticence of Moses on this subject was owing to the strong and ever-present conviction of the people, over whom he was set as a lawgiver, not only that there was a world of spiritual beings separated from this, as it were, only by a thin veil, but that their own souls would survive their bodies, and enter into that world at death; just as many discourses, and extended works, in our day, proceed on the assumed knowledge and admission, on the part of readers, of a future state, without its being proved, or so much as mentioned. This certainly would have been better than to say, as Warburton was compelled to do, that "Moses both knew and believed the immortality of Enoch, and purposely obscured the fact, from whence it might have been collected," and that his allusions to the subject of a future state are to be distinguished from those of the Old Testament writers subsequent to the time of David, in that he, merely as a faithful historian, records facts from which the future separate existence of the soul might be inferred, but which inference he purposely designed to conceal; while the others "concluded for this existence of the soul from its very nature."*

The German neologists have, as might be expected, failed to discover any trace of a knowledge of future existence among the ancient Hebrews. All the passages which appear to teach the doctrine of a future state of rewards and punishments, are either adroitly explained away by them, or are pronounced surreptitious, and referred for their origin to a later period.

Having endeavored to bestow a patient and careful examination on this question, and to give full weight to all the

* Div. Leg., B. v., § 5; B. vi., § 1.

arguments and reasonings of those who contend that the writings of Moses do not reveal a future state, and that such a state is only revealed, in the most indistinct manner, in any portion of the Hebrew Scriptures, I would solicit attention to the following attempt to show that while the doctrine of a future state is not brought to light as it is in the Gospel of Christ, yet it is clearly and distinctly revealed in the writings of Moses and the prophets.

1. The argument employed by Bishop Whately, and which had been employed by Dean Warburton before him, meets us at the outset; viz., that if Christ brought life and immortality to light, then, it is contradictory to say that immortality is revealed in the Old Testament. The soundness of this argument depends, of course, upon the correctness of the interpretation of 2 Tim. i. 10, from which it is avowedly drawn. If the interpretation fails, of course, the argument which has been based upon it, falls to the ground. The *appearing* of Christ, here spoken of, evidently denotes his first appearance in the flesh—his incarnation—whereby he was made visible to men, and became subject to death. *Who hath abolished death; i. e.,* put it away, brought it to nought, does not mean, as we can all testify, that Christ banished death from the world, in the sense that men are no longer subject to it. The ravages of death, so far as we can see, have in no way been mitigated since the death of Christ. Even his most devoted and useful disciples are no more favoured than the rest of mankind. The word, therefore, is not to be taken in its absolute sense. He has abolished death by depriving it of its final power in respect to all who believe on him; and at length he will abolish it altogether; but until then, so complete was his victory when he arose from the dead, that to all whom he assures of a final rescue from it, the power of death is, in an important sense, as if it did not exist at all. And no more is the expression, *brought life and immortality to light* to be taken in its strictly absolute sense, as meaning the

revelation or discovery of that which was perfectly unknown before; but it also must be understood in a comparative sense. The doctrine of immortal life was made so much clearer by our Saviour Jesus Christ, that he may be said to have brought it to light; he brought it out of comparative darkness into clear light. He illustrated, *illuminated* it. This is very different from saying that the doctrine of immortality is not found at all in the Old Testament, or that it was not known at all, before the appearing of Christ. But we should do great injustice to the Apostle's language, if we supposed that it means no more than simply to declare that the doctrine of the soul's immortality was made more clear by Christ. It was immortal life which the Redeemer brought to light; that is, he made more clear the way in which an immortal soul might become partaker of salvation. To limit the passage to the immortality of the soul, is, therefore, greatly to impoverish its intent and meaning. Christ came in the flesh, and died, and revived, not merely to confirm the doctrine of the soul's immortality, but to atone for sin, to open a way whereby immortal souls might be delivered from eternal death, to teach the world pure doctrine, and to send his Spirit, to lead his disciples into all truth, and to convince the world of sin, of righteousness, and of judgment. This being the full meaning of the passage, to take the expression *brought to light*, as Warburton and Whately do, in its most unqualified absolute sense, would require us to regard the passage as teaching that there is no revelation whatever, or only that which is faint and uncertain, respecting the way of salvation in the Old Testament, *i. e.*, that the Old Testament can hardly claim to be in any sense regarded as a revelation.

2. Before proceeding to show, by a direct examination of distinct passages, the clear manner in which a future state is revealed in the Scriptures of the Old Testament, it is important first to show that the light which we have from the Scriptures, in relation to this doctrine, is not exclusive of some

light even from nature or reason. It will not be necessary to appeal to Socrates, nor to examine the writings of Plato and Cicero, to ascertain by what arguments they endeavoured to establish themselves in the belief of the immortality of the soul. We might only discover that many of their reasonings were vague and fanciful, their sentiments inconsistent with one another, and their conclusions uncertain. Nay, we think that without the least loss to the argument upon this point, we might freely admit what Warburton takes so much pains to prove, that the ancient philosophers did not themselves believe the doctrine of a future state of rewards and punishments, which they inculcated on the people, for the sake merely of its conservative influence; and that on account of their philosophical speculations and metaphysical principles respecting the nature of God, and of the human soul, it was impossible for them to believe this doctrine.* For the natural evidence in favor of this doctrine, is not that which philosophers alone are capable of discovering, but which is addressed to the common sense and apprehension of mankind. One of the greatest of ancient philosophers† has told us, *Omnium consensus naturæ vox est :* the consent of all is nature's voice. The common belief of the world as·to the continued existence of the soul, after the death of the body, is of unspeakably greater importance, in proof of its existence, than the speculations of a few philosophers, however ingenious or renowned. These very philosophers, in their writings upon this subject, appeal to this common belief, in proof of the immortality of the soul, thus proving that men in general were not indebted to them for this notion, and that it did not arise from abstract reasoning. Nor were mankind indebted to the poets for the idea of immortality ; rather were the poets indebted to this natural notion ; they built upon it ; it was the foundation which supported the fictions and inventions, which, at length, became incorporated in the religious belief of the common

* Div. Leg., B. iii., § 2 and 4. † Cicero.

people. The most barbarous nations which have yet been discovered, with hardly an exception, all appear to have a firm persuasion of the immortality of the soul. Now it is in this widely diffused, if not universal persuasion of the human race, rather than in the speculations of philosophy, that we are to look for the natural evidence in favor of the immortality of the soul.

Whence does this common consent of all men, in respect to the existence of the soul, arise? whence but from something which is common to them all? You may call it an intuitive sentiment, a primitive judgment, an instinct of nature; Cicero calls it (*quoddam augurium*) a certain kind of presage of a future state, which sticks (*inhæret*) in the mind. Mankind shrink from the idea of annihilation; they yearn for continued existence. God has thus planted in the human mind the idea of immortality. We are conscious of our personal being now, and our moral nature points to the continuance of our conscious personality hereafter; the mind is so constituted that belief in such continuance becomes a sort of intellectual necessity. "This belief and persuasion of the certainty of a future life," remarks Bishop Sherlock, "arose from the common sense that men have of the difference of good and evil, and of every man's being accountable for the things done in this world, as the least degree of observation will enable men to see—they concluded, or rather they felt, from the very force of reason and conscience, that there was an account to be given hereafter. *Such an internal argument as this, which springs up in the heart, and from the heart of every man,* has a greater weight in it, than all the reasonings of philosophy put together, and will tie men down, if not to hope for, yet at least to fear, a future immortality; either of which is the silent voice of nature, testifying the reality of a life to come."* "It is not the expectation of living," he adds, "that makes men infer the reasonableness or necessity of a judgment; but it is

* Sherlock's Sermons, Discourse vi.

the reasonable and natural expectation of judgment which makes them infer the necessity and reality of a future life."

When philosophers began to reason and speculate upon the subject, they only darkened counsel by words without knowledge. The main difficulty with which they had to contend, as Cicero informs us, was, that they could not conceive of a disembodied spirit. The idea of the common people was that they should live, and be just the same flesh and blood in the world to come which they now are. But reason, as the philosophers plainly saw, did not support such a hope; and they could not understand how the existence of the same individuals could be continued after their bodies had perished in the grave. They needed the Gospel to bring immortality to light by revealing and demonstrating the resurrection of the body in the person of Christ. Their speculations turned upon the exclusion of the body as being any part of the man, and upon the nature of the soul; they sought to distinguish between the man—that is, his body and sensitive soul, and the pure intellectual mind; to the latter alone they attributed immortality. All who could not follow, or could not be satisfied with these distinctions and refined, subtle reasonings, could not satisfy themselves from mere abstract reasonings, that the soul of man exists after the death of his body. All that philosophy did, was to obscure this great doctrine, and beget unbelief. And this was all it could do. Some analogy exists between the light which mere philosophy sought to shed on the being and character of God, and the light which it sought to shed on the immortality of the soul. How came it to pass that the God of natural theology, and of a boasted philosophy was no better than the dumb idol which the blind multitude worshipped. To solve this problem, it is not necessary to deny that there is any clear light of nature, which, of itself, without the Bible, is sufficient to prove there is a God. The Apostle has given us a true answer;* an an-

* Rom. i.

2

swer which points to the ruined and depraved state of the human faculties. The reason why the heathen do not know the true God, who is manifest in them, and the invisible things of whom are seen in the things that are made, is because they hold the truth in unrighteousness. The truth is bound or stifled by their depravity; or they substitute their own vain imaginations and false reasonings for the truth. Precisely so, in respect to the immortality of the soul; the natural evidence of this truth, that which springs up in the heart itself, which arises from a reasonable expectation of a state of retribution to succeed the present, has been obscured, and the minds of men puzzled and confounded by the vain imaginations and false reasonings of philosophers. Some of them even reasoned themselves into the denial of the Divine existence; as the Epicureans among the Greeks, and the Sadducees among the Jews, reasoned themselves into the denial of the soul's immortality. But they could not erase from the soul of man—not even from their own—the signature impressed upon it by its Maker, the pre-assurance of a future existence. It remained among the common people, both of Greece and Rome, clear and distinct. It has been found among the most barbarous tribes of men yet discovered on the earth. The ancient Hebrews were men—sharers in the principles of our common nature; and how can it be supposed, even if they had had no inspired teachers to instruct them, that they were inferior in respect to their knowledge of a future state of existence to the Egyptians, the Greeks, the Romans, or the savage aborigines of this continent.

3. It is directly asserted in the New Testament, that not merely does the Old Testament in general, but the writings of Moses, in particular, afford proof of a future life. We have the words of Christ himself in his argument against the Sadducees: "Now that the dead are raised, even Moses showed at the bush, when he calleth the Lord the God of Abraham, and the God of Isaac, and the God of Jacob. For he is not a God of

the dead, but of the living; for all live unto him." Luke xx. 37, 38. "But as touching the resurrection of the dead, have ye not read that which was spoken unto you by God, saying, I am the God of Abraham, and the God of Isaac, and the God of Jacob? God is not the God of the dead, but of the living." Matt. xxii. 31, 32. These patriarchs had been long dead when these words were spoken. God says, "I am," not "I was" the God of Abraham, etc.; and as he is not the God of the dead, but of the living, the words imply that they were in an important sense still alive. Their bodies were lifeless in the grave; our Lord must therefore have meant to teach that God's address to Moses, Ex. iii. 16, proved the separate existence of the soul in another state. The Sadducees denied the resurrection of the body, and the separate existence of the soul, and maintained that the soul perished with the body. Our Lord charges them with ignorance of the Scriptures, and of the law of Moses particularly, which they admitted was good authority, and which directly asserts that the soul does not die with the body, but exists in another state.

In Christ's parable of the rich man and Lazarus, he also clearly taught that the doctrine of a future state was revealed not only in the writings of the prophets, but in the books of Moses. When Dives sees Abraham afar off, and Lazarus in his bosom, and desires him to send Lazarus to his father's house, that he may testify to his brethren, lest they too should come into that place of torment, he is told, "If they hear not Moses and the prophets, neither will they be persuaded though one rose from the dead." Luke xvi. 31. The rich man is described as living in an entirely thoughtless manner, in the gratification of his sensual appetites, in the possession of every luxury, and altogether heedless of a state of rewards and punishments; after he was dead, he wished his brethren, who were probably spending their lives as he had spent his, to be warned of their danger, by being assured of the reality of a place of torment for all who thus spend life, and die impenitent. He was told that they had Moses and the prophets to give them all needed information and warning respecting a future state; and that the return of Lazarus from that state would fail to convince those who were not convinced by what is contained in the writings of Moses and the prophets.

"Your father Abraham," said Christ to the unbelieving Jews, "rejoiced (earnestly desired) to see my day, and he saw it and was glad." John viii. 5, 6. A remarkable promise had been given to him (Gen. xii. 3), that in him all the families of the earth should be blessed. The promise was made " to Abraham and his seed," " which is Christ." (Gal. iii. 16.) He wished to have the purport of the promise which had been made to him more clearly revealed. His ardent longings were gratified. In the command to offer up his son Isaac, and the events consequent thereupon, God graciously granted a clear revelation of the great sacrifice of Christ, for the redemption of mankind. He saw the day of Christ, by seeing a type of the Victim, which, in due time, should be offered for the sins of the world, to give to all possessed of the righteousness of faith, eternal life. That life and immortality which Jesus Christ brought clearly to light, were shadowed forth to him; and the history of the transaction, recorded by Moses, became a direct prophecy of the advent of the Redeemer, and the great purpose of his advent to the world.

But in the Epistles of Paul, as well as in the discourses of Christ, it is every where implied, and in many places directly asserted, that the doctrine of a future state of rewards and punishments was perfectly well known to the Jewish patriarchs and prophets. His argument, in the Epistles to the Romans and the Galatians, proceeds on the principle that under the first covenant, the covenant of works, mankind had eternal life offered to them upon condition of perfect and perpetual obedience to the law of God; but having broken the law, and forfeited the blessings of that covenant, the only way in which men, whether Jews or Gentiles, can now be made partakers of eternal life, is by faith in Jesus Christ. He shows that Abraham, and all that were saved before the advent of Christ, were saved by the righteousness of faith; and that, for this end, the Gospel was preached before unto Abraham (Gal. iii. 6, 8); that the covenant of works having failed, the covenant of grace was revealed to all who were " blessed with faithful Abraham;" and that eternal life was revealed as the promise or blessing of both covenants. "Moses describeth the righteousness which is of the law; that the man which doeth those things shall live by them. But the righteousness which is of faith speaketh on this wise, That if thou shalt confess with thy mouth the Lord Jesus, and shalt believe in thy heart that God raised him from the dead, thou shalt be saved." Rom. x. 5–9. The Apostle contrasts the two methods of justification, or ways of obtaining eternal life. The former had utterly failed, for " cursed is every one that continueth not in all things written in the book of the law to do them." " And the law is not of faith; but the man that doeth them shall live in them. Christ hath redeemed us from the curse of the law, being made a curse for us." Gal. iii. 10–13. As there is no man who does all that the law of God, by which he is to be tried, demands, he can not be made a partaker of eternal life on the ground of such obedience, but only by faith in Him who was made a curse for us, to redeem us from the curse of the law. The great promise of the first covenant was ETERNAL LIFE, as it is of the second. It is not indeed explicitly mentioned by Moses, in the second chapter of Genesis, where he gives an account of the law under which our first parents were placed in Paradise; but it may be inferred from the threatening of death, which it would be absurd to suppose was only temporal death. From the death which was denounced against disobedience, man had reason to hope for eternal life as the reward of obedience. Unless eternal life was included in that " Gospel" which was preached unto Abraham, and Moses, and all the patriarchs, how could the

Apostle with propriety designate it as a gospel at all? What a perfect enigma the whole religious economy of the Jews becomes, when we ignore the doctrine of a future life as a part of it! But all is made clear by the Apostle, in his Epistle to the Hebrews, where he shows that the very ceremonies of the law were figurative, and the law itself "a shadow of good things to come." (x. 11.) The whole economy of their worship and temple, of their Sabbaths, and their coming into possession of the land of Canaan, pointed out to a heavenly temple, a heavenly inheritance and rest.

But in the eleventh chapter of Hebrews, it is again and again asserted that the ancient Hebrews believed in the continued existence of the soul, after death. By faith Abraham is said to have "looked for (forward to) a city which hath foundations, whose builder and maker is God." (ver. 10.) It was this that made him contented to leave his native country, and to sojourn as a foreigner in a land which was to be the inheritance of his posterity, or to lead the roving, unsettled life of a nomad. The city to which he looked forward was the heavenly city, the New Jerusalem, mentioned in the next chapter, and described at large, in the most glowing terms, by John in the Apocalypse—the same to which Christians are looking forward. Nor was Abraham alone in this; but all who, in like manner, were persuaded of the truth of the promises which they saw afar off, and embraced them, confessing that they were pilgrims and strangers on earth, and dying in faith, declared plainly that they sought a country, not in the earthly Canaan, in which they were strangers, tented or roving nomads, nor in their ancestral land, Chaldea, to which they might have returned, but "a better country, that is, a heavenly." (vs. 13–16.) Again he refers to the faith of Abraham as exemplified in another incident of his life, his offering of Isaac, and represents it as so strong that he accounted "God was able to raise him up even from the dead," proving that not only was the immortality of the soul known to him, but that the doctrine of the resurrection of the body had not been entirely concealed. (ver. 19.) The faith of Moses is next brought to view, who, in preference to the honours that awaited him in the court of Pharaoh, preferred to suffer affliction with the people of God, " esteeming the reproach of Christ greater riches than the treasures in Egypt; for he had respect unto the recompense of reward." [vs. 24–26.] He preferred the recompense of reward, the everlasting blessings of the heavenly kingdom, to the wealth, luxury, and honours of the most powerful of earthly kingdoms. And among the believing Jews, there were those whose faith was so strong, that they " were tortured, not accepting deliverance; that they might obtain a better resurrection. (ver. 35.) But what was this faith? The Apostle himself has given us a definition—it " is the substance (the firm assurance) of things hoped for, the evidence (demonstration) of things not seen;" i. e., it is an unshaken confidence in the promises of God. It was such confidence on the part of Abraham, Moses, and other patriarchs, in the promise of God, that he would prepare for them a city, a heavenly and eternal city, which enabled them to practice self-denial, and cheerfully submit to the trials of their condition. The promises seen afar off, of which they were persuaded, which they embraced, could not have been promises of earthly good, but, gave the prospect of a better country, that is, an heavenly, which enabled them cheerfully to consent to remain pilgrims and strangers, and suffer persecution with the people of God in this world.

4. We are now prepared to go directly to the Old Testament, to show that it clearly reveals a future state of existence. In addition to the natural evidence of the soul's immortality, which the ancient Hebrews had, in common with the Egyptians and other idolatrous nations, they lived under the light of an immediate revelation from heaven. They were vastly more enlightened, in respect to the existence and nature of the supreme Being. That He is a spirit, for whom it would be

one of the greatest of sins to form, or imagine any likeness whatever, was one of the first lessons taught them. It being once understood that such a Being as the God of the Hebrews existed, and that He is not matter, "thus much is gained, that there is such a thing as spirit, an immaterial substance, that is not liable to die or perish ; and though there be this difference between God and all other spirits, that He is an infinite Spirit, whereas others are but finite; yet no man that grants the existence of an infinite spirit, can with any pretense or color of reason deny the possibility of a finite spirit."* Again, as the economy under which they lived was administered by angels, they had evidence of the existence of spiritual beings, and of a spiritual world, distinct from, yet closely connected with this. Indeed it is not unreasonable to conclude that, in consequence of this supernatural ministry, their convictions, as to the reality of such beings, and of such a world, were far more vivid and strong than the convictions of those who lived after this ministry had ceased. Nay, the alleged reticence of the books of Moses, in respect to the future separate existence of the soul of man, as suggested before, might be accounted for, from the full and ever present belief of this doctrine by the ancient Hebrews, rather than from any supposed attempt of Moses to conceal it. The name of God is not found in the book of Esther ; and why would it not be as rational to say that its author was ignorant of the Divine existence, when the book was written to illustrate and confirm the wonderful providence of God, for the deliverance of his people, as to say that because the revelation of a future life is not made more prominent in the Pentateuch, the ancient Hebrews were ignorant of the doctrine ?

(1.) " And God said, Let us make man in our image, after our likeness, etc. So God created man in his own image, in the image of God created he him." Gen. i. 26, 27. Anthropomorphites alone would say that this image of God, in which

* Archbishop Tillotson's Sermons, vol. ix., Serm. i.

man was created, consisted in his shape, or the form of his body. Nor have we any warrant for singling out his intelligence or reason, and saying that it consisted in that. It is the immortality of man, more than his reason, which distinguishes him from the lower animals ; but we would not single out even that as entirely constituting the image of his Maker in which he was created. We would rather say that while the image of God principally consisted in the qualities of man's soul, which were similar to the perfections of his Maker, it referred also to the essence of his soul as spiritual, like the Divine essence. The matter, which God created, was not made after his image, but the human soul was, because it is spiritual and immortal. The immortality of the soul is clearly implied, if not directly asserted by Moses, under the guidance of the Spirit of inspiration, in what he says in these passages, respecting the original creation of man in the image, and after the likeness of God.

" And the Lord God formed man of the dust of the ground, and breathed into his nostrils the breath of life ; and man became a living soul." Gen. ii. 7. It is not necessary to deny that the original *nephish*, translated *soul* is sometimes used for the *principle of animal or natural life*. But it means more than this here. He not only gave man life in common with other animals formed out of the dust, but he communicated to him a rational, living, immortal soul. There is a great number of passages in which *nephish* is used for the rational soul in man—that which constitutes *the me*, which is capable of rejoicing in God, trusting in God, praising God, and of cultivating piety and holiness. (Vide Deut. iv. 29 ; vi. 5 ; Ps. xix. 8 ; xlii. 2, 3 ; xliii. 5 ; ciii. 1, 2 ; cxix. 20, 81, 129, 167, et al.) The above passage, therefore, declaring that "the first Adam was made a living soul," taken in connection with those which declare that he was made in the image of God, teaches the immortality of the soul. That the *nephish* in man is a very different thing, and far more excellent than the *nephish* in animals,

2*

Moses himself shows in the respective accounts he gives of the creation of man and of the other animals. The Spirit that created them is one and the same; but the difference in the products is made very striking, by the different manner in which they were created. The animals were produced (Gen. i. 20, 24 ; ii. 19,) by the brooding of the Divine Spirit upon the waters and the ground, as it had brooded upon the chaos (Gen. i. 2,) at the formation of the world ; but man, his body having been made out of the ground, received his soul from the breath of the Almighty, that he might exist in the image and likeness of God.

Archbishop Tillotson makes this just and striking comment on the account of the murder of Abel, contained in Gen. iv. : " Now if the immortality of the soul and a future state be not supposed and taken for granted in this story, this very passage is enough to cut the sinews, and pluck up the roots of all religion. For if there were no rewards after this life, it were obvious for every man to argue from this story, that it was a dangerous thing to please God ; if this were all that Abel got by it to be knocked on the head by his brother, who offended God."*

" And Enoch walked with God ; and he was not, for God took him." Gen. v. 24. A premature death was not the reward, as some have endeavoured to persuade themselves, which was bestowed on Enoch for his remarkable piety. Such an interpretation is little better than trifling with the word of God. For while a good man may be taken away by death from the evil to come (Is. lvii. 1), Enoch's removal is spoken of in a different manner from that of the other patriarchs (v. 5, 8, 11, 14, etc.), and the same word is used which is applied to the removal of the prophet Elijah (2 Kings ii. 3, 5), who was carried visibly, by a chariot of fire and horses of fire, into heaven. It was demonstrated to the ancient Hebrews, by the translation of Enoch and Elijah, that there is a heaven, a defined place of residence, where the pious departed enjoy eternal felicity. Even Warburton is compelled to admit that "Moses both knew and believed the immortality of Enoch;" but he strangely adds, that he "purposely obscured the fact (*i. e.*, in narrating his translation), from whence it might have been collected." He also gives as a reason why the history of the translation of Elijah more clearly reveals a future state, that "when the latter history was written, it was thought expedient to make a preparation for the dawning of a future state of reward and punishment, which in the time of Moses had been highly improper."* It is not so easy to see why it would have been highly improper to make as clear a revelation of a future state in the time of Moses, as was made in the time of Elijah. The translation of these eminent servants of God was to their cotemporaries a more palpable and impressive evidence of a state of future reward than could have been given by the plainest and most direct assertion of the doctrine by Moses and the prophets. The narratives, as given by the inspired historians, were precisely what men needed to give them assurance of a blessed immortality, as the reward of piety, before Christ came to bring life and immortality to light by his resurrection from the dead, and ascension into heaven. Their translation typified that resurrection and ascension.

The vision of the patriarch Jacob (Gen. xxviii. 10–15), was equally well fitted to assure men of the existence of a heavenly world, the abode of angels, and of the pious departed like Enoch, who was translated, and Abraham, who had been gathered to his fathers in peace. In his vision he saw "a ladder set up on the earth, and the top of it reached to heaven: and behold the angels of God ascending and descending upon it. And, behold, the Lord stood above it, and said, I am the Lord God of Abraham thy father, and the God of Isaac." I

* Div. Leg., B. v., § 5.

am, not I *was*, the God of Abraham; *i. e.*, he was the God of the living, of Abraham, who was still alive, although his body was seeing corruption in the grave.

"Then Abraham gave up the ghost, and died in a good old age, an old man and full of years; and was gathered to his people," Gen. xxv. 8. (Comp. xxxv. 29; xlix. 33; Numb. xx. 24.) To the fact that these patriarchs died, it is added, that they were gathered to their people, which is not to be regarded as a repetition of the same fact, by another merely pleonastic expression. The language implies that there was a place or receptacle of departed souls, where their pious ancestors were gathered before them. Jacob expected (Gen. xxxvii. 35,) to go to his son Joseph, of whose place of burial he was ignorant, or rather whose body he believed had been torn in pieces by wild beasts. In respect to the separate existence of the soul in another state, the doctrine of the ancient Hebrews was far in advance of that of the Egyptians, who believed that unless the body was embalmed, and received the rites of sepulture, the soul would be subject to transmigration from one body to another. But Jacob, although he had reason to believe that the body of his favourite son had been torn in pieces, expected to meet his spirit in another world. The prophets Isaiah (xiv. 15 sq.) and Ezekiel (xxxii. 17 sq.), at a later period, describe those, whose bodies had been cast out unburied, as joining the spirits of the dead in another world. The former prophet (v. 18 sq.) speaks of the King of Babylon whose body was not buried, but was cast out among the corpses of the slain. It seems marvelous indeed how it ever came to be questioned that the ancients believed in the doctrine of a world of departed spirits. This was the world in which Abraham, and Isaac, and Jacob were gathered to their people. This was the world from which David did not expect the spirit of his departed child to return, but whither he expected, in due time, to go to it (2 Sam. xii. 23). If *Sheol* does not mean the grave, but a place where souls after death exist, separate from their bodies, in Is. xiv. 11, and elsewhere in the prophets, then we have a warrant for supposing that it has the same import in Gen. xlii. 38; xliv. 29, 31, especially when taken in connection with Gen. xxxvii. 35.

Is it then possible that the ancient Hebrews, who had no other revelation than that contained in the Law of Moses, could believe that man, created in the image of God, and placed under the ministry of angels, taught how to worship God acceptably, and to whom the history of the translation of one, in body and spirit, to another world was well known, ceased to exist when his short life on earth was terminated? It is impossible.

2. From the books of Moses, let us pass to a piece of writing undoubtedly somewhat earlier in date, the book of Job. He was a patriarch of Abrahamic descent, although not in the line of the covenanted seed. He was probably a great-grandson of Esau. Eliphaz, Bildad, and Zophar were no doubt of the same descent. Job and his three friends were probably emirs, or Idumean princes, of great wealth and authority. The Septuagint translators make him one of those kings of Edom who are mentioned (Gen. xxxvi. 31), as reigning before there was any king over Israel. They make him the same as Jobab, the second in the list of kings there mentioned. I think we have good reason for placing the era of Job about 1600 years B. C. The chief topic discussed in the book relates to the distribution of good and evil in the world. It is an inquiry whether there is a righteous and equal retribution in the present life. In the discussion the three friends of Job maintain the affirmative, contending that men are placed under that equal providence, which, according to Warburton's theory, was exercised exclusively over the Israelitish nation. Job maintains the opposite opinion, and shows that the afflictions of men do not certainly prove that they are bad, as their prosperity does not certainly prove that they are good men. But the particular question which we wish to ex-

amine, is whether the doctrine of a future state is revealed in this, undoubtedly the oldest book, in the world.

It is evident that the Hebrew doctrine of a *Sheol*, an invisible world to which the dead depart, was perfectly familiar to his mind. He describes it (iii. 13–19) as the place where kings, princes, and counsellors of the earth are congregated; where the weary are at rest, and the wicked cease from troubling; where the prisoners rest together, and hear not the voice of the oppressor, and the slave is free from his master. The idea that the soul perished with the body did not enter into the belief of Job. The souls of the small as well as the great, of infants who died at their birth, would survive the body. To him the grave was but the entrance to a world of spirits, of conscious existence, of happiness or woe.

But the passage, xix. 25–27, is the one which has the most important bearing on the question under consideration: " For I know that my Redeemer liveth, and that he shall stand at the latter day upon the earth : and though after my skin worms destroy this body, yet in my flesh shall I see God : whom I shall see for myself, and mine eyes shall behold, and not another; though my reins be consumed within me." It would require a long dissertation to state the conflicting interpretations of this passage. There are of these four, from which, doubtless, we are to select the true one: 1. That it relates to the resurrection of the dead. 2. That it expresses the expectation of Job that he would, in this life, be restored to his former prosperity and happiness. 3. That it expresses the confidence of Job that before the disease which was then wasting his body should bring him to the grave, God would appear as the vindicator of his innocence. 4. That God would become his vindicator after his death, when he himself, his body being left behind, should be rejoicing in his presence. The word translated *Redeemer*, *Goël*, properly denotes a redeemer or vindicator; and there is nothing in the meaning of the term, or its use, which would prevent its application to the Messiah. And there is nothing in a fair construction of what is said about his manifestation inconsistent with understanding it to be a visible appearance. Whether Job meant he should have a vision of his Redeemer, in his living body, on the morning of the resurrection, according to the first interpretation, or that he should enter, a disembodied spirit, joyful and accepted, into his presence in heaven, according to the fourth interpretation specified above, must depend upon the true sense of the words translated *in my flesh*. That sense, we think, has been given by Rosenmüller, who translates, "without my flesh," *i. e.*, "my whole body being consumed, I shall see God." Other Hebrew scholars, however, (*e. g.*, Herder,) translate it, in "my living body." And, perhaps, it may well be asked, if so clear a revelation was given to Job of the advent of the Messiah, (Goël,) why we should hesitate to suppose that the resurrection of the body, which that Messiah was more clearly to make known, was not also, indistinctly, at least, revealed to him as it had been to Abraham. Our choice obviously must lie between the first and the last of the interpretations specified above ; and, as to the main question before us, it is immaterial which we prefer. Ambrose, Epiphanius, Augustine, and all the Latin Fathers, adopted the first interpretation, viz., that Job is speaking of the resurrection of his body. The great body of English interpreters, and among the Germans, A. Schultens, Kosegarten, and J. H. and J. D. Michaelis,* have referred the passage to the resurrection. Ewald, Vaihinger, and Oehler,† have defended the fourth interpretation. viz., that after his death, when he was enjoying the beatific vision in heaven, God would vindicate his innocence in the eyes of men on earth. Some distinguished critics, however, have held that Job does not refer to a resurrection nor a

---

* See Hahn's "De Spe Immortalitatis sub Vet. Test.," etc., pp. 34, 35, Note.

† See Oehler's "Vet. Test. sententia de rebus post mortem futuris illustrata," p. 81.

future life, such as Grotius, Warburton, Patrick, Knapp, and Hahn. Mr. Barnes, in his Notes on Job—one of the ablest of his productions—tells us with what pain he came to the conclusion which he has adopted in respect to this passage, that it means no more than that God would come forth as the vindicator of Job, which he afterward did, as recorded in the close of the book. The chief argument which is urged against that interpretation which makes the passage refer to a future state, is, that Job made no more use of it in his controversy with his three friends. But these three friends denied, certainly they ignored, a future state, and contended that men were placed under an equal providence in this life, a doctrine which, if true, would supersede the necessity of a future state of rewards and punishments. Job met them on their own ground, and contented himself with denying their premises, and stating facts, drawn from every day life, in refutation of them. It was enough for him once, most emphatically, to make a declaration of his belief that the day would come when God would compensate men for all the inequalities of his providence in this world, and express the wish that this declaration were graven with an iron pen, and laid in the rock forever. Its importance well entitled it to such an honour. "O that my words were now written! O that they were inscribed in a book! That they were graven with an iron pen, and laid in the rock forever! For I KNOW THAT MY RE-DEEMER LIVETH, AND THAT HE SHALL APPEAR AT A FUTURE DAY UPON THE EARTH: AND THOUGH AFTER MY SKIN THIS (FLESH) BE DESTROYED, YET IN MY LIVING BODY (OR WITHOUT MY FLESH) SHALL I SEE GOD." What further use could Job make of his belief in the doctrine of a future existence, in his controversy with men who virtually denied it, beyond this emphatic declaration of it? He must first convince them of the truth of this doctrine; he therefore wisely preferred to meet them on their own ground, and oppose the facts, which meet men on all sides, to their false theory.

3. Let us pass to the Psalms, and inquire whether they do not contain some clear, distinct, revelations of a future state. "Therefore my heart is glad, and my glory rejoiceth; my flesh also shall rest in hope. For thou wilt not leave my soul in hell; neither wilt thou suffer thine Holy One to see corruption. Thou shalt show me the path of life: in thy presence is fullness of joy; at thy right hand there are pleasures for evermore." Ps. xvi. 9–11. The Psalm is Messianic; for while it expresses the strong confidence which every pious sufferer reposes in God, there are some parts of it which can have their *complete* fulfillment only in Christ. *My flesh shall rest in hope*," (dwell in security,) "is applicable," says J. A. Alexander,* " both to preservation from death, and preservation in death, and may therefore without violence be understood, in a lower sense, of David, who did die and see corruption, but whose body is to rise again, as well as in a higher sense of Christ, whose body, though it died, was raised again before it saw corruption." We follow the same eminent critic, in determining the meaning of the rest of the passage. The Hebrew, translated *Holy One*, in the original text is plural (holy ones); in the margin singular. The Jews contend for the former, the New Testament retains the latter. " To both (David and Christ) the words contain a promise of deliverance from death; but in the case of Christ, with specific reference to his actual escape from the corruption which is otherwise inseparable from dissolution. Believers in general are saved from the perpetual dominion of death, but Christ was saved even from the first approach of putrefaction. In this peculiar and most pregnant sense, the words are applied to Christ exclusively by two apostles, and in that sense declared to be inapplicable to David (Acts ii. 29–31; xiii. 35–37). Their reasoning would utterly forbid the application to any lower subject, were it not for the ambiguity or twofold meaning of the Hebrew, which can not therefore be explained away with-

* The Psalms Translated and Explained.

out embarrassing the interpretation of this signal prophecy."
The *path of life* is the way to a blessed immortality, which
God will show to the pious sufferer. His presence, in which
is the fullness of joy, is his blissful presence in heaven ; the
pleasures which are for evermore at his right hand, are the
eternal joys which he dispenses.

" As for me, I will behold thy face in righteousness : I shall
be satisfied, when I awake, with thy likeness." Ps. xvii. 15.
Rosenmüller and Stuart think it can scarcely be otherwise than
that this passage should be interpreted of a future life. If
David looked no further than the present world, where lies
the force of the antithesis, "*As for me*" ? He had been speaking of men of the world, who have their portion in this life,
i. e., in the present state as distinguished from futurity. " True
they have all that heart can wish of the blessings of the present
life, but I shall behold the face of God in righteousness ; I shall
be satisfied with that vision, when I open my eyes in eternity,
or when I awake from the sleep of death." Professor Alexander, who thinks that the interpretation which puts the higher
sense upon the phrase as referring to the act of awaking from
the sleep of death, excludes too much from view the enjoyment of God's favor and protection even here, which is the
burden of the whole prayer, nevertheless adds, that " the same
state of mind and heart which enables a man now to be contented with the partial views which he enjoys of God will prepare him to be satisfied hereafter with the beatific vision
through eternity."

" For this God is our God forever and ever ; he will be our
guide even unto death." Ps. xlviii. 14. *Forever and ever*
literally means eternity, everlasting duration. " This is to be
our God for eternity." *Unto death, i. e.*, at death, and beyond
death. The meaning is, that God will not only guide his people even to the end of life, but to a happy immortality beyond
the grave. The second clause carries out to its full sense the

first, that God is the God of those who trust in him for eternity.

" Thou shalt guide me with thy counsel, and afterward receive me to glory. Whom have I in heaven but thee ? and there is none upon earth that I desire besides thee. My flesh and my heart faileth ; but God is the strength of my heart, and my portion forever." Ps. lxxiii. 24–26. Asaph, a cotemporary of David, and his chief musician, in this celebrated composition, adopts as his theme that *God is good, only and always good to Israel*, that is, the " true Israel," the sincere and spiritual members of the church. He had been tempted, by the apparent inequalities of God's providential dealings, to think otherwise ; and in the psalm he describes the manner in which his mind had been brought from its state of fearful conflict and dark misgivings. He had viewed the righteous and the wicked from the wrong stand-point. But when he came into the sanctuary of God, or into the holy places where God reveals himself, and contemplated these seeming inequalities by the light of Divine revelation, all the darkness which had perplexed his mind was dissipated. He saw the wicked standing on slippery places ; he saw them fall into destruction. He saw the righteous, however sorrowful their present allotment, guided by Divine counsel, and afterward received into glory. *After glory or honor thou wilt take me ; i. e.*, after honoring or vindicating me here, thou wilt receive me to glory. Reference to a future state " is as evident," says Professor Alexander, " in this verse (24) as it is in verses 16–19, if interpreted in any natural and reasonable manner : *God is the rock of my heart and my portion to eternity.*"

4. It will be seen to be especially pertinent in an introduction to a work on the book of Ecclesiastes, to inquire what traces may be found of the doctrine of a future life in the Proverbs of Solomon. The separate existence of the soul is recognized throughout this book, in the Hebrew doctrine of Sheol, as a place in which the souls of men are gathered after

death. If we except one or two places (i. 12 ; xxx. 16,) where it appears to mean simply the grave, Sheol in the Proverbs is used with reference to a place where the souls of the dead are still alive and conscious. (Comp. ii. 18 ; v. 5 sq. ; vii. 26 sq. ; ix. 18 ; xxi. 16.)

" The way of life is above to the wise that he may depart from hell beneath." xv. 24. With which compare xii. 28. " In the way of righteousness is life ; and in the pathway thereof there is no death." These passages not only point to a future state, but to a future state of rewards and punishments. There is a way of life, of everlasting life, by which the truly wise may depart from hell beneath. There is a way of righteousness, of which everlasting life is the goal ; and there is a pathway of which the end is death. Even Oehler, who endeavors to explain away almost every other passage in which there has been supposed to be reference to the doctrine of a future state, is compelled to admit that these passages may teach, that some better portion after death awaits the righteous than awaits the wicked. This way, he says, which conducts the wise above that they may escape hell beneath (orcum), can scarcely be referred to the happiness of this life, and we must conclude that there was not wanting some better hope to the pious Israelites.*

" The wicked is driven away in his wickedness : but the righteous hath hope in his death." Prov. xiv. 32. The wicked man who supremely loves the present world, who has laid up all his good things here, is described at death as being *driven away*, because he has no treasure laid up in heaven ; he clings to the world, and releases his grasp only because he is compelled so to do ; but the good man leaves the world with joy ; he has hope in his death. If the Hebrews had not any hope of a future state, " then what is the ground," Professor Stuart well asks, " or source of hope or confidence in a dying hour ? This verse must be a real problem for those who have such

* Vet. Test. Sententia de rebus, etc., pp. 79, 80.

views of the state of knowledge among the Hebrews.   If there was nothing beyond the grave, in their view, on what is the hope or confidence here fixed ?"

"Correction is grievous unto him that forsaketh the way : and he that hateth reproof shall die." Prov. xv. 10.   To say that the phrase *shall die* threatens punishment, "is saying only what lies of course upon the face of it.   But what punishment, and how much ?   Clearly all sinners are not punished in this world, either with sudden, or violent, or premature death. Can we make out any thing significant, or really intelligible, in the passage before us, and in other like passages, without supposing the Hebrews to have looked to some future retribution ?   To say to the wicked man : *Thou shalt die,* if we mean merely a natural and ordinary death, is saying no more than Providence says, every day, to the good as well as to the wicked.   To say that all of the wicked die, or shall die a sudden, violent, premature death, is saying what is most evidently not a matter of fact or truth.   What then did or could a Hebrew mean by such phraseology ?   If it has a meaning which is intelligible, it would seem to be that the idea of future retribution must have entered into the minds of those who employed this language.   Otherwise no meaning, which is at the same time both significant and true, can well be attached to it."*

Such being the prominence given to the doctrine of a future existence and future retribution in the Proverbs of Solomon, we need not be surprised at the greater prominence given to it in another book, Ecclesiastes, written (as will be shown in the sequel) by the same author.   "And moreover, I saw under the sun the place of judgment, that wickedness was there ; and the place of righteousness that wickedness was there.   I said in mine heart God shall judge the righteous and the wicked : for there is a time there for every purpose and for every work." Eccl. iii. 16, 17.   "Because sentence against an evil work is

* Stuart's Commentary on Prov. *in loco.*

not executed speedily, therefore the heart of the sons of men is fully set in them to do evil. Though a sinner do evil a hundred times, and his days be prolonged, yet surely I know that it shall be well with them that fear God, which fear before him; but it shall not be well with the wicked, neither shall he prolong his days, which are as a shadow; because he feareth not before God." (viii. 11–13.) "Rejoice, O young man, in thy youth; and let thy heart cheer thee in the days of thy youth, and walk in the ways of thine heart, and in the sight of thine eyes; but know thou, that for all these things God will bring thee into judgment." (xi. 9.) "For God shall bring every work into judgment, with every secret thing, whether it be good, or whether it be evil." (xii. 14.) It is shown, at the proper places, in the following pages, that these passages can only be fairly interpreted, by referring them to a future state of retribution. Indeed, it is the object of this work on Ecclesiastes, which is here offered to the public, to show that it is the doctrine of this inspired book, as stated by the writer of it himself (Comp. ch. i. 2, with ch. xii. 13, 14.), that A DAY OF FUTURE RETRIBUTION ALONE CAN REDEEM ALL THINGS IN THIS WORLD, WHICH ARE EITHER MATTERS OF OBSERVATION OR EXPERIENCE—MAN AND HIS AFFAIRS, AND EVEN THE MATERIAL WORLD, IN WHICH HE SPENDS HIS BRIEF EXISTENCE—FROM BEING REGARDED AS AN INEXPLICABLE MYSTERY, OR AS THE GREATEST VANITY IMAGINABLE.

5. As it is generally conceded even by those who are most strenuous in denying that the ancient Hebrews possessed any knowledge of a future state, that it might be expected some traces of this doctrine would be found in the writings of the prophets, whose most important office was "to prepare the way for the approach of the Messiah's kingdom, and give hints of the nature of his glorious Gospel which brought life and immortality to light,"[*] I shall not detain the reader with any lengthy expositions of passages from the prophets, touching the

* Whately's Future State, p. 20.

immortality of the soul and the resurrection of the body, but will dismiss the subject, by merely citing a few of these passages. And I shall leave the subject, confident that most readers who have patiently followed me, will agree that the denial to the ancient Hebrew Scriptures of the revelation of the doctrine of a future state, is environed with insuperable difficulties.

" He will swallow up death in victory ; and the Lord God will wipe away tears from off all faces." Is. xxv. 8. Comp. 1 Cor. xv. 54. " Thy dead men shall live; together with my dead body shall they arise. Awake, and sing, ye that dwell in the dust : for thy dew is as the dew of herbs, and the earth shall cast out the dead." Is. xxvi. 19. " And as I prophesied there was a noise, and behold a shaking, and the bones came together, bone to his bone," etc. " Behold, O my people, I will open your graves, and cause you to come up out of your graves," etc. Ezek. xxxvii. 1–14. " And many of them that sleep in the dust of the earth shall awake ; some to everlasting life, and some to shame and everlasting contempt." Dan. xii. 2. The imagery of the resurrection is employed to illustrate the wonderful deliverances which God would accomplish for his people; and its employment proves that the Jews must have been well acquainted with the doctrine from which the imagery is derived. Isaiah and Ezekiel were predicting the release of the Jews from their captivity in Babylon ; Daniel was predicting their deliverance, at a later period, from the oppressions of Antiochus. The same power which could raise their bodies from the grave, and cause their dew to be as the dew of herbs, could open the tomb of oppression, and raise them from their civil death, i. e., could pluck them from the hand of oppressors who had despoiled them of their liberty.

II. Authorship of the Book of Ecclesiastes.

1. The book claims to be the production of King Solomon, the son of David. "The words of the Preacher, the son of David, King of Jerusalem." Chap. i. 1. The words are those of a son of David; but as David had many sons, we have the further information, to prevent any possible mistake, that the writer was king in Jerusalem. Now Solomon was the only son of David who was king in Jerusalem; therefore Solomon must be meant. "I the Preacher was king over Israel in Jerusalem." i. 12. The claim set up in the title is here repeated in the body of the work. It is therefore indisputable that the book claims to be the production of Solomon. No candid critic will venture to call this in question. Those who deny that Solomon was the author, are compelled to take the ground that the writer, who, they assume, lived at a much later age, personates Solomon, or says what he might have been supposed to say. But this is nowhere said or intimated in the book itself; it affords not the least warrant for any such assumption. The assumption is therefore perfectly gratuitous, and is demanded only for the support of a theory which, it is the object of the following pages to show, is equally groundless. Nothing, absolutely nothing, can be inferred from the expression "I was king," rather than "I am," in favour of the ground that Ecclesiastes was written by a pseudo-Solomon, posterior to the age of Solomon. Solomon was writing not for his own age alone, nor for his own nation alone. He expected that his words would be read long after he was dead; the most natural expression, therefore, which he could employ was that which he does employ, "I was king." Nor does he use this expression because the men of his times, or of any times, needed to be informed that he was a king; but he was about to give to the world certain results of his experience, observation, and reflection, which were truly remarkable as

proceeding from a king. "I was king when I had this experience, when I made these observations, when I was led to these reflections on the vanity of the world, and came to the conclusion stated in the final words, xii. 13, 14." It is to be considered, moreover, that he was unquestionably very far advanced in life when he composed this book, and expected shortly to leave the stage of action; it was natural, therefore, that he should speak or write more as in the presence of posterity, men who would read his words after he was dead, than in the presence of his own generation.

But that there may be no mistake, the author clearly identifies himself as Solomon, near the close of the book: "And moreover, because the Preacher was wise, he still taught the people knowledge; yea, he gave good heed, and sought out, and set in order many proverbs. The Preacher sought to find out acceptable words: and that which was written was upright, even words of truth." Eccl. xii. 9, 10. Here the Preacher, *i. e.,* the author of Ecclesiastes, describes himself as the author of other writings, viz., Proverbs. We have the fact recorded (1 Kings iv. 32,) that Solomon wrote three thousand proverbs; and we have a book in the sacred canon, bearing this title, *The Proverbs of Solomon, the son of David, King of Jerusalem,* containing unquestionably a part, at least, of the proverbs which we are expressly told he wrote. How could the author of Ecclesiastes more emphatically declare that he was no other than Solomon, than when he claimed to be the author of that monument of wisdom, the Book of Proverbs?

2. The personal descriptions of the author, which the book contains, are applicable in an eminent degree to Solomon. "I applied mine heart to know and to search, and to seek out wisdom and the reason of things," etc. vii. 25. "And I gave my heart to seek and search out by wisdom concerning all things that are done under heaven." i. 13. This accords with what the sacred historians tell us respecting Solomon, that his 'wisdom excelled the wisdom of all the children of the east

country, and all the wisdom of Egypt. For he was wiser than all men ; than Ethan the Ezrahite, and Heman, and Chalcol, and Darda, the sons of Mahol, and his fame was in all nations round about." 1 Kings iv. 30, 31. Compare 1 Kings i. 12, " I have given thee a wise and understanding heart; so that there was none like thee before thee ; neither after shall any arise like unto thee," with Eccl. i. 12, " Lo, I am come to great estate, and have gotten more wisdom than all they that have been before me in Jerusalem." Compare Eccl. ii. 7–9, " I had great possessions of great and small cattle above all that were in Jerusalem before me : I gathered me also silver and gold, and the peculiar treasure of kings and of the provinces : I was great and increased more than all that were before me in Jerusalem : also my wisdom remained with me," with 1 Kings iv. 23 ; ix. 28 ; x. 14, 23, 27, in which Solomon is described as exceeding all the kings of the earth for riches as well as for wisdom.

3. Ecclesiastes attributes the construction of great works to its author, which accord well with the edifices, cities, and other public works which occupied the attention of Solomon during a great part of his reign. " I made me great works ; I builded me houses; I planted me vineyards : I made me gardens and orchards, I planted me trees in them of all kind of fruits : I made me pools of water, to water therewith the wood that bringeth forth trees." ii. 4–6. Besides the Temple, he built palaces on which his workmen were occupied for many years, a navy, and several fortified cities in remote parts of his empire. (See 1 Kings, chs. ix and x).

4. The book contains passages which can not be interpreted more naturally than by applying them to Rehoboam, the son and successor of Solomon, and to Jeroboam, the first king of the ten revolting tribes. " Yea, I hated all my labour which I had taken under the sun : because I should leave it unto the man that shall be after me. And who knoweth whether he shall be a wise man or a fool ?" ii. 18, 19. Rehoboam quickly showed after he ascended the throne, that he had small capacity

for government. The pain which the speaker in Ecclesiastes expresses, in view of leaving his estate and kingdom to his heir, and the doubt which his question implies, might all very naturally be applied to Solomon, if he had been led to question the ability of the heir apparent to sustain the great affairs of state which were to devolve upon him when he should come to the throne. The language well expresses the sadness and disappointment of the father, if he had hitherto failed to discover promising talents in the son on whom his hopes were placed. "Better is a poor and a wise child than an old and foolish king, who will no more be admonished. For out of prison he cometh to reign; whereas also he that is born in his kingdom becometh poor. I considered all the living which walk under the sun, with the second child that shall stand up in his stead," etc. Ecc. iv. 13–16. The description of the "poor and wise child" or youth, here mentioned, strikingly applies to Jeroboam. He was of humble origin, the son of one of Solomon's servants, but early developed fine talents. The allusion to himself as an "old and foolish king," is not to be taken as an acknowledgment that he considered Jeroboam as better qualified to be king than himself; but this was what he foresaw the people would be ready to say. The "prison," or house of captives, is Egypt into which Jeroboam fled to escape from the vengeance of Solomon. His own kingdom, in which he was born a poor man, was the kingdom of Israel. "The second child" or young man, again refers to Jeroboam, who stood up in the stead of him who had the *first*, or rightful claim, *i. e.*, Rehoboam.

5. Although Ecclesiastes is evidently designed to be a connected, philosophical discourse, the writer continually falls into a proverbial style, strikingly similar to the Proverbs of Solomon; *e. g.*, "In much wisdom is much grief: and he that increaseth knowledge increaseth sorrow," i. 18. "The wise man's eyes are in his head; but the fool walketh in darkness," ii. 14. "Better is a handful with quietness, than both the

hands full, with travail and vexation of spirit," iv. 6. "The sleep of a labouring man is sweet, whether he eat little or much: but the abundance of the rich will not suffer him to sleep." v. 12. "A good name is better than precious ointment: and the day of death than the day of one's birth." vii. 1, etc. It is not surprising that a man who had written "three thousand proverbs," should fall into this proverbial style. And here it may be worth mentioning that, including all that are contained in this book, with those which are ascribed to him, contained in other parts of the sacred canon, it would still be difficult to make out the number which the inspired historian expressly declares he wrote.

6. Finally, ancient tradition, with one voice, ascribed the book to Solomon. "If this question," says Professor Stuart, "be referred to the decision of past times, then is it easily answered. One and all of the older writers declare for Solomon." Among all the objections which some of the learned Jews made to this book, none of them appear to have called in question its genuineness as the work of Solomon. This fact will go far to remove the objections to considering it the work of Solomon, drawn from the Hebrew style and diction; and the opinion of the ancients, on the general question, will go very far to outweigh all that the moderns have or can allege against attributing the authorship to Solomon. Some of these objections let us now proceed to consider.

Grotius appears to have been the first who called in question the ancient and common opinion that Ecclesiastes was the production of Solomon. In this he has been followed by Eichhorn, Bauer, Augusti, Umbreit, De Wette, Gesenius, Jahn, Hitzig, Kurtz, Professor Stuart, Burger, and others. Their theory is that it is the work of a later writer, who introduces Solomon as speaking in it. It would be sufficient, perhaps, to say, that the work itself contains no intimation that such was its origin; but on the contrary claims to contain the words of the real Solomon, the son of David, king in Jerusalem. Would it not be better to deny the canonicity of the book altogether, than to attempt to convict it of setting up a spurious claim in respect to its authorship. If the title or inscription is false—if the writer spoke falsely in i. 12—what confidence can we have in any of his statements, which involve matters of fact, or record the results of his observation and experience? Then, again, those who contend that it was not written by king Solomon, find it necessary to attempt to show that the *pseudo-*Solomon, the supposed author, attributes opinions to the wise king, whom he personates, which it would be ridiculous and absurd to suppose that he ever held. But what becomes of the inspiration and authority of a writer who could fall into such egregious mistakes and blunders, as it regards truth to nature and history, mistakes which uninspired men, living so many centuries later, could easily correct? But we will, nevertheless, consider, as proposed, some of the objections which those who have followed Grotius have made to the claim which the book itself sets up to be the work of Solomon, the son of David, and to the whole testimony of antiquity that it is his work.

It is objected that what the author says i. 9, that there is no new thing under the sun, could not have been said by Solomon, since the temple which he had built at Jerusalem was something altogether new. But surely it was no new thing for men to build temples of worship, although it undoubtedly was a new thing for a temple to be built to the one living and true God. The temple, however, was, after all, but an enlarged copy of the tabernacle. But it is .of human experience, of the events which happen to men, and not of inventors in art, and discoveries in science, of which the author is speaking in this verse. In one age we see the outlines of every other. In human experience and striving there is constant change, and yet there is nothing new.

It is also objected, that in the whole book no mention whatever is made of the temple built by Solomon, which would have scarcely been omitted by him in a discourse concerning his own experience. If Ecclesiastes professed to be a life of Solomon, written by himself, the objection might be valid. But he is merely giving the results of his experiments, and of the inquiries which he instituted to ascertain whether the present world is capable of affording solid and lasting happiness, irrespective of an hereafter. His discourse refers mainly to his experience after he forsook the Lord's right way; an experience which eventually led him to sincere repentance. The temple was built during the earlier years of his reign, which were distinguished for his piety, and devotion to the service of God, and its erection formed no part of any of those experiments on which he entered, to test the efficacy of worldly magnificence, pleasures, and appliances, to impart real happiness. There was no occasion for his making special mention of it; indeed, it would have been out of place for him to have introduced it—and for the same purpose—in connection with the other great works, the palaces and cities which he built.

It is further contended, that Solomon could not have written the book of Ecclesiastes, because it contains no allusions to his singular wisdom in administering justice. The meaning is, it may be supposed, that he makes no allusion to his memorable decision between the two women, who both claimed to be mothers of the same child. But surely his wisdom as a judge may be presumed to be included in that wisdom in which he professes to have excelled all who had preceded him in Jerusalem. See chap. i. 16, and compare with 1 Kings iii. 12 : "Lo, I have given thee a wise and an understanding heart; so that there was none like thee before thee, neither after thee shall any arise like unto thee."

It is objected, that the author of Ecclesiastes claims (i. 16, ii. 9) to have been wiser and richer than all who had ruled or lived before him in Jerusalem, and that a son of David could not have so spoken. But the claim set up in these passages is in perfect accordance with what the inspired historian has put on record in respect to Solomon, 1 Kings iii. 12, x. 23–25, etc. The objection would lie almost as strongly against applying these latter historical passages to Solomon, as against applying the former. It can only be said, that, when speaking of himself, modesty, and veneration for his father ought to have restrained him; but it is to be remembered that it was necessary to Solomon's argument, and the full effect of what he was saying, that the world should understand that it was no mere child, or ignorant, weak-minded person, but a man, celebrated for wisdom, who was speaking.

Again it is said that in many places, *e. g.*, chap. iii. 16; iv. 1; v. 8; viii. 11, etc., the author complains of the injustice of judges; that a king who should thus express himself would confess his impotence, or his own injustice; and that it was especially impossible for Solomon, who was celebrated throughout the world for his administration of justice, to have spoken in this manner. But are we to suppose that Solomon's knowledge of the manner in which justice may be perverted, was confined to what took place in his own dominions? Or is it too much for us to believe that as he looked back upon that portion of his life when he had forsaken the way of piety, he may have seen injustice sometimes sitting on his own judgment-seat? But the same objection lies equally against attributing the book of Proverbs to Solomon, for it refers to acts of bribery "to pervert the ways of judgment," xvii. 2, 3; to false witnesses, xix. 9; to wicked rulers, who are compared to "a roaring lion and a ranging bear," xxviii. 15, etc.

Other similar objections, but of even less weight, have been advanced. Much more reliance, however, seems to be placed upon an objection of a different sort, first advanced by the same writer, Grotius, who is entitled to the honour of originating the idea that Solomon could not have written Ecclesiastes; viz., THE DICTION OF THE BOOK. But of the four words which Grotius has specified as foreign, viz., (sir) a thorn, vii. 6; (abjonah) desire, xii. 5; (pashar) to interpret, viii. 1; (gumatz) a pit, x. 8., Witsius has well shown two only can at all be considered as belonging to his argument; and in respect to them he remarks, that because they are at present found only in the Chaldee, it does not necessarily follow that they are not Hebrew, for how many other words are there in the Hebrew language, the roots of which are to be found only in the kindred Arabic or Chaldee dialect? Even Professor Stuart, familiar as he was with the philological speculations of the modern Germans, following in the main Herzfeld, whose accuracy and diligence he praises, admits that there are only some ten or eleven cases which can fairly be said to belong to the later Hebrew; and in respect to these cases, that there is room to doubt. "Where the words are normally constructed," he says, "and where following analogy, they might have been easily constructed and readily used in ancient times, although they do not now appear in the Hebrew Scriptures, we can hardly affirm with confidence that this word and that belong only to the later Hebrew." And in like manner of the small list of "probable Chaldaisms," "amounting to only some eight or ten words at most," he says, "it is impossible to prove that more or less of this last class of words were not extant in the older Hebrew, or that they are not normal derivations of the Hebrew." The philological speculations of such men as Eichhorn and Knobel, it will therefore be seen, so far as both these classes of words are concerned, amount to but very little, as it respects the argument in question. Stuart, however, contends that in passing from a critical reading of the book of Proverbs to Ecclesiastes, one finds himself in a new and different region; "this is a thing, however, which can only be *felt* by a reader familiar with the Hebrew; and therefore one of which an adequate description can not well be given." But may not this difference in the style of these two books be accounted for by the difference in the nature of the compositions; one being a collection of sentences or apothegms, which are to a great extent, independent of one another; the other being a connected discourse, having one great subject running throughout, and partaking somewhat of the nature of a philosophical discussion? If this difference in the nature of the compositions fails to meet the whole case, may not the advanced age of Solomon, and his long familiarity with foreign ambassadors and residents at his court, and his heathen wives, account for whatever Aramæan complexion the book can in truth be said to possess? The objection derived from the diction of the book is the only one which appears to have any force; but if learned Jews did not, on this ground, reject it as the production of Solomon, and if such scholars as Witsius, Van der Palm, Le Clerc, J. D. Michaelis, L. Ewald, and Schelling failed to feel the force of it, and if it is impossible to prove that the "probable Chaldaisms," and words which are said to belong to the later Hebrew, were not extant in the older Hebrew, it is, to say the least, the feeblest of all grounds on which to call in question Solomon's authorship, in the face of the claim which the book itself sets up, and the testimony of all antiquity. Indeed the argument that Solomon did not write the book of Ecclesiastes, comes to no less than this, that the book is not inspired, and ought not to be included in the sacred canon.

III. Solomon.

Solomon was born at Jerusalem 1033 years before the birth of Christ. His mother's name was Bathsheba. His name was derived from the Hebrew word, *shelemah*, which means *peaceable*, and has been supposed to point to the state of peace which was to characterize his reign. Nathan the prophet was sent with an express command from God, that another name should also be conferred on him, Jedediah, which means *beloved of the Lord*. (2 Sam. xii. 24, 25.) In the year 1015 B. C., David died; but some months before this event, the aged monarch, to defeat the conspiracy of Adonijah, who regarded the right to the succession as falling to him, after the death of the ill-fated Absalom, caused Solomon, then scarcely twenty years of age, to be inaugurated as his successor. He flourished before the era of authentic profane history had its beginning—long before Nebuchadnezzar, Alexander, and Hannibal entered upon the stage of action. Arabia, Egypt, and Tyre were the only important countries, except that over which he bore sway, of the entire known world. The wise statesmanship and prowess of his father had made his kingdom second to no other then existing. Of the Psusennes and Shishaks of Egypt we know comparatively nothing, except as they are brought into notice by the Scripture history; and the same is true of the King of Tyre, made famous principally by his friendship for David and treaties with Solomon, and his co-operation in building the temple.

It having been shown that Ecclesiastes was written by Solomon, it becomes important—especially as in this book he makes use of the results of his own experience and observation of the world—in an attempt to explain that book, to preface it with an outline of the leading facts in his history. In order to appreciate the writings of any author, it is necessary to understand something respecting his history and character; and the more we know of the leading circumstances of his life, and of his country, and age, the more correct will be our estimate of his writings, and our understanding of them. And if, in addition, we can so far fix the date of any writing, as to be able to refer it either to a man's early life, or to his old age, we have another clew to guide us to its true intent and import. Never did the peculiarities in the history and character of an author more strikingly impress themselves on the productions of his mind than we find to have been the case with Solomon in writing the book of Ecclesiastes. It is by keeping this in view that we are furnished with a key to this remarkable book, which removes its obscurities and apparent solecisms, and shows it to be one of the most impressive and practical portions of the Bible.

His parentage was illustrious. His father was the most renowned of the race of Hebrew kings, who came to the throne when the enemies of the Israelites were numerous and powerful, and had just gained a signal victory, in which Saul and several of his sons fell. David, soon after he was proclaimed king over all Israel, retrieved the sinking fortunes of the nation. He at length conquered the Philistines and the Moabites; he subdued all Syria, and carried his expeditions as far as the Euphrates, and conquered the Edomites. He fought the Ammonites, besieged Rabbah their capital, laid it waste, and carried away the spoils. His fame went abroad through the surrounding nations. He was not only a brave and successful warrior, but a great statesman. He formed a treaty of commerce with the Tyrians, those ancient lords of the sea, which was highly advantageous to the agricultural and domestic interests of his people, and greatly increased the wealth of the nation. He imported not only building materials for his own palace at Jerusalem, but made most extensive preparations for the erection of a magnificent temple for the worship of God. It was the cherished purpose of his heart to erect this building himself; but God informed him, by the prophet, that the time had not arrived, and that this honour was reserved for another. He did not, however, relax his efforts to accumulate the necessary materials for so vast a work. According to the present supply of the precious metals, and their present standard of value, the quantity of gold and silver which he amassed, would seem to be almost incredible. One learned writer,* in his table of ancient currency, makes the total amount £800,-000,000. But the standard of value among ancient oriental nations is too uncertain, and has too much changed to justify any great degree of certainty. It is certain, however, that immense treasures, from the commerce established with Tyre,

* Dr. Arbuthnot.

and the spoils and tribute of conquered nations, must have been accumulated.

Such were the treasures which Solomon inherited, and such was the great work allotted him—the building of the temple —which was to spread his fame through the earth, and signalize his reign in all coming time. When his father, in order to defeat the attempt of an elder son to supplant Solomon, some months before his death, abdicated in his favour, the people appear to have hailed the event with rapturous joy. They shouted, "GOD SAVE KING SOLOMON. And all the people came up after him, and the people piped with pipes, and rejoiced with great joy, so that earth rent with the sound of them." We are not to infer that King David had lost his place in the affections of the people; for it was by his influence that the threatened insurrection was so easily suppressed, and the prince whom he had designated as his successor securely established upon the throne. The nation must still have been proud of his warlike achievements, and were ready to honour him as the chief instrument of their national prosperity. But he had become old; his trembling limbs could no longer bear him as their leader into the thickest of the conflict; he could no longer wield the spear and the sword in the mortal fray with their enemies. Perhaps, however, we have in this case an illustration of that propensity which is said to prevail among the subjects of monarchical governments, to prefer the heir-apparent to the old king. Solomon most feelingly alludes to this in his own case—as I shall have occasion to notice in the exposition which is to follow—when he became aged, and was about to be succeeded by another, or rather by others in his kingdom: "Better is a poor and wise child than an old and foolish king."

SOLOMON'S LEARNING.

His father was a poet of the highest order. His sublime, pathetic, and pious strains, which will always be dear to the

Church of God, sufficiently attest that he possessed an intellect
of the first order. But he can not be regarded as a learned
man. He spent his childhood and early youth about his
father's sheepcotes, and leading his flocks over Judea's hills.
But he doubtless felt all the more keenly the importance of
mental culture, and, therefore, spared no pains in the education
of his son. He became his instructor. Solomon afterward
paid this beautiful tribute to the parental care and faithful-
ness of which he was the favoured object: "For I was my
father's son, tender and only beloved in the sight of my mother.
He taught me also, and said unto me, Let thine heart retain
my words: keep my commandments, and live. Get wisdom,
get understanding: forget it not: neither decline from the
words of my mouth." Prov. iv. 3–5. We are not to infer
that he confined himself to moral instruction; nor are we to
infer that he was his only teacher. All the most learned men
of the nation were doubtless employed; and there is every
reason to suppose that the assistance of the wise men and
literati of Egypt, then the cradle of learning, was, as far as
possible, put into requisition. We may rationally suppose that
he not only had the first of Israelitish scholars, such as Ethan
and Heman, but the most distinguished Egyptian and Phenician *savans*, for his tutors. The sacred historian expressly informs us that "Solomon's wisdom excelled the wisdom of all
the children of the east country (meaning probably the Chaldeans) and all the wisdom of Egypt. For he was wiser than
all men; than Ethan the Ezrahite, and Heman, Chalcol, and
Darda, the sons of Mahol; and his fame was in all nations
round about. And he spake three thousand proverbs; and his
songs were a thousand and five. And he spake of trees, from
the cedar-tree that is in Lebanon, even unto the hyssop that
springeth out of the wall; he spake also of beasts, and of
fowl, and of creeping things, and of fishes. And there came
of all people (or nations) to hear the wisdom of Solomon,
from all kings of the earth, which had heard of his wis-

dom." It was from the valley of the Nile that civilzation traveled into Greece; and it was thither that such men as Pythagoras, Herodotus, and Plato resorted for instruction. But we are expressly told that the wisdom of Solomon excelled all the wisdom of Egypt in his day. Ambassadors came from other courts to listen to his wisdom, and report to their sovereigns. In addition to his proverbs and lyrics, in which departments he appears to have been a copious writer, his acquaintance with natural history was most extensive and accurate. He was able more perfectly than any preceding philosopher to explain the laws and processes " which govern and distinguish the tribes, classes, families, and habits of the vegetable and animal creation." He possessed talents of the first order, and his natural faculties had received the highest cultivation. " He possessed," it has been truly said, " more accurate and extensive knowledge, on an immense variety of subjects, than any other mere man in any age or nation of the world." " He had a mind," says Bishop Patrick, " very comprehensive of all sorts of knowledge, and a heart to do a vast deal of good." He possessed not only knowledge, but wisdom; two things which are quite distinct. That is, he was possessed not only of learning, but of practical wisdom, a knowledge of mankind, and of the most effective way of employing his talents for the general good. He had not only Heman and Ethan, and Chaldean, and Egyptian philosophers for his tutors, God himself was his instructor. " God gave him wisdom and understanding exceeding much, and largeness of heart, even as the sand that is on the sea-shore." Soon after the commencement of his reign, God appeared to him at Gibeon, and said, " Ask what I shall give thee !" The young monarch did not ask for long life, nor for riches and power, nor for the destruction of his enemies. He said, " I am but a little child: I know not how to go out or come in." He asked for wisdom, or an understanding heart. God was well pleased, and granted his request. " I have given thee a wise and understanding heart; so that there was none like thee before thee, neither after thee shall any arise like unto thee. And I have also given thee that which thou hast not asked, both riches and honour." The practical wisdom or the understanding heart, for which Solomon prayed, was very soon called into exercise, in judging between the two women who appeared before him, with a living and a dead infant, each claiming the living one as her own. He directed a sword to be brought, and commanded one of his officers to sever the child in two, and give half to each claimant; instantly the affection of the true mother pointed her out to the king.

THE EARLY PIETY OF SOLOMON.

He had been favoured with the pious, though far from perfect example of his illustrious father, who had been careful to instruct him most religiously. The prophets and pious priests, it is fair to presume, took the deepest interest in his religious education. When David was about to resign the throne to him, he addressed a most affectionate and earnest exhortation to him to know the God of his father, and to serve him with a perfect heart, and a willing mind; adding, "If thou seek him, he will be found by thee; but if thou forsake him, he will cast thee off forever." These instructions and entreaties, it is evident, were not lost upon the prince. His marriage, shortly after he ascended the throne, with an Egyptian princess, is not to be interpreted, as has sometimes been done, to his disadvantage. If we are to suppose that he resided in Egypt for a season, in the process of his education, we may also suppose that he then became acquainted with this princess, and that, through his instruction and influence, she embraced the religion of Israel. Immediately after his marriage, it is distinctly mentioned that "Solomon loved the Lord, walking in the statutes of David his father." On the altar in Gibeon, a favourite place of worship, he offered a thousand burnt-offerings. It was there that God appeared to him in a vision, saying,

"Ask what I shall give thee," and, in answer to his prayer, promised to give him an understanding heart. The zeal with which he prosecuted the great work of building the temple, and ordering its worship, attests the earnestness of his early piety. Read his prayer at the dedication of the temple. The ark had been deposited in the designated place, and the priests had withdrawn from the apartment. On the east of the altar the vast choir had taken its station, all of them dressed in white linen. One hundred and twenty priests, with silver trumpets, stood with them. When they sounded, the voices of the multitude were lifted, accompanied with cymbals, psalteries, and harps:

"PRAISE THE LORD FOR HE IS GOOD;
FOR HIS MERCY ENDURETH FOREVER."

Suddenly a cloud of glory, the symbol of the presence of DEITY, filled the temple, so that the priests could not stand to minister because of the cloud. The king addressed the people, recapitulating the leading events in the erection of the edifice, and then, ascending the brazen platform, prepared for the occasion, offered his sublime and memorable prayer of dedication. At the close of the solemn benediction he pronounced on the people, there was another manifestation of the Divine presence. Fire descended from heaven, and consumed to ashes the sacrifices which had been prepared and laid upon the altars. Thus did God signify his acceptance of the temple of Solomon, and of the nation, in this great public transaction.

SOLOMON'S POWER AND THE EXTENT OF HIS DOMINION.

David, as before observed, had quelled the enemies of the nation, and made several of them tributary to his kingdom. Syria, Moab, and Ammon, were little more than provinces of Israel. Solomon succeeded to the same power. The territory over which he swayed the sceptre, extended eastwardly to the Euphrates, westwardly to the shores of the Mediterranean, and southwardly to the frontiers of Egypt, in breadth about three hundred, and in length four hundred miles. David having been severely punished for taking a census of the people, no census was taken during the reign of Solomon; and therefore it is impossible to state the actual population of the country; but we are told that "it was like the sand which is by the sea in multitude." The national importance of the Israelitish nation, during the reign of Solomon, appears from his commercial treaties, and the enterprises he carried on in connection with the Tyrians, the great maritime people of early antiquity. He had control of the trade of the immense caravans from India, which annually traversed the desert to the Euphrates; and by way of the Red Sea he had access to the precious metals and rare productions of the east African coast. He made a treaty with Hiram, by which he undertook, conjointly with the Tyrians, an expedition from Ezion-Geber on the Red Sea, through the straits of Babel-Mandel to Ophir. The articles of commerce which were brought from Ophir, were gold and silver, sandal-wood, precious stones, ivory, apes, and peacocks. It would appear highly probable that the Phenicians must have visited the western coasts of the Indian peninsula. But as it appears difficult to form an idea of western India as a fruitful source of gold, it is probable that these expeditions visited southern Arabia, and the auriferous coast of Sofala, in eastern Africa. The inhabitants of India from the earliest times had made settlements in the eastern part of Africa, and on the coast immediately opposite the coasts of their native country; and the traders to Ophir might have found in the basin of the Erythreian and Indian Seas other sources of gold besides India itself.*

WEALTH OF SOLOMON.

He appears to have been greatly enriched by his foreign trade. It is probable that commerce had never been carried

* See Humboldt's Cosmos, vol. ii., pp. 137, 138. Harp. Ed.

on before on so grand a scale. Pharaoh, his father-in-law, appears to have reserved to him, to the exclusion of other nations, the advantages of the lucrative trade of Egypt. Subject princes, the governors of provinces, and merchants, paid him a heavy tribute, and a large revenue flowed from ordinary taxes, payable in gold and silver, in articles of luxury, armour, and rich stuffs for clothing and ornament. Of course it is impossible to attach a specific value to these various commodities. The gold amounted to 666 talents in a year, exclusive of the tribute paid by traders and foreign princes. It is difficult, if not impossible, to reduce this sum to modern currency, with accuracy; but those who have made the subject a study inform us that the value of this single item of Solomon's revenue was not less than $25,000,000. The king had two hundred targets and three hundred shields, all of wrought gold, provided for his body-guard. One author estimates his daily income at nearly $2,000,000. The nation at large appears to have shared in the great wealth of their monarch. A very large proportion of his vast revenues was derived from ordinary taxation, as well as from the immense contributions of the people to the public works. It is also expressly stated that the king made silver at Jerusalem as plenty as stones. The ruins of those ancient cities, which still excite the wonder of travelers in oriental countries, attest the almost boundless wealth of Solomon, and the people over whom he wielded the sceptre. Palmyra or Tadmour of the desert, was situated in the midst of the Syrian desert. It now lies in ruins; but the broken columns and immense stones which lie scattered over the ground, afford evidence of its former magnificence. Baalbec lies at the base of Mount Lebanon. Of its ruins, in comparison with those of ancient cities in Greece and Egypt, travelers assert that "we can not help thinking of them as the remains of the boldest plan that appears ever to have been attempted in architecture." On the sites of these ancient cities may doubtless be seen some of the stones which were shaped and hewn by the masons whom Solomon employed.

But the greatest of the public works, that which affords the best evidence of the resources of his kingdom, was the Temple at Jerusalem, the building of which was specially to signalize his reign, and spread his fame in the earth. Large portions of the sacred edifice were literally overlaid with gold and silver; and in addition to the time occupied in collecting the materials, its construction occupied between seven and eight years.

The Royal State of Solomon.

Surveying his palace, we should have seen a building composed of stones, massive and beautiful beyond precedent. They were "hewed stones, sawed with saws within and without." Josephus informs us that "the walls of the palace were wainscoted with sawn stones, or slabs of great value, such as are dug out of the earth for the ornaments of the temples, or to make fine prospects in royal palaces and so beautiful and curious are they as to make the mines whence they are dug, famous." Had we entered that palace in the retinue of the Queen of Sheba, who came in great state to Jerusalem, to hear the wisdom of Solomon, we should have beheld a scene of splendour which perhaps has had no parallel in any age or country. We should have seen the ministers of the king in their splendid robes, his body-guard in their costly armour, with their targets and shields of gold, the vessels for domestic use of the same precious metal—silver being too common and cheap a material for such a purpose. 1 Kings x. 21. We should have seen the most wonderful and imposing of all the structures connected with the palace, the THRONE, on which the king sat to give audience to the ambassadors, philosophers, and royal visitors of other countries. It was carved out of ivory, and overlaid with the purest gold. Two carved lions stood on either side, and twelve lions, such as had never been made in any other kingdom, stood on the steps leading up to the throne—six on either side. His resources enabled him to gratify every taste and appetite—to adorn his palace and his pleasure-grounds with all that luxury could desire, or art devise. To this he refers in Ecclesiastes: "I made me great works; I builded me houses; I planted me vineyards; I made me gardens and orchards; I made me pools of water," etc.

Solomon's Sin and Shame.

The luxury and splendour in which he lived, tended no doubt, as they do in the case of men in general, to beget effeminacy. But it is a strange spectacle to see one who had been so greatly honoured and beloved of God—a Jedediah—and employed in services so sacred, polluting himself with such vices and crimes, and bringing such disgrace on true religion. The painful story is briefly but honestly related on the pages of the Bible. Solomon became a dissolute man. He wearied of one pleasure after another, of one luxury after another, and finally he turned to the love of many strange women. He filled a harem, after the manner of other licentious monarchs of the East, with the women of the Moabites, Ammonites, Edomites, Zidonians, and Hittites. As every thing with him was on a grand scale—his cities, his palace, his throne, his entire establishment—so the means which he provided for sensual gratification were on the same liberal scale. "He had seven hundred wives, princesses, and three hundred concubines." As his head grew gray, his passions seemed to gather strength. His wives seduced him to idolatry. He went after Ashtoreth, the goddess of the Zidonians, and after Milcom, the abomination of the Ammonites. He built a high place for Chemosh, the idol of the Moabites, and for Moloch, another idol of the Ammonites. He burned incense, and sacrificed unto the idols of all his strange wives. He who had built God's temples, and his altars, now builds altars to Moloch and Chemosh. He who had offered a thousand burnt-offerings on the altar at Gibeon to the true God, now offers sacrifices to Ashtoreth and Milcom. How is the gold become dim, and the most fine gold changed! And Solomon, having reigned in Jerusalem forty years, slept with his fathers.

SOLOMON'S REPENTANCE.

But did he die without giving evidence of repentance? This has been thought, by some, to be a difficult question. Nothing is said of his repentance in Kings, and nothing of his idolatry in Chronicles. But we undoubtedly have the proof and monument of his repentance in the book of Ecclesiastes. The means, however, which awakened him to repentance, are sufficiently intimated by the inspired historian. "And the Lord was angry with Solomon, because his heart was turned from the Lord God of Israel, which appeared unto him twice, and had commanded him concerning this thing, that he should not go after other gods : but he kept not that which the Lord commanded. Wherefore the Lord said unto Solomon, Forasmuch as this is done of thee, and thou hast not kept my covenant, and my statutes, which I have commanded thee, I will surely rend the kingdom from thee, and will give it to thy servant. Notwithstanding, in thy days I will not do it, for David thy father's sake ; but I will rend it out of the hand of thy son." This threatening must have startled the sensual monarch ; he was reminded of God's early favour toward him, and of his youthful piety. It could not have failed to arrest him in his sinful career. It must have been a most poignant thought to him, that, on account of his sin, all the kingdom, save one tribe—spared not for his sake, but for David's sake— was to be wrested out of his son's hand, and given to a servant. But this threatening of future calamity was not the only means employed to awaken Solomon to reflection and repentance. The Lord stirred up adversaries against him, Hadad a prince of Edom, who had fled before the victorious Joab to Egypt, where he married the sister of the Queen, but had now returned to his own land, that he might be avenged on his conquerors ; Rezon, the King of Syria, who cherished a peculiar hatred to Israel : but Solomon had an enemy at home capable of doing him greater evil than all his foreign foes. This was Jeroboam the son of Nebat, a servant of the king. He had, on account of his fine talents, been promoted to an honourable office by his royal master ; but this only served to fan the flame of his ambition to be a king, and afforded him an excellent opportunity to plot against the government, and carry out his aspiring views. It must have proved a most bitter trial to him, one well suited to awaken him to repentance, that the man whom he had raised from a servile condition to a post of honour, should have lifted up his hand against him. The book of Ecclesiastes is just the production which we might have expected Solomon would pen in the state of mind produced by the Divine threatening, and these adverse events. It becomes therefore a book of the greatest interest, as the work of a man of threescore years, who had enjoyed the greatest worldly prosperity, who fell into great sin, the evening of whose days was marked by some mortifying reverses, and the most bitter, heartfelt repentance. It is of especial interest, because like the fifty-first Psalm of David, which, by reason of his eminent position, and grievous sin, it is the will of God should be read and sung in the Church to the latest ages, it records and perpetuates the repentance and confession of one whom God greatly honoured, and by whom he was greatly dishonoured. On this confession the author engrafts an admirable argument for a future judgment, and a state of rewards and punishments. At the outset, he seems to admit for the sake of argument, the monstrous doctrine of the skeptic, or the implied position of the thoughtless worldling, whose conduct is an emphatic disavowal of belief in a future state, and then employs the *argumentum ex absurdo*, with overwhelming effect: " All is vanity," or would indeed be vanity, if there be no hereafter, if life has no higher end than sensual or worldly pleasure; and at length arrives at the conclusion of the whole matter; "Fear God, and keep his commandments; for this is the whole duty of man. For God shall bring every work into judgment, with every secret thing, whether it be good, or whether it be evil." The subject of the entire book may be expressed in a single sentence thus; (comp. Eccl. i. 2, with xii. 13, 14.)

It is that great day when "God shall bring every work into judgment," which alone redeems "all" things—man and his affairs, and the world in which he spends his brief existence—from being regarded as an inexplicable mystery, or as the greatest "vanity" imaginable.

ECCLESIASTES; OR, THE PREACHER.

CHAPTER I.

1 *The Preacher sheweth that all human courses are vain: 4 because the creatures are restless in their courses, 9 they bring forth nothing new, and all old things are forgotten, 12 and because he hath found it so in the studies of wisdom.*

THE words of the Preacher, the son of David, king in Jerusalem.

2 Vanity of vanities, saith the Preacher, vanity of vanities; all *is* vanity.

3 What profit hath a man of all his labour which he taketh under the sun?

4 *One* generation passeth away, and *another* generation cometh: but the earth abideth for ever.

5 The sun also ariseth, and the sun goeth down, and hasteth [*panteth*] to his place where he arose.

6 The wind goeth toward the south, and turneth about unto the north; it whirleth about continually, and the wind returneth again according to his circuits.

All things would be vanity, if life had no higher object than present worldly happiness, and God had not appointed a day in which to rectify the inequalities of Providence which distinguish the present state. Ch. i. 2—ch. xii. 13, 14,

THE words of the Preacher, [Convener,] the son of David, king in Jerusalem.

Vanity of vanities, saith the Preacher, vanity of vanities; all is vanity.

What profit hath a man from all his labour, in which he toils under the sun.

A generation goeth off, and a generation cometh on: while the earth abideth forever.

The sun ariseth, and the sun goeth down, and panteth to the place where it ariseth: it goeth to the south, and turneth about unto the north.

The wind whirleth and whirleth about, and returneth to its circuits.

7 All the rivers run into the sea; yet the sea *is* not full: unto the place from whence the rivers come, thither they return [*return to go*] again.

8 All things *are* full of labour; men cannot utter *it:* the eye is not satisfied with seeing, nor the ear filled with hearing.

9 The thing that hath been, it *is that* which shall be; and that which is done *is* that which shall be done: and *there is* no new *thing* under the sun.

10 Is there *any* thing whereof it may be said, See, this *is* new? it hath been already of old time, which was before us.

11 *There is* no remembrance of former *things;* neither shall there be *any* remembrance of *things* that are to come with *those* that shall come after.

12 ¶ I the Preacher was king over Israel in Jerusalem.

13 And I gave my heart to seek and search out by wisdom concerning all *things* that are done under heaven: this sore travail hath God given to the sons of man [*to afflict them*] to be exercised therewith.

14 I have seen all the works that are done under the sun: and behold, all *is* vanity and vexation of spirit.

All the rivers run into the sea, yet the sea is not full; unto the place whence the rivers come, thither they return again.

All things are full of labour, no man can express it; the eye is not satisfied with seeing, nor the ear filled with hearing.

The thing that hath been that will be; and that which hath been done, that will be done; and there is no new thing under the sun.

Is there any thing concerning which one may say, "See, this is new?" It hath been long ago in ancient times which were before us.

There is no remembrance of former things, and of things that are to come there shall be no remembrance among those who shall live afterwards.

I, the Preacher, was king over Israel in Jerusalem.

And I gave my heart to seek, and search out, by wisdom, concerning all things which are done under heaven,—this difficult employment which God hath given to the sons of men, that they may busy themselves therein.

I surveyed all things which are done under the sun; and, behold, all are vanity and a fruitless striving after wind.

15 *That which is* crooked cannot be made straight: and [*defect*] that which is wanting cannot be numbered.

16 I communed with mine own heart, saying, Lo, I am come to great estate, and have gotten more wisdom than all *they* that have been before me in Jerusalem: yea, my heart [*had seen much*] had great experience of wisdom and knowledge.

17 And I gave my heart to know wisdom, and to know madness and folly: I perceived that this also is vexation of spirit.

18 For in much wisdom *is* much grief: and he that increaseth knowledge increaseth sorrow.

CHAPTER II.

1 *The vanity of human courses in the works of pleasure.* 12 *Though the wise be better than the fool, yet both have one event.* 18 *The vanity of human labour, in leaving it they know not to whom.* 24 *Nothing better than joy in our labour; but that is God's gift.*

I SAID in mine heart, Go to now, I will prove thee with mirth; therefore enjoy pleasure: and behold, this also *is* vanity.

2 I said of laughter, *It is* mad: and of mirth, What doeth it?

3 I sought in mine heart [*to draw my flesh with wine*] to give

That which is crooked cannot be made straight: and that which is wanting cannot be numbered.

I communed with my own heart, saying, Lo, I have increased and added to wisdom more than all who have been before me in Jerusalem; yea my heart has much considered wisdom and knowledge.

And I gave my heart to know wisdom, and to know madness and folly : I perceived that this also is striving after wind.

For in much wisdom is much dissatisfaction, and he that increaseth knowledge increaseth sorrow.

I SAID in my heart, Come now, I will try thee with mirth, and do thou enjoy good, and behold this also was vanity.

Of laughter I said, It is mad: and of pleasure, What avails it?

I resolved to stimulate my body with wine and to lay hold

myself unto wine, yet acquainting mine heart with wisdom; and to lay hold on folly, till I might see what *was* that good for the sons of men, which they should do under the heaven [*the number of the days of their life*] all the days of their life.

4 I made me great works; I builded me houses; I planted me vineyards:

5 I made me gardens and orchards, and I planted trees in them of all *kind of* fruits:

6 I made me pools of water, to water therewith the wood that bringeth forth trees:

7 I got *me* servants and maidens, and had [*sons of my house*] servants born in my house; also I had great possessions of great and small cattle above all that were in Jerusalem before me;

8 I gathered me also silver and gold, and the peculiar treasure of kings and of the provinces: I gat me men-singers and women-singers, and the delights of the sons of men, *as* [*musical instrument and instruments*] musical instruments, and that of all sorts.

9 So I was great, and increased more than all that were before me in Jerusalem: also my wisdom remained with me.

10 And whatsoever mine

on folly, while my mind should still continue to guide with wisdom; until I should see whether this is the good for the sons of men, which they should pursue under heaven, all the days of their life.

I made me great works; I builded me houses; I planted me vineyards.

I made me gardens and pleasure-grounds, in which I planted fruit-trees of every kind.

I made me reservoirs from which to water the grove, producing trees.

I purchased servants and maidens, and had servants born in my house; and much wealth in herds and cattle belonged to me, more than all who were before me in Jerusalem.

I amassed for myself also silver and gold and the treasures of kings and the provinces; I procured for myself men-singers and women-singers, and the delights of the sons of men—musical instruments and that of all sorts.

So I waxed great and increased more than all that were before me in Jerusalem: my wisdom also remained with me.

And whatever my eyes de-

eyes desired I kept not from them, I withheld not my heart from any joy; for my heart rejoiced in all my labour: and this was my portion of all my labour.

11 Then I looked on all the works that my hands had wrought, and on the labour that I had laboured to do: and behold, all *was* vanity and vexation of spirit, and *there was* no profit under the sun.

12 ¶ And I turned myself to behold wisdom, and madness, and folly: for what *can* the man *do* that cometh after the king? [*in those things which have been already done*] ev n that which hath been already done.

13 Then I saw [*that there is an excellency in wisdom more than in folly, &c.*] that wisdom excelleth folly, as far as light excelleth darkness.

14 The wise man's eyes *are* in his head; but the fool walketh in darkness: and I myself perceived also that one event happeneth to them all.

15 Then said I in my heart, As it happeneth to the fool, so it [*happeneth to me, even to me*] happeneth even to me; and why was I then more wise? Then I said in my heart, that this also *is* vanity.

16 For *there is* no remembrance of the wise more than

sired I kept not from them, I withheld not my heart from any joy; for my heart rejoiced in all my labour, and this was my portion from all my labour.

Then I surveyed all my works which my hands had wrought, and the labour which I had toiled in performing: and behold it was all vanity and striving after wind and there was no profit under the sun.

Then I turned myself to consider wisdom and madness and folly: for what can the man do that cometh after the king? even that which has been already done.

And I saw that wisdom excelleth folly, as far as light excelleth darkness.

The wise man's eyes are in his head; but the fool walketh in darkness, yet still I myself perceived also that one event happeneth to all.

Then I said in my heart, As it happeneth to the fool, so it happeneth to me; then why was I more wise? Then I said in my heart that this also is vanity.

For there is no remembrance of the wise man more than of

of the fool for ever; seeing that which now *is* in the days to come shall all be forgotten. And how dieth the wise *man?* as the fool.

17 Therefore I hated life; because the work that is wrought under the sun *is* grievous unto me: for all *is* vanity and vexation of spirit.

18 ¶ Yea, I hated all my labour which I had [*laboured*] taken under the sun: because I should leave it unto the man that shall be after me.

19 And who knoweth whether he shall be a wise *man* or a fool? yet shall he have rule over all my labour wherein I have laboured, and wherein I have shewed myself wise under the sun. This *is* also vanity.

20 Therefore I went about to cause my heart to despair of all the labour which I took under the sun.

21 For there is a man whose labour *is* in wisdom, and in knowledge, and in equity; yet to a man that hath not laboured therein shall he [*give*] leave it *for* his portion. This also *is* vanity and a great evil.

22 For what hath man of all his labour, and of the vexation of his heart, wherein he hath laboured under the sun?

the fool for ever; seeing that in the days to come shall all that now is be forgotten. And how dieth the wise man? as the fool.

Therefore I hated life because what is done under the sun appeared evil unto me; for all is vanity and striving after wind.

Yea, I hated all my labour which I had performed under the sun; which I should leave to the man who shall be after me.

And who knoweth whether he shall be a wise man or a fool? And yet shall he have dominion over all my work in which I have toiled, and which I have wisely performed under the sun. This also is vanity.

Then I came even to give up my heart to despair in respect to all my work in which I had toiled under the sun.

For there is a man whose labour hath been with wisdom, and knowledge, and gratifying success; but to a man who hath bestowed no labour on it, he must leave it as his portion. This also is vanity and a great evil.

For what hath man of all his labours and the chafing of his spirit, with which he wearies himself under the sun.

23 For all his days *are* sorrows, and his travail grief; yea, his heart taketh not rest in the night. This is also vanity.

24 ¶ *There is* nothing better for a man *than* that he should eat and drink, and *that* he should make his soul enjoy good in his labour. This also I saw, that it *was* from the hand of God.

25 For who can eat, or who else can hasten *hereunto* more than I?

26 For *God* giveth to a man that *is* good [*before him*] in his sight, wisdom, and knowledge, and joy: but to the sinner he giveth travail, to gather and to heap up, that he may give to *him that is* good before God. This also *is* vanity and vexation of spirit.

CHAPTER III.

1 *By the necessary change of times, vanity is added to human travail.* 11 *There is an excellency in God's works.* 16 *But as for man, God shall judge his works there, and here he shall be like a beast.*

TO every *thing there is* a season, and a time to every purpose under the heaven:

2 A time [*to bear*] to be born, and a time to die; a time to plant, and a time to pluck up *that which is* planted;

3 A time to kill, and a time to

For all his days are sorrows, and his business a vexation; yea, his heart findeth not rest in the night. This also is vanity.

There is no good for a man unless he should eat and drink, and let his soul enjoy good in his labour. Even this, I have seen, comes from the hand of God.

For who can feast, and who can enjoy himself more than I.

For to the man who is well pleasing in his sight God giveth wisdom, and knowledge, and joy; but to the sinner he giveth the unsatisfying toil of gathering and amassing, that he may give it to him who is well pleasing in the sight of God. This also is vanity and grasping at wind.

TO every thing there is a fixed season, and an appointed time to every event under heaven.

There is a time of being born, and a time of dying; a time of planting and a time of plucking up that which is planted.

A time of killing, and a time

heal; a time to break down, and a time to build up;

4 A time to weep, and a time to laugh; a time to mourn, and a time to dance;

5 A time to cast away stones, and a time to gather stones together; a time to embrace, and a time [*to be far from*] to refrain from embracing;

6 A time [*to seek*] to get, and a time to lose; a time to keep, and a time to cast away;

7 A time to rend, and a time to sew; a time to keep silence, and a time to speak;

8 A time to love, and a time to hate; a time of war, and a time of peace.

9 What profit hath he that worketh in that wherein he laboureth?

10 I have seen the travail, which God hath given to the sons of men to be exercised in it.

11 He hath made every *thing* beautiful in his time: also he hath set the world in their heart, so that no man can find out the work that God maketh from the beginning to the end.

12 I know that *there is* no good in them, but for *a man* to rejoice, and to do good in his life.

13 And also that every man should eat and drink, and enjoy

of healing; a time of demolishing, and a time of building.

A time of weeping, and a time of laughing; a time of mourning, and a time of dancing.

A time of casting abroad stones, and a time of collecting them together; a time of embracing and a time of abstaining from embracing.

A time of seeking, and a time of losing; a time of keeping, and a time of casting away.

A time of rending, and a time of sewing; a time of keeping silence, and a time of speaking.

A time of loving, and a time of hating; a time of war, and a time of peace.

What profit hath the toiler from that in which he toils?

I have surveyed the allotment which God hath assigned to the sons of men to be exercised therewith.

He hath made every thing beautiful in its time; also he hath put eternity in their heart, without which no man can find out the work which God doeth from the beginning to the end.

I know that there is no good in them, but for a man to rejoice, and enjoy good during his life.

And moreover [I know] that as often as any man eats and

the good of all his labour; it *is* the gift of God.

14 I know that, whatsoever God doeth, it shall be for ever; nothing can be put to it, nor any thing taken from it: and God doeth *it*, that *men* should fear before him.

15 That which hath been is now; and that which is to be hath already been; and God requireth [*that which is driven away*] that which is past.

16 ¶ And moreover I saw under the sun the place of judgment, *that* wickedness *was* there; and the place of righteousness, *that* iniquity *was* there.

17 I said in mine heart, God shall judge the righteous and the wicked: for *there is* a time there for every purpose and for every work.

18 I said in mine heart concerning the estate of the sons of men, [*that they might clear God and see*] that God might manifest them, and that they might see that they themselves are beasts.

19 For that which befalleth the sons of men befalleth beasts; even one thing befalleth them: as the one dieth, so dieth the other; yea, they have all one breath; so that a man hath no pre-eminence above a beast: for all *is* vanity.

20 All go unto one place; all

drinks and enjoys the good of all his labour, it is the gift of God.

I know that all which God doeth shall be for eternity; nothing can be added to it, nor any thing taken from it; and God doeth it that men may fear before him.

That which hath been is now; and that which is to be hath already been; and God seeketh out that which is past.

Moreover, I saw under the sun that in the place of judgment iniquity was there, and in the place of justice, injustice was there.

I said in my heart, God will judge the righteous and the wicked; since there is a time appointed for every purpose and every work.

I said in my heart (this happens) on account of the sons of men that God might search them and make them see that left to themselves they are beasts.

For as to the lot of men, and the lot of beasts, one and the same lot befalleth them; as the one dieth so dieth the other, and there is one breath to all; and there is no pre-eminence of man above a beast; for all is vanity.

All go unto one place; all are

AUTHORIZED VERSION.

are of the dust, and all turn to dust again.

21 Who knoweth the spirit [*of the sons of man*] of man that [*is ascending*] goeth upward, and the spirit of the beast that goeth downward to the earth?

22 Wherefore I perceive that *there is* nothing better, than that a man should rejoice in his own works; for that *is* his portion: for who shall bring him to see what shall be after him?

CHAPTER IV.

1 *Vanity is increased unto men by oppression,* 4 *by envy,* 5 *by idleness,* 7 *by covetousness,* 9 *by solitariness,* 13 *by wilfulness.*

SO I returned, and considered all the oppressions that are done under the sun: and behold the tears of *such as were* oppressed, and they had no comforter; and on the [*hand*] side of their oppressors *there was* power; but they had no comforter.

2 Wherefore I praised the dead which are already dead more than the living which are yet alive.

3 Yea, better *is he* than both they, which hath not yet been, who hath not seen the evil work that is done under the sun.

4 ¶ Again, I considered all travail, and [*all the righteousness*

REVISED VERSION.

of the dust and all return to dust again.

Who knoweth whether the spirit of the sons of men goeth upward (to God) and the spirit of beasts, whether it goeth downward to the earth?

Then I saw that there is nothing better than that a man should rejoice in such actions as please him; for that is his inheritance: for who shall bring him to see what shall be after him?

THEN I turned and surveyed all the oppressions which are done under the sun; and behold, the tears of the oppressed! and they had no avenger; and from the hand of their oppressors, there was violence, but to them no avenger.

Therefore I pronounced the dead happy, who have been long since dead, more than the living, who are yet alive.

Yea, better off than both of them is he, who doth not yet exist, who hath not seen the evil work which is done under the sun.

Again I saw that all toil, and every successful enterprise, that

of work] every right work, that [*this* is *the envy of a man from his neighbour*] for this a man is envied of his neighbour. This *is* also vanity and vexation of spirit.

5 The fool foldeth his hands together, and eateth his own flesh.

6 Better *is* an handful *with* quietness, than both the hands full *with* travail and vexation of spirit.

7 ¶ Then I returned, and I saw vanity under the sun.

8 There is one *alone*, and *there is* not a second; yea, he hath neither child nor brother: yet *is there* no end of all his labour; neither is his eye satisfied with riches: neither *saith he*, For whom do I labour, and bereave my soul of good? This *is* also vanity, yea, it *is* a sore travail.

9 ¶ Two *are* better than one; because they have a good reward for their labour.

10 For if they fall, the one will lift up his fellow: but woe to him *that is* alone when he falleth; for *he hath* not another to help him up.

11 Again, if two lie together, then they have heat: but how can one be warm *alone?*

12 And if one prevail against him, two shall withstand him;

for this a man is envied by his fellows. This also is vanity and grasping at wind.

The fool foldeth his hands together, and eateth his own flesh; (saying),

Better is a handful with quietness, than both the hands full of toil and striving after wind.

Then I turned and saw another vanity under the sun.

There is one alone and no one with him; yea he hath neither son nor brother; yet there is no end to all his toil; neither are his eyes satisfied with riches; neither saith he, For whom do I toil, and bereave my soul of good? This also is vanity, yea it is an evil thing.

Two are better than one; because they have a good reward for their labour.

For if they fall, the one shall lift up his fellow; but woe to him who is alone, when he falleth, and hath not another to lift him up!

Again, if two lie together, then they have warmth; but how can one be warm alone?

And if one prevail against one, two shall withstand him; and a and a threefold cord is not quickly broken.

13 ¶ Better *is* a poor and a wise child, than an old and foolish king, [*who knoweth not to be admonished*] who will no more be admonished.

14 For out of prison he cometh to reign; whereas also *he that is* born in his kingdom becometh poor.

15 I considered all the living which walk under the sun, with the second child that shall stand up in his stead.

16 *There is* no end of all the people, *even* of all that have been before them: they also that come after shall not rejoice in him. Surely this also *is* vanity and vexation of spirit.

CHAPTER V.

1 *Vanities in divine service,* 8 *in murmuring against oppression,* 9 *and in riches.* 18 *Joy in riches is the gift of God.*

KEEP thy foot when thou goest to the house of God, and be more ready to hear, than to give the sacrifice of fools: for they consider not that they do evil.

2 Be not rash with thy mouth, and let not thine heart be hasty to utter *any* [*word*] thing before God: for God *is* in heaven, and thou upon earth: therefore let thy words be few.

threefold cord is not quickly broken.

Better is a youth, poor and wise, than a king old and foolish, who will not any more be counseled.

For from the house of captives he comes forth to reign; whereas, even in his own kingdom, he was born a poor man.

I saw all the living, who walk under the sun with the young man, the second, who stood up in his stead.

There was no end to all the people before whom he went forth; yet they that come afterward shall not rejoice in him. Yea, this also is vanity and grasping at wind.

KEEP thy foot when thou goest to the house of God; and it is better to draw nigh to hear than to offer the sacrifice of fools; for they know not that they do evil.

Be not rash with thy mouth, and let not thy heart be swift to utter a thing before God: for God is in heaven, and thou upon earth; therefore let thy words be few.

3 For a dream cometh through the multitude of business; and a fool's voice *is known* by multitude of words.

4 When thou vowest a vow unto God, defer not to pay it; for *he hath* no pleasure in fools: pay that which thou hast vowed.

5 Better *is it* that thou shouldest not vow, than that thou shouldest vow and not pay.

6 Suffer not thy mouth to cause thy flesh to sin; neither say thou before the angel, that it *was* an error; wherefore should God be angry at thy voice, and destroy the work of thine hands?

7 For in the multitude of dreams and many words *there are* also *divers* vanities: but fear thou God.

8 ¶ If thou seest the oppression of the poor, and violent perverting of judgment and justice in a province, marvel not [*at the will*, or, *purpose*] at the matter: for *he that is* higher than the highest regardeth; and *there be* higher than they.

9 ¶ Moreover, the profit of the earth is for all: the king *himself* is served by the field.

10 He that loveth silver shall not be satisfied with silver; nor he that loveth abundance with increase: this *is* also vanity.

11 When goods increase, they

For a dream cometh through much business; and a fool's voice is known by a multitude of words.

When thou vowest a vow to God defer not to pay it; for he hath no pleasure in fools: that which thou hast vowed, pay.

It is better not to vow, than to vow and not to perform.

Let not thy mouth expose thy flesh to punishment; neither say before the angel, that it was a mistake; wherefore should God be angry on account of thy utterance, and destroy the work of thy hands.

For in a multitude of dreams there are indeed vanities; so also in a multitude of words; but fear thou God.

If thou seest the oppression of the poor, and perversion of judgment and justice in a province, be not disturbed on account of this; for over the high officer, a higher one watches, and over both of them the highest ONE.

Moreover, the profit of the land is for all; the king is served by the field.

He that loveth silver shall not be satisfied with silver; nor he that loveth abundance with increase. This is also vanity.

When property is increased,

are increased that eat them; and what good *is there* to the owners thereof, saving the beholding *of them* with their eyes?

12 The sleep of a labouring man *is* sweet, whether he eat little or much: but the abundance of the rich will not suffer him to sleep.

13 There is a sore evil *which* I have seen under the sun, *namely*, riches kept for the owners thereof to their hurt.

14 But those riches perish by evil travail: and he begetteth a son, and *there is* nothing in his hand.

15 As he came forth of his mother's womb, naked shall he return to go as he came, and shall take nothing of his labour, which he may carry away in his hand.

16 And this also *is* a sore evil, *that* in all points as he came, so shall he go: and what profit hath he that hath laboured for the wind?

17 All his days also he eateth in darkness, and *he hath* much sorrow and wrath with his sickness.

18 ¶ Behold *that* which I have seen: [*there is a good which is comely, &c.*] *it is* good and comely *for one* to eat and to drink, and to enjoy the good of all his labour that he taketh

they are increased who consume it: and what profit is there to the owners thereof, save the beholding of it with their eyes?

The sleep of the labouring man is sweet, whether he eat little or much; but the superabundance of the rich will not suffer him to sleep.

There is a sore evil which I have seen under the sun, riches kept to the hurt of the owner thereof.

And those riches perish in fruitless speculations, and he hath begotten a son, and there is nothing in his hand.

As he came forth from his mother's womb, naked shall he return, so that he may depart as he came, and shall take nothing of his labour which he may carry away in his hand.

And this also is a sore evil, that in all points as he came, so shall he go: and what profit is there to him who hath toiled for the wind?

All his days also he consumes in darkness, and in much vexation, infirmity, and irritation.

Behold what I have seen which is good and comely! to eat and drink, and enjoy the good of all one's labour, which he takes under the sun all the days of his life, which God

under the sun [*the number of the days*] all the days of his life, which God giveth him: for it *is* his portion.

19 Every man also to whom God hath given riches and wealth, and hath given him power to eat thereof, and to take his portion, and to rejoice in his labour; this *is* the gift of God.

20 For he shall not much remember the days of his life; because God answereth *him* in the joy of his heart.

CHAPTER VI.

1 *The vanity of riches without use.* 3 *Of children,* 6 *and old age without riches.* 9 *The vanity of sight and wandering desires.* 11 *The conclusion of vanities.*

THERE is an evil which I have seen under the sun, and it *is* common among men:

2 A man to whom God hath given riches, wealth, and honour, so that he wanted nothing for his soul of all that he desireth, yet God giveth him not power to eat thereof, but a stranger eateth it: this *is* vanity, and it *is* an evil disease.

3 ¶ If a man beget an hundred *children*, and live many years, so that the days of his years be many, and his soul be not filled with good, and also *that* he have no burial; I say,

giveth him; for it is his portion.

Moreover, if to any man God hath given riches and wealth, he hath given him also to enjoy them and take his portion, and to rejoice in his labour; this is the gift of God.

For he will not much remember the days of his life, when God answereth to the joy of his heart.

THERE is an evil which I have seen under the sun which presses heavily upon men;

A man to whom God hath given riches, wealth and honour; neither doth he lack any thing which he desireth; yet God giveth him not power to eat thereof, but another eateth it. This is vanity, and a sore evil.

If a man beget a hundred children and live many years, so that the days of his years be many, and moreover there be no burial to him, and his soul be not satisfied with good;

that an untimely birth *is* better than he.

4 For he cometh in with vanity, and departeth in darkness, and his name shall be covered with darkness.

5 Moreover he hath not seen the sun, nor known *any thing :* this hath more rest than the other.

6 ¶ Yea, though he live a thousand years twice *told*, yet hath he seen no good: do not all go to one place?

7 All the labour of man *is* for his mouth, and yet the [*soul*] appetite is not filled.

8 For what hath the wise more than the fool? what hath the poor, that knoweth to walk before the living?

9 ¶ Better *is* the sight of the eyes [*than the walking of the soul*] than the wandering of the desire: this *is* also vanity and vexation of spirit.

10 That which hath been is named already, and it is known that it *is* man: neither may he contend with him that is mightier than he.

11 ¶ Seeing there be many things that increase vanity, what *is* man the better?

12 For who knoweth what *is* good for man in *this* life, [*the*

I say that an untimely birth is better than he.

For this cometh in vanity and departeth in darkness, and its name is concealed in darkness:

Moreover it hath not seen the sun, nor known; this hath rest rather than the other.

Yea, though he live a thousand years twice told, and see no good: do not all go to one place?

All the labour of man is for his mouth, and yet the appetite is not satisfied.

What advantage, then, is there to the wise man over the fool? What hath the poor who knoweth how to walk before the living?

Better is the sight of the eyes than the wandering of desire. This is also vanity and striving after wind.

That which hath been—his name hath already been pronounced, and it is known that he is a man, and that he can not contend with Him who is mightier than he.

Seeing there are many things which increase vanity, what advantage hath man?

For who knoweth what is good for man all the days of his

number of the days of the life of his vanity] all the days of his vain life which he spendeth as a shadow ? for who can tell a man what shall be after him under the sun ?

CHAPTER VII.

1 *Remedies against vanity are, a good name,* 2 *mortification,* 7 *patience.* 11 *wisdom.* 23 *The difficulty of getting wisdom.*

A GOOD name *is* better than precious ointment ; and the day of death than the day of one's birth.

2 ¶ *It is* better to go to the house of mourning, than to go to the house of feasting : for that *is* the end of all men ; and the living will lay *it* to his heart.

3 [*Anger*] Sorrow *is* better than laughter : for by the sadness of the countenance the heart is made better.

4 The heart of the wise *is* in the house of mourning ; but the heart of fools *is* in the house of mirth.

5 *It is* better to hear the rebuke of the wise, than for a man to hear the song of fools :

6 For as the [*sound*] crackling of thorns under a pot, so *is* the laughter of the fool : this also *is* vanity.

7 Surely oppression maketh a wise man mad ; and a gift destroyeth the heart.

vain life which he spendeth as a shadow ? for who can tell man what shall be after him under the sun ?

A GOOD name is better than precious ointment, and the day of one's death than the day of his birth.

It is better to go to the house of mourning, than to go to the house of feasting ; for that is the end of all men ; and the living will lay it to heart.

Sorrow is better than laughter ; for by the sadness of the countenance the heart is made better.

The heart of the wise is in the house of mourning ; but the heart of fools is in the house of mirth.

It is better for a man to hear the rebuke of the wise than to hear the song of fools.

For as the crackling of thorns under a pot, so is the laughter of the fool. This, also, is vanity.

Surely oppression maketh a wise man mad ; and a bribe corrupteth the heart.

8 Better *is* the end of a thing than the beginning thereof: *and* the patient in spirit *is* better than the proud in spirit.

9 Be not hasty in thy spirit to be angry: for anger resteth in the bosom of fools.

10 Say not thou, What is *the* cause that the former days were better than these ? for thou dost not inquire [*out of wisdom*] wisely concerning this.

11 Wisdom [*is as good as an inheritance, yea, better too*] *is* good with an inheritance : and *by it there is* profit to them that see the sun.

12 For wisdom *is* a [*shadow*] defence, *and* money *is* a defence : but the excellency of knowledge *is, that* wisdom giveth life to them that have it.

13 Consider the work of God : for who can make *that* straight, which he hath made crooked ?

14 In the day of prosperity be joyful, but in the day of adversity consider : God also hath [*made*] set the one over against the other, to the end that man should find nothing after him.

15 All *things* have I seen in the days of my vanity : there is a just *man* that perisheth in his righteousness, and there is a wicked *man* that prolongeth *his life* in his wickedness.

Better is the end of a thing than the beginning thereof: better is the patient in spirit than the proud in spirit.

Be not hasty in thy spirit to be angry ; for anger resteth in the bosom of fools.

Say not, Why is it that the former days were better than these ? for thou dost not inquire wisely concerning this.

Wisdom is good as well as an inheritance ; yea, it is better to them that see the sun.

For wisdom is a defence, and money is a defence ; but the excellence of wisdom is, that it giveth life to them that have it.

Consider the work of God ; for who can make that straight which he hath made crooked ?

In the day of prosperity be joyful, but look for the day of adversity ; for God hath set one over against the other, in order that man should not discover any thing which shall be after him.

All this have I considered in the days of my vanity ; there is a righteous man that perisheth in his righteousness, and there is a wicked man who liveth long in his wickedness.

16 Be not righteous over much; neither make thyself over wise: why shouldest thou [*be desolate*] destroy thyself?

17 Be not over much wicked, neither be thou foolish: why shouldest thou die [*not in thy time*] before thy time?

18 *It is* good that thou shouldest take hold of this; yea, also from this withdraw not thine hand: for he that feareth God shall come forth of them all.

19 Wisdom strengtheneth the wise man more than ten mighty *men* which are in the city.

20 For *there is* not a just man upon earth, that doeth good, and sinneth not.

21 Also [*give not thine heart*] take no heed unto all words that are spoken; lest thou hear thy servant curse thee:

22 For oftentimes also thine own heart knoweth that thou thyself likewise hast cursed others.

23 All this have I proved by wisdom. I said, I will be wise; but it *was* far from me.

24 That which is far off, and exceeding deep, who can find it out?

25 [*I and my heart compassed*] I applied mine heart to know, and to search, and to seek out wisdom, and the reason *of*

Be not righteous over much, neither make thyself over wise; why shouldest thou make thyself desolate?

Be not wicked over much; neither be thou a fool: why shouldest thou die before thy time?

It is good that thou shouldest take hold of this; yea also from that withdraw not thine hand: for he that feareth God shall come forth of them all.

Wisdom strengtheneth the wise more than ten mighty men who are in the city.

Truly there is not a just man upon earth who doeth good and sinneth not.

Moreover, give no heed unto all the words that are spoken; lest thou hear thy servant cursing thee.

For thine own heart also knoweth that oftentimes thou thyself hast cursed others.

All this have I tried by wisdom: I said, Let me become wise; but it was far from me.

That which is far off, and very deep, who can find it out?

I applied my heart to know, and to explore, and to seek out wisdom and intelligence, and to know wickedness and

things, and to know the wickedness of folly, even of foolishness *and* madness :

26 And I find more bitter than death the woman whose heart *is* snares and nets, *and* her hands *as* bands : [*he that is good before God*] whoso pleaseth God shall escape from her; but the sinner shall be taken by her.

27 Behold, this have I found, saith the Preacher [*weighing one thing after another, to find out the reason*], *counting* one by one, to find out the account;

28 Which yet my soul seeketh, but I find not; one man among a thousand have I found; but a woman among all those have I not found.

29 Lo, this only have I found, that God hath made man upright; but they have sought out many inventions.

CHAPTER VIII.

1 *Kings are greatly to be respected.* 6 *The divine providence is to be observed.* 12 *It is better with the godly in adversity, than with the wicked in prosperity.* 16 *The work of God is unsearchable.*

WHO *is* as the wise *man?* and who knoweth the interpretation of a thing? a man's wisdom maketh his face to shine, and [*the strength*] the boldness of his face shall be changed.

folly, even foolishness and madness.

And I found more bitter than death the woman whose heart is snares and nets, and her hands, bands; whoso pleaseth God shall be delivered from her; but the sinner shall be taken by her.

Behold, this I have found, saith the Preacher, adding one thing to another, to find out knowledge;

That which my soul perseveringly sought, I have not found; One man among a thousand have I found, but a woman among all these have I not found.

Lo, this only have I found, that God made man upright; but they have sought out many devices.

WHO is as the wise man who knoweth the explanation of a thing? A man's wisdom maketh his face to shine, but haughty arrogance disfigureth his countenance.

2 I *counsel thee* to keep the king's commandment, and *that* in regard of the oath of God.

3 Be not hasty to go out of his sight: stand not in an evil thing; for he doeth whatsoever pleaseth him.

4 Where the word of a king *is, there is* power: and who may say unto him, What doest thou?

5 Whoso keepeth the commandment [*shall know*] shall feel no evil thing: and a wise man's heart discerneth both time and judgment.

6 ¶ Because to every purpose there is time and judgment, therefore the misery of man *is* great upon him.

7 For he knoweth not that which shall be: for who can tell him [*how it shall be*] when it shall be?

8 *There is* no man that hath power over the spirit to retain the spirit: neither *hath he* power in the day of death: and *there is* no [*casting off weapons*] discharge in *that* war; neither shall wickedness deliver those that are given to it.

9 All this have I seen, and applied my heart unto every work that is done under the sun: *there is* a time wherein one man ruleth over another to his own hurt.

10 And so I saw the wicked

I counsel thee to keep the king's commandment, and that on account of the oath of God.

Do not hastily go out of his sight; do not persist in an evil thing, for he doeth whatsoever pleaseth him.

Where the word of a king is there is power; and who may say unto him, What doest thou?

Whoso obeyeth the command shall feel no evil thing; and the wise man's heart regardeth both time and judgment.

For to every thing there is a time and judgment; for injustice toward man presses heavily upon him.

For no one knoweth that which shall be; for who can tell him when it shall take place?

No man hath power over the wind to restrain the wind, nor hath power in the day of death, neither is there any discharge in that war; neither shall wickedness deliver those that are given to it.

All this have I seen, and I gave heed to every work that is done under the sun; there is a time when a man ruleth over another to his own hurt.

And so I saw the wicked

buried, who had come and gone from the place of the holy, and they were forgotten in the city where they had so done: this *is* also vanity.

11 Because sentence against an evil work is not executed speedily, therefore the heart of the sons of men is fully set in them to do evil.

12 Though a sinner do evil an hundred times, and his *days* be prolonged, yet surely I know that it shall be well with them that fear God, which fear before him:

13 But it shall not be well with the wicked, neither shall he prolong *his* days, *which are* as a shadow; because he feareth not before God.

14 There is a vanity which is done upon the earth; that there be just *men*, unto whom it happeneth according to the work of the wicked: again, there be wicked *men*, to whom it happeneth according to the work of the righteous: I said that this also *is* vanity.

15 Then I commended mirth, because a man hath no better thing under the sun, than to eat, and to drink, and to be merry: for that shall abide with him of his labour the days of his life, which God giveth him under the sun.

buried who had gone to and from the place of the holy, and they were forgotten in the city where they had so done. This also is vanity.

Because sentence against an evil work is not executed speedily, therefore the heart of the sons of men is fully set in them to do evil.

Though a sinner do evil a hundred times and prolong his days, yet surely I know that it shall be well with them that fear God, that fear before him;

But it shall not be well with the wicked, neither shall he prolong his days; as a shadow is he that feareth not God.

There is a vanity which is done on the earth; there are righteous men to whom it happeneth according to the work of the wicked, and there are wicked men to whom it happeneth according to the work of the righteous; I said that this surely is vanity.

Then I commended joy, because it is good for a man under the sun to eat, and to drink, and to be joyful; for this shall abide with him in his toil all the days of his life which God giveth him under the sun.

AUTHORIZED VERSION.

16 When I applied mine heart to know wisdom, and to see the business that is done upon the earth: (for also *there is that* neither day nor night seeth sleep with his eyes:)

17 Then I beheld all the work of God, that a man cannot find out the work that is done under the sun: because though a man labour to seek *it* out, yet he shall not find *it;* yea further, though a wise *man* think to know *it*, yet shall he not be able to find *it*.

CHAPTER IX.

1 *Like things happen to good and bad.* 4. *There is a necessity of death unto men.* 7 *Comfort is all their portion in this life.* 11 *God's providence ruleth over all.* 13 *Wisdom is better than strength.*

FOR all this [*I gave*, or, *set to my heart*] I considered in my heart even to declare all this, that the righteous, and the wise, and their works, *are* in the hand of God: no man knoweth either love or hatred *by* all *that is* before them.

2 All *things come* alike to all: *there is* one event to the righteous and to the wicked; to the good, and to the clean, and to the unclean; to him that sacrificeth, and to him that sacrificeth not: as *is* the good, so *is* the sinner; *and* he that sweareth, as *he* that feareth an oath.

REVISED VERSION.

When I applied my heart to know wisdom, and to consider the business which is done on the earth—for neither day nor night does one sleep with his eyes—

Then I saw the whole work of God, that a man can not find out the work that is done under the sun; how much soever he may labour to search it out, yet shall he not comprehend it; yea, though a wise man resolve to know it, yet shall he not be able to find it out.

FOR all this I considered in my heart, and searched out all this, that the righteous and the wise, and their works, are in the hands of God; also love and hatred; neither do men know all that is before them.

All things happen alike to all; there is one event to the righteous, and to the wicked; to the good, to the clean, and the unclean; to him that sacrificeth, and to him that sacrificeth not: as is the good, so is the sinner; he that sweareth as he that feareth an oath.

AUTHORIZED VERSION.

3 This *is* an evil among all *things* that are done under the sun, that *there is* one event unto all; yea, also the heart of the sons of men is full of evil, and madness *is* in their heart while they live, and after that *they go* to the dead.

4 ¶ For to him that is joined to all the living there is hope: for a living dog is better than a dead lion.

5 For the living know that they shall die: but the dead know not any thing, neither have they any more a reward; for the memory of them is forgotten.

6 Also their love, and their hatred, and their envy, is now perished; neither have they any more a portion for ever in any *thing* that is done under the sun.

7 ¶ Go thy way, eat thy bread with joy, and drink thy wine with a merry heart; for God now accepteth thy works.

8 Let thy garments be always white; and let thy head lack no ointment.

9 [*See*, or, *enjoy life*] Live joyfully with the wife whom thou lovest all the days of the life of thy vanity, which he hath given thee under the sun, all the days of thy vanity: for that *is* thy

REVISED VERSION.

This is an evil among all things which are done under the sun, that there is one event to all; therefore, also, the heart of the sons of men is full of evil, and madness is in their heart while they live, and after that they go to the dead.

For there is hope for him that is joined to all the living; a living dog is better than a dead lion.

For the living know that they must die, but the dead know not any thing, neither is there any more reward for them, for the memory of them is forgotten.

Their love also, as well as their hatred, and their envy is now perished; neither have they a portion any more forever in any thing which is done under the sun.

Go thy way, eat thy bread with joy, and drink thy wine with a cheerful heart; for now God is pleased with thy work.

At all times let thy garments be white; and let not thy head lack precious ointment.

Enjoy life with the wife whom thou lovest all the days of thy vain life, which he (God) hath given thee under the sun, all the days of thy vanity: for that is thy portion in life, and in thy portion in *this* life, and in thy labour which thou takest under the sun.

10 Whatsoever thy hand findeth to do, do *it* with thy might; for *there is* no work, nor device, nor knowledge, nor wisdom, in the grave, whither thou goest.

11 ¶ I returned, and saw under the sun, that the race *is* not to the swift, nor the battle to the strong, neither yet bread to the wise, nor yet riches to men of understanding, nor yet favour to men of skill; but time and chance happeneth to them all.

12 For man also knoweth not his time: as the fishes that are taken in an evil net, and as the birds that are caught in the snare; so *are* the sons of men snared in an evil time, when it falleth suddenly upon them.

13 This wisdom have I seen also under the sun, and it *seemed* great unto me:

14 *There was* a little city, and few men within it; and there came a great king against it, and beseiged it, and built great bulwarks against it.

15 Now there was found in it a poor wise man, and he by his wisdom delivered the city; yet no man remembered that same poor man.

toil which thou takest under the sun.

Whatsoever thy hand findeth to do, do it with thy might; for there is no work, nor device, nor knowledge, nor wisdom in the grave (or the world beyond), whither thou goest.

I turned and saw under the sun, that the race is not to the swift, nor the battle to the strong, nor yet bread to the wise, nor riches to men of understanding, nor favour to men of knowledge; but time and opportunity happen to all of them.

For man also knoweth not his time; as fishes which are caught in an evil net, and as birds which are caught in a snare, so are the sons of men snared in an evil time, when it falleth suddenly upon them.

Even this wisdom have I seen under the sun, and it seemed great to me:

There was a little city, and the men in it were few, and there came against it a great king, and besieged it, and built over against it great bulwarks;

And there was found within it a poor wise man, and he by his wisdom delivered the city; yet no one remembered that same poor man.

16 Then said I, Wisdom *is* better than strength : nevertheless the poor man's wisdom *is* despised, and his words are not heard.

17 The words of wise *men are* heard in quiet more than the cry of him that ruleth among fools.

18 Wisdom *is* better than weapons of war : but one sinner destroyeth much good.

CHAPTER X.

1 *Observations of wisdom and folly: 16 of riot, 18 slothfulness, 19 and money. 20 Men's thoughts of kings ought to be reverent.*

DEAD [*Flies of death*] flies cause the ointment of the apothecary to send forth a stinking savour : so *doth* a little folly him that is in reputation for wisdom *and* honour.

2 A wise man's heart *is* at his right hand; but a fool's heart at his left.

3 Yea also, when he that is a fool walketh by the way, [*his heart*] his wisdom faileth *him,* and he saith to every one *that* he *is* a fool.

4 If the spirit of the ruler rise up against thee, leave not thy place ; for yielding pacifieth great offences.

5 There is an evil *which* I have seen under the sun, as an

Then said I, Wisdom is better than strength, yet the poor man's wisdom is despised, and his words are not listened to.

The words of the wise, heard in quiet, are better than the clamorous voice of a ruler among fools.

Wisdom is better than weapons of war; but one sinner destroyeth much good.

A DEAD fly causeth the ointment of the apothecary to ferment and send forth an offensive odour; so a little folly is often more weighty than wisdom and honour.

A wise man's heart is at his right hand; but a fool's heart at his left.

And even when a fool walketh by the way, his understanding faileth him, and he saith to every one that he is a fool.

If the spirit of a ruler rise up against thee, leave not thy place; for gentleness quieteth great offenses.

There is an evil which I have seen under the sun, as an error

error *which* proceedeth [*from before*] from the ruler:

6 Folly is set [*in great heights*] in great dignity, and the rich sit in low place.

7 I have seen servants upon horses, and princes walking as servants upon the earth.

8 He that diggeth a pit shall fall into it; and whoso breaketh an hedge, a serpent shall bite him.

9 Whoso removeth stones shall be hurt therewith; *and* he that cleaveth wood shall be endangered thereby.

10 If the iron be blunt, and he do not whet the edge, then must he put to more strength: but wisdom *is* profitable to direct.

11 Surely the serpent will bite without enchantment; and a [*the master of the tongue*] babbler is no better.

12 The words of a wise man's mouth are [*grace*] gracious; but the lips of a fool will swallow up himself.

13 The beginning of the words of his mouth *is* foolishness: and the end of [*his mouth*] his talk *is* mischievous madness.

14 A fool also [*multiplieth words*] is full of words: a man cannot tell what shall be; and what shall be after him, who can tell him?

which proceedeth from the ruler:

Folly is set in high places and the rich sit in obscurity.

I have seen servants upon horses, and princes walking as servants upon the earth.

He that diggeth a ditch shall fall into it; and whoso breaketh through a hedge a serpent shall bite him.

Whoso removeth stones shall be hurt therewith; and he that cleaveth wood shall be endangered thereby.

If the iron be blunt, and he do not whet the edge, then must he put forth more strength; but wisdom is preferable to give success.

Surely a serpent, if not enchanted, will bite; and a flatterer is no better.

The words of a wise man's mouth are gracious; but the lips of a fool destroy him.

The beginning of the words of his mouth is folly; and the end of his talk is mischievous madness.

The fool also multiplieth words, when man knoweth not what shall be; and what shall be after him, who can tell?

15 The labour of the foolish wearieth every one of them, because he knoweth not how to go to the city.

16 Wo to thee, O land, when thy king *is* a child, and thy princes eat in the morning!

17 Blessed *art* thou, O land, when thy king *is* the son of nobles, and thy princes eat in due season, for strength, and not for drunkenness!

18 By much slothfulness the building decayeth; and through idleness of the hands the house droppeth through.

19 A feast is made for laughter, and wine [*maketh glad the life*] maketh merry: but money answereth all *things*.

20 Curse not the king, no, not in thy [*conscience*] thought; and curse not the rich in thy bedchamber: for a bird of the air shall carry the voice, and that which hath wings shall tell the matter.

CHAPTER XI.

1 *Directions for charity.* 7 *Death in life,* 9 *and the day of judgment in the days of youth, are to be thought on.*

CAST thy bread [*upon the face of the waters*] upon the waters: for thou shalt find it after many days.

2 Give a portion to seven,

The toil of fools wearieth him who knoweth not how to go to (*is not at home in*) the city.

Woe to thee, O land, whose king is a child, and whose princes revel in the morning!

Hail to thee, O land, whose king is the son of nobles, and whose princes feast in due season, for strength, and not for reveling!

By much slothfulness the building decayeth, and by the slackness of the hands the house leaketh.

For reveling, they make a feast; and wine maketh merry, and money provideth every pleasure.

Curse not the king, no, not in thy thought; and curse not the rich in thy bed-chamber; for a bird of the air shall carry the voice, and that which hath wings shall tell the matter.

CAST thy bread upon the waters; for thou shalt find it after many days.

Divide a portion to seven, and

and also to eight; for thou knowest not what evil shall be upon the earth.

3 If the clouds be full of rain, they empty *themselves* upon the earth : and if the tree fall toward the south, or toward the north, in the place where the tree falleth, there it shall be.

4 He that observeth the wind shall not sow; and he that regardeth the clouds shall not reap.

5 As thou knowest not what *is* the way of the spirit, *nor* how the bones *do grow* in the womb of her that is with child : even so thou knowest not the works of God who maketh all.

6 In the morning sow thy seed, and in the evening withhold not thine hand: for thou knowest not whether [*shall be right*] shall prosper, either this or that, or whether they both *shall be* alike good.

7 Truly the light *is* sweet, and a pleasant *thing it is* for the eyes to behold the sun :

8 But if a man live many years, *and* rejoice in them all; yet let him remember the days of darkness; for they shall be many. All that cometh *is* vanity.

9 Rejoice, O young man, in thy youth; and let thy heart

also to eight; for thou knowest not what evil shall be upon the earth.

When the clouds are full of rain, they empty themselves upon the earth; and when a tree falleth toward the south, or toward the north, in the place where the tree falleth, there it shall be.

He that observeth the wind shall not sow; and he that regardeth the clouds shall not reap.

As thou knowest not what is the way of the spirit, nor how the bones are formed in the womb of her that is with child; so thou knowest not the works of God, who causeth all things.

In the morning sow thy seed, and in the evening withhold not thy hand; for thou knowest not which shall prosper, whether this or that, or whether they both shall be alike good.

Truly the light is sweet, and a pleasant thing it is for the eyes to behold the sun.

For if a man live many years, let him rejoice in them all; but let him remember the days of darkness, for they shall be many. All that cometh is vanity.

Rejoice, O young man, in thy youth; and let thy heart cheer

cheer thee in the days of thy youth, and walk in the ways of thine heart, and in the sight of thine eyes: but know thou, that for these *things* God will bring thee into judgment.

10 Therefore remove [*anger*] sorrow from thy heart, and put away evil from thy flesh; for childhood and youth *are* vanity.

CHAPTER XII.

1 *The Creator is to be remembered in due time.* 8 *The preacher's care to edify.* 13 *The fear of God is the chief antidote of vanity.*

REMEMBER now thy Creator in the days of thy youth, while the evil days come not, nor the years draw nigh, when thou shalt say, I have no pleasure in them:

2 While the sun, or the light, or the moon, or the stars, be not darkened, nor the clouds return after the rain:

3 In the day when the keepers of the house shall tremble, and the strong men shall bow themselves, and [*the grinders fail, because they grind little*] the grinders cease because they are few, and those that look out of the windows be darkened,

4 And the doors shall be shut in the streets, when the sound of the grinding is low, and he shall rise up at the voice of the

thee in the days of thy youth, and walk in the ways of thy heart, and in the sight of thine eyes: but know thou that for all these things God will bring thee into judgment.

Therefore remove sorrow from thy heart, and put away evil from thy flesh; for childhood and youth are vanity.

REMEMBER thy Creator in the days of thy youth, before the evil days come, and the years draw nigh when thou shalt say, I have no pleasure in them;

Before the sun, and the light, and the moon and the stars grow dim, and the clouds return after the rain;

In the day when the keepers of the house tremble, and the strong men bow themselves, and the grinders cease because they are few, and those that look out of the windows are darkened,

And the doors shall be shut in the streets;—and while the sound of the grinding is low they rise up at the voice of the bird,

bird, and all the daughters of music shall be brought low;

5 Also *when* they shall be afraid of *that which is* high, and fears *shall be* in the way, and the almond-tree shall flourish, and the grasshopper be a burden, and desire shall fail: because man goeth to his long home, and the mourners go about the streets:

6 Or ever the silver cord be loosed, or the golden bowl be broken, or the pitcher be broken at the fountain, or the wheel broken at the cistern.

7 Then shall the dust return to the earth as it was: and the spirit shall return unto God who gave it.

8 Vanity of vanities, saith the Preacher; all *is* vanity.

9 And [*the more wise the Preacher was*] moreover, because the Preacher was wise, he still taught the people knowledge: yea, he gave good heed, and sought out, *and* set in order many proverbs.

10 The Preacher sought to find out [*words of delight*] acceptable words: and *that which was* written, *was* upright, *even* words of truth.

11 The words of the wise *are* as goads, and as nails fastened *by* the masters of assemblies,

and all the daughters of music are brought low;

When also they shall be afraid of that which is high, and the almond shall be refused, and the locust a burden, and the caperberry shall be in vain; since man goeth to his everlasting home, and the mourners go about the streets;

Before the silver cord is loosed, or the golden bowl is broken, or the pitcher is shivered at the fountain, or the wheel broken at the cistern,

And the dust shall return to the earth as it was, and the spirit shall return unto God who gave it.

Vanity of vanities, saith the Preacher [Convener]; all is vanity.

And since the Preacher was wise, he moreover taught the people knowledge; yea he gave good heed, and searched out, and set in order many proverbs.

The Preacher sought to find out acceptable words, and to write down correctly words of truth.

The words of the wise are as goads, and as nails driven are those who collect the sayings of

which are given from one shepherd.

12 And further, by these, my son, be admonished : of making many books *there is* no end ; and much [*reading*] study *is* a weariness of the flesh.

13 [*The end of the matter, even all that hath been heard, is*] Let us hear the conclusion of the whole matter : Fear God, and keep his commandments : for this *is* the whole *duty* of man.

14 For God shall bring every work into judgment, with every secret thing, whether *it be* good, or whether *it be* evil.

the wise, which are given from one Shepherd.

And further, by these, my son, be admonished : of making many books there is no end, and much study is a weariness of the flesh.

Let us have the conclusion of the whole matter : Fear God, and keep his commandments ; for this is the whole duty of man ;

For God will bring every work into judgment, with every secret thing, whether it be good or whether it be evil.

ANALYSIS OF PART FIRST.

I.—VANITY OF THE MATERIAL UNIVERSE, AND OF THE EXISTENCE OF THE HUMAN RACE, IF THERE BE NO STATE BEYOND THE PRESENT; Chap. i. 1—11.

II.—VANITY OF LEARNING; Chap. i. 12—18.

III.—THE MOCKERY OF MIRTH, LUXURY, AND WORLDLY SPLENDOUR; Chap. ii. 1—17.

IV.—VANITY OF GREAT ENTERPRISES, OR OF ACTIVITY AND SUCCESS IN BUSINESS; Chap. ii. 18—26.

V.—THE BEAUTY OF DIVINE PROVIDENCE SEEN ONLY IN THE LIGHT OF A FUTURE STATE; Chap. iii. 1—15.

VI.—THE INEFFICACY OF HUMAN LAWS, OR OF JUSTICE AS ADMINISTERED AMONG MEN, TO REDEEM THE WORLD FROM THE REPROACH OF VANITY; Chap. iii. 16—22.

ECCLESEASTES EXPLAINED

§ I. Chap. I. 1–11.

VANITY OF THE MATERIAL UNIVERSE, AND OF THE EXIST-
ENCE OF THE HUMAN RACE, IF THERE BE NO STATE BE-
YOND THE PRESENT.

(1.) *The Words of the Preacher (Convener),
the son of David, King in Jerusalem.*

In this, its title, the book clearly purports to be the
production of Solomon. *King* is in apposition with
Preacher, and not with *David*; and as Solomon was
the only son of David who was king in Jerusalem, he
must be meant. The same claim is set up in the
body of the work. The learned among the Jews and
the more ancient Christian writers, one and all, attribute the authorship of the book to Solomon. Speaking in his own person, he describes the greatness and
splendour of his works. He alludes to his son, the
heir-apparent, and to Jeroboam. (Chap. iv. 13–16.)
He speaks in the style of an aged man, who had had
large experience of the world, and made trial of all
its sources of happiness, and had occasion bitterly to
lament many follies.

The book contains proverbs in every part, which
render the style strikingly analogous to the book of

Proverbs. Inasmuch as it claims to be the work of Solomon, to deny it is to assail its inspiration, destroy its canonicity, and place it among the Apocryphal books. [For a more complete consideration of the question respecting the authorship of Ecclesiastes, see the Introduction.]

The Hebrew word Koheleth, which our translators have rendered *the Preacher*, is derived from a verb which signifies *to gather, to assemble, to come to another person*. The Septuagint renders it Ecclesiastes, *i. e., assembly*. Our translators adopted a word which refers to the purpose for which an assembly meets ; viz., to be addressed. *Convener* would better preserve the etymological analogy, and would perhaps more strictly express the sense of the original. It is not merely the idea of preaching which is contained in Koheleth, but that of turning or drawing men unto God, by example as well as precept. Koheleth seems to combine the two ideas of the Penitent and the Preacher ; that is, he presents himself to those whom he addresses, as one who, having departed from the Lord, and having been brought to him again, penitently seeks to counteract his pernicious example, and to gather other wanderers to the same gracious, forgiving God. It will be obvious that such is the full meaning of the word translated Preacher, when we take into consideration the object of the book or writing in the title of which it occurs.

In early life Solomon " loved the Lord, walking in the statutes of David his father." (1 Kings iii. 3.) On the altar in Gibeon, a favourite place of worship, he offered a thousand burnt-offerings. The zeal with which he prosecuted the great work of building the temple, and ordering its worship, attests the earnestness of his piety. But the painful story of his fall is briefly yet honestly related on the pages of the Bible. Solomon became a dissolute man. He wearied of one pleasure after another, of one luxury after another, and finally imitated the example of the licentious monarchs of the East, in some of its most disgusting features. (1 Kings xi. 1–12.) He who had built God's temple and his altars, and had offered burnt-offerings at Gibeon, now builds altars to Moloch and Chemosh, and offers sacrifices to Ashtoreth and Milcom. In his old age judgments began to come, but there is no record in the books of Kings or of Chronicles of his repentance. May not the reason of this silence be found in the fact that the evidence of his heartfelt contrition had been put on record by himself in this book of Ecclesiastes ?

The book becomes one of great interest as the production of an aged man, who, in early life, gave evidence of piety, who had enjoyed the greatest worldly prosperity, who fell into great sin, but the evening of whose life was marked by the most sincere repentance. Like the fifty-first Psalm of his father David, which it is the will of God should be read and sung from age to age, it presents Solomon in the Church of God, in the perpetual attitude of a penitent confessing and deploring, and thus counteracting his corrupt example.

(2.) *Vanity of vanities, saith the Preacher ; vanity of vanities ; all is vanity.*

That of which he predicates unsubstantial nothingness is the το παν, the universe ; including in this *all* not only what is done or happens among men, but the great objects of material nature. He does not mean, however, to pronounce the works and ways of God as defective ; but he means to say that to the mind of a rational creature, who seeks in the present world the means of solid happiness, "all" must prove the merest vanity. That is, he aims to show—as will be made evident when we apply the rule of interpretation of making one part of a book determine the meaning of another, or the meaning of the parts be determined by the scope of the whole—that if the future be left entirely out of view, then all things which relate to man and time are one complex vanity. The *argumentum ex absurdo* underlies a large portion of his discourse. The use which Solomon makes of this argument will account for many, if not all, those instances in which he seems to doubt or deny a future existence. Apparent inconsistencies and sentiments, which in themselves appear objectionable, are all easily explained, when we remember that the author is telling us what he thought, and what every rational being must think, when considering things under a certain aspect ; viz., that man must find his whole happiness and the great end of his existence, in the present world. If it be said that there is nothing in the text which indicates that he is pointing out the absurdity which must arise on the denial of a future state, and that, therefore, this view of the case is a gratuitous assumption ; it may be replied that this is a question which can be decided only from considering the scope and bearing of the whole composition. If in this second verse, as has been said, "the main subject of the book is at once announced," we can ascertain what meaning the Preacher attached to his text, only by attending to the discourse which he founded upon it. To interpret this book in accordance with the theory suggested above, and by a rigid process of exegetical inquiry, is what is proposed in the following pages. As we proceed, we shall find the author dropping all mere hypothesis and his favourite *argumentum ex absurdo*, and proclaiming with solemn emphasis a future judgment, as in iii. 17, where he declares that a time will come, when God will judge the wicked ; and in xi. 9, where he solemnly warns the young man who is resolved to walk in the ways of his heart, and in the sight of his eyes, that God will bring him into judgment. And in the very last words of the book, he sums up all by declaring that " God will bring every work into judgment, with every secret thing, whether it be good or whether it be evil." Even neology is constrained to admit that this last passage has reference to a future judgment ; but in order to break its force, it denies the genuineness of the passage ; and this denial is made on the bold and groundless assumption that the author of Ecclesiastes was ignorant of a future state.*

(3.) *What profit hath a man from all his labour, in which he toils under the sun ?*

What real advantage hath a man from all his toilsome labour, in this world, if there be no hereafter ? He seems to challenge the whole world to answer this question. He did not mean to discourage an industrious application to one's calling, or to say that no advantage can arise from the efforts which men make in the affairs of this life. But his question is the

* *Vide* Knobel.

strongest kind of affirmation that it is impossible to show any real purpose answered or profit gained, if there be nothing beyond this life.

(4.) *A generation goeth off, and a generation cometh on : while the earth abideth for ever.*

There is no lasting good in the present world ; even men themselves do not last ; their stay here is too brief for them to reap any real advantage from all their hard toil. Just as one generation are ready to enter on the enjoyment of the fruits of their labours, they must give way to another. While the earth, which he seems to view as a stage on which these successive generations appear and disappear, abides forever, *i. e.*, outlasts them all. If there be no hereafter, what is this but vanity—aye, vanity of vanities ?

(5.) *The sun ariseth and the sun goeth down, and panteth (hasteneth) to the place where it ariseth.*

Having spoken of the earth as the fixed and immovable stage on which the generations of men appear, he proceeds to describe the extent and grandeur of its scenery and equipments ; for what purpose we shall see in the sequel. He first lifts his eyes to the heavens, sees the sun coming out of his chamber in the east, rejoicing as a strong man that panteth in a race. (Ps. xix. 5.) In speaking as he does of the sun's rising and setting, we are not to infer that the writer of Ecclesiastes necessarily supposed that the sun revolved around the earth. He speaks just as we, just as learned philosophers now speak. He adopted a parlance suited to what appears to be. Nor have we any right, from the expression "hasteth to the place whence he ariseth," to conclude that he supposed the sun went round or under the world, by some subterranean passage, in order to return to the place of his rising. There is nothing in this book nor in any other book of the Old Testament which proves that the ancient Hebrews held to such a belief. On the contrary, we know that in the age of Daniel and Ezekiel, the Chaldean or Egyptian theory placed the sun, instead of the earth, in the centre ;* for it was in that age that Pythagoras visited Egypt and perhaps Chaldea, and introduced the astronomical theory of the Egyptians into Greece. Egypt received her first lessons in astronomy from Chaldea, and it was from the valley of the Nile that science and civilization traveled into Greece. Now it seems impossible to account for the existence of a true theory of the universe in a remote antiquity, which possessed neither telescopes nor the differential calculus, except we attribute it to some tradition of a more perfect science, divinely revealed to man in his state of innocence, which had survived the fall. To say that this theory was the result of surmise or guess, without the least scientific basis for its support, is incredible ; certainly far more incredible than that God should have imparted some knowledge to the first man before his fall, of the true theory of the universe. But if any such theory existed in Pythagoras's day, it must have existed in Solomon's, who lived several hundred years earlier. The Scriptures expressly assert that he excelled in learning all the scholars of both Egypt and Chaldea. (1 Kings iv.

* Arist., de Cœl., ii. 13.

30.) It is not, however, essential to the force and impressiveness of Solomon's words in this high argument, to prove that he was acquainted with the Pythagorean or Egyptian, which, as far as it went, was substantially the same as the Copernican, theory of the universe. All I am solicitous about is, to guard against an undue lessening of the field which he contemplated, by denying to him a knowledge of things with which we may fairly suppose him to have been acquainted. Even supposing that he regarded the earth as the centre around which the sun revolved, the figurative illustration, which he here employs for the purpose of making the vanity of the creation, and continued existence of such a universe appear the greater, remains the same. It may well be doubted whether the emotional effect in his case would have been any greater, if he could have measured the distances and diameters of the planets, and calculated the relative weight of bodies at their surface.

(6.) *It goeth to the south and turneth about unto the north. The wind whirleth and whirleth about, and returneth to its circuits.*

It is suggested by Dr. Adam Clark that the fifth and sixth verses should be divided thus, " his place where he ariseth ; going to the south and circulating to the north. The wind is continually whirling about, and the wind returneth upon its whirlings." Thus v. 5 refers to the approximations of the sun to the north and south tropics, viz., of Cancer and Capricorn. " All the versions," he says, " except ours, apply the clause (I add to v. 5) to the sun and not to the wind. My old MS. Bible is quite correct : " The sunne riiseth up and goth doun, and to his place turnith again ; and there again riising, goth about bi the south, and then again to the north." The author points out, 1. The sun's daily course ; 2. His yearly course, through the twelve signs of the zodiac.

Solomon turns from the astronomical to the atmospherical heavens. He particularly notices the constant motion of the air. In referring to the motions of the sun, or his change of place, what he particularly observed was, that it was constantly going on, and yet the same identical phenomena were constantly recurring. He seems to refer to the shiftings of the wind for the same purpose. It is continually veering from point to point, and returning to that from which it started, forever repeating its endless circuits. Changing ever, it can never blow in any direction in which it has not often blown before. Thus whether we look to the solar heavens, or to the region of our own atmosphere, there is a repetition everywhere of the same phenomena.

(7.) *All the rivers run into the sea, yet the sea is not full ; into the place whence the rivers come, thither they return again.*

He comes down to the surface of the earth, to objects nearer, which may be subjected to a closer examination, in search of the same thing ; that is, to discover whether, in the midst of perpetual changes, there is ever any thing new. His eye fixes upon the rivers. They are constantly in motion ; they are constantly changing. Away in the hills a little brook runs along, over which a child can pass at a single bound. But it unites with others in its onward flow ; it is constantly widening and deepening, until it reaches the ocean. There it pours its mighty, constant tribute, but is never exhausted. And this for centuries on centuries, its course determined, and its channel fixed, without any essential variation. And although a multitude of other similar rivers pour their waters into the same sea, yet it is not full, nor its volume sensibly increased. They do but supply the place of the drops which are constantly taken up by evaporation, to fall in rain from the clouds to feed the little brooks among the hills ; in other words, they do but return from the place whence they came. The ocean, where they are discharged, is the real place of their origin or source. When they leave it they first float in the cloud ; they descend in the shower ; they feed the springs among the hills ; they flow in the streamlet ; they course on the river, and are re-embosomed in the mighty reservoir, only to renew their circulating, ceaseless motion. Here, too, is constant change, but no new phenomena ; and this goes on age after age.

(8.) *All things are full of labour, no man can express it ; the eye is not satisfied with seeing, nor the ear filled with hearing.*

All such things as have been described before—the sun, the wind, the streams, *i. e.*, all material things are undergoing perpetual change, without producing any thing new. It would weary the mind to follow them, or the tongue to describe them, steadfast only in the same round of change, and in the recurrence of the same phenomena. Even those senses, or organs, the eye and the ear, which experience the least fatigue from exercise, although surfeited with the number of these changes, are not satisfied ; they, too, grow weary of seeing and hearing the same things over and over again.

(9.) *The thing that hath been, that will be ; and that which hath been done, that will be done ; and there is no new thing under the sun.*

From the field of material, unconscious nature, he passes to the scene of human activity and experience ; and the result of his observations is the same. As the earth revolves day after day on its axis, and goes round year after year, in its orbit—as the wind whirls round and round, blowing from every point of the compass, but from no one point long—as the streams keep up their circulating motion from the ocean, through the clouds and the valleys, to the ocean again, from age to age, and all these and other parts of material nature not only present constant change, but a repetition of the same changes ; so in life, in human experience and striving there is constant vicissitude, and yet there is nothing new. The events which happen to men are substantially the same as have happened to others before them ; the pursuits in which they engage are the same, from age to age. Here, too, the tongue of one who would describe them, would grow weary ; for it would be but an enumeration of the same occurrences, and the same actions. In one age we see the grand outlines and lineaments of every other. There are changes, there is progress, and there are retrograde movements. But human nature is the same in every age and in every country ; and its wants, physical and moral, are the same. No discoveries are made which do away with the necessity of eating, drinking, and sleeping, or supersede toil, pain, and sickness.

(10.) *Is there any thing concerning which one may say, " See, this is new?"   It hath been long ago in ancient times which were before us.*

He appeals to observing men, and challenges them to point out any thing new in the great characteristical features of human experience. He does not mean to deny that men may make discoveries and inventions, which shall give them certain advantages over all who have preceded them ; but he considers them as creatures of hopes, of fears, and of wants, and asserts that the experience and general pursuits of one generation are precisely those of generations which lived long before. The great laws of the kingdoms of nature and providence remain the same.

(11.) *There is no remembrance of former things, and of things that are to come there shall be no remembrance among those who shall live afterwards.*

A reason seems to be here assigned against too soon concluding that any thing which takes place is really new ; viz., our ignorance of the past. In the absence of a full record of what has happened to those who have lived before us, it soon passes from the memories of men ; and when the same thing happens to them they may be tempted to think that none ever had such an experience before. Moreover, as we are ignorant of, or forget what happened to generations which have preceded us, so generations which come after us will forget, or be ignorant of what has happened to us, and will perhaps think that something new has befallen them, when their trials, their successes, and their disappointments are substantially the same as ours. There is no new thing under the sun.

But what is the meaning of all this? What is its bearing upon the principal subject of the book? How does the fact that there is nothing new in the kingdom of nature or of providence, illustrate to the mind of a reasoning man the vanity of the present world, as affording the means of real and lasting happiness? In this way: men have never yet been made truly happy by the things of this world; and hence we conclude that while their nature remains the same, and their experience of the world the same, they never can be. We have no right to conclude that it will afford any greater satisfaction to us than it afforded to others, constituted just as we are, who have tried it in all conceivable forms, and under all conceivable circumstances during the ages that are passed. Well then, might Solomon inscribe upon it, " Vanity of vanities; all is vanity." It is indeed a tissue, a complication of vanities, if men are not to look above or beyond it, for their chief happiness and end of existence. It is only when we look at the conclusion of the whole matter, xii. 13, 14, that the reproach of vanity is wiped from the face of creation, and from human striving and labour. Look no higher than this world, and true happiness is not to be found; the mind of man receives no satisfaction, but is painfully impressed with the unprofitableness of all his labours, and of all the great changes and movements in the natural world, of which he is the witness, or of which he is made the subject. But Solomon did look beyond. He looked forward to a day, when men will read clearly the great purpose of the creation ; when they will understand why they suffered ; and when all the seeming inequalities of Divine Providence, which now perplex the faith, will be rectified, by every work being brought into judgment, whether good or evil.

SCOPE OF ARGUMENT IN SECTION I.

The king of Jerusalem, startled by the threatenings and judgments of heaven, and the fearful length to which he had gone in idolatry and sensuality, and recurring to the day of his espousals, when God's banner over him was love (Cant. ii. 4), opens his discourse in earnest, impassioned language. From his lofty pinnacle of power, of philosophy, of pleasure, and of riches, he looks out upon the stage of human action. Never did a man enjoy better advantages for forming a true estimate of the worth of the world, and all it contains, viewed irrespectively of the destiny of its intelligent inhabitants. He sees generation follow generation,

"Like shadows o'er the plain,"

and asks what purpose—if this be the only stage on which these beings are to flourish—worthy of their creation, or of the toil and suffering to which they are subjected, is answered ? Is this state of things to continue on without change ? Is this earth to abide forever, merely as a great theater where this empty pageant, this mock tragedy, is to be enacted without end ? He glances at the vast machinery and movements of the universe ; the sun making his daily and annual course through the heavens ; the wind, veering from point to point of the compass ; the rivers coursing through almost every valley of the earth ; the ocean, ebbing and flowing, and sending up its exhalations to supply the rills and mighty streams which feed, but never fill it. " All things are full of labour ; man can not express it," or describe the mighty movements, or the curious, minute mechanism of the universe. And age after age, the same thing is enacted over and over again ; nothing is new. If it be but a theatrical show, gotten up and maintained, at so vast an expense, why not, like players, change the scene ? why this perpetual, dull uniformity ? But who can believe that God created this great universe ; lighted up the sun to rise and set, to go from tropic to tropic ; adorned the heavens with stars ; channeled out the rivers ; set to the heaving ocean its bounds ; and gave ordinances to the shifting wind, only to build and embellish a splendid stage, on which poor, short-lived men, generation after generation might labour, and struggle, and die ; or only to erect a stately mausoleum for entombed and forgotten nations ? Is this universe so aimless a thing, and its mighty Maker so blind a trifler ?

Solomon does not deem it essential to the completeness of his argument to premise the proof that there is a God, and that the universe had a Maker, and that God was its Maker. His skepticism had never proceeded so far, and the skepticism of other minds, with which he had become acquainted, had never proceeded so far as to call these truths in question. Polytheism, rather than Atheism, was the great error of his times ; and even the belief that matter is eternal, and that the earth has existed, in nearly its present state, from everlasting, or that it was formed by the progressive concentration of phosphorescent matter, such as is supposed now to constitute *nebulæ,* which no telescopic power has yet resolved, concentrating itself by the effect of its own gravity into masses—such a belief, I say, was too low a form of skepticism for the age in which Solomon lived. Without stopping to prove that there is a God, and that the earth and man were made, and are governed by him, he grappled at once with the skepticism which perhaps had haunted, and for a time, overmastered him, and to which he knew that others, especially the learned, the rich, the gay, and the young, were exposed. He applied himself at once to prove the unspeakable vanity of all created things, and all human striving, if man is to find his entire happiness and chief end in this world—that the universe is no better than a magnificent toy.

We shall better feel the force of his words, if we are able to obtain a clear idea of the Cosmos which was addressed to the eye of his contemplation—or that assemblage of things with which space is filled, from the remotest dimly-shining star to the hyssop that springeth out of the wall, and the creeping thing which to him as a philosopher, constituted the το παν of the universe.

But so imperfect are the traces which are left to us of the state of science, in remote antiquity, that peculiar caution is here demanded. On the one hand, we may be in danger of ascribing to him a knowledge of some natural things, of which he was ignorant ; and on the other, of ascribing to him an ignorance of some things with which he was well acquainted. He possessed neither the telescope nor the microscope ; he knew nothing of the differential calculus ; but he had an observing eye, and a mind of most remarkable acuteness, and his knowledge was extensive and accurate on a great variety of subjects.

How far may we suppose he had an acquaintance with the true theory of the universe, in respect to its astronomical wonders ? That he was acquainted with the spherical form of the earth can not be well doubted ; for his sailors, on their long three years' voyages to Ophir, could not have failed to notice the great changes which must have taken place in the appearance of the polar constellations ; and he must have well understood a doctrine which is known to have been so familiar to Chaldean and Egyptian astronomers, whom the Bible expressly affirms he excelled in learning, *viz.*, that the round shadow on the disc of the moon in eclipses was the shadow of the earth. The sphericity of the earth, and even its motion on its axis, and in its orbit around the sun, were maintained many centuries before Copernicus and Galileo were born. That the earth is round and not an extended plain, was proved by Aristotle, Pliny, and others, by the same arguments which are still introduced into our school-books, *viz.*, the curved shadow of the earth on the moon, and the varying heights of the stars, in respect to the horizon, by a small change of distance, either to the north or to the south. " It would seem to be naturally suggested by some of the simplest and most obvious aspects of the visible universe ; and that, too, independent of the phenomena to which we have alluded, and which must have forced it upon the thoughts of all who had ever traveled by land or sea, over any considerable extent of the earth's surface.*

But the true principles of astronomy had been propounded and held in Greece, long before the days of Aristotle. Pythagoras taught the doctrine that the sun was the centre around which the earth, and other planets, revolved ; and one of his disciples is said to have also taught that the earth turns on its axis, producing all the phenomena of day and night.† But whence was this theory, which modern science has demonstrated to be the true one, derived ? And how is it to be accounted for that it approached the truth so much nearer than that adopted by their later and more learned countrymen ?

In answer to the first of these questions, I reply, that there can be no doubt he derived it from the same countries whence a knowledge of the method of calculating eclipses of the sun and moon were introduced into Greece, or rather from the same traditions. In his extraordinary desire for knowledge, Pythagoras early traveled to Egypt, where he put himself under the instruction of the priests. He afterward visited the country of the Chaldeans, to acquire the learning

* See "Astron. Views of the Ancients," by T. Lewis, LL. D., Bib. Repos., April and July, 1849.

† Hicetas of Syracuse, Theophrastus, Heraclides Pontiacus, and Ecphantus, all appear to have had a knowledge of the rotation of the earth on its axis. But Aristarchus of Samos, and more particularly Seleucus of Babylon, who lived one hundred and fifty years after Alexander, taught that the earth rotated on its axis.—Humboldt's Cosmos (Harper's), vol. ii., p. 109.

of their wise men ; and it is even supposed by some
that he there may have seen Daniel and Ezekiel, and
received instruction from them. But while the Egyptian or Pythagorean doctrine was the true one, the
arguments by which it was supported by its ancient
advocates, were so unsubstantial and inconclusive,
that it was rejected by the later philosophers, and the
earth, instead of the sun, was taken by them as the
centre of the system. And the very insufficiency of
their arguments renders the conviction irresistible, that
so grand a conception as the true theory of the universe could not possibly have been suggested by these
arguments, but must have been the result of some
traditionary wreck of a more perfect science, which
had survived the flood. A tradition of the true astronomical theory, but no tradition of the philosophy
which could explain and establish it, survived. It was
doubtless from Chaldea that Egypt received its astronomy. Solomon possessed all the learning of both
these countries. He lived nearly five hundred years
before Pythagoras, when if there was a tradition
which had been brought out of Chaldea into Egypt,
which placed the sun in the centre of the system, it
must have been much more distinct than in the days
of the Grecian philosopher.

But even if we are to suppose that he considered
the earth on which he stood as the centre, around
which the sun and stars revolved, still his impressions
of the vastness of the universe, probably did not fall
short of those of the most accomplished modern astronomer. It would have added nothing to these impressions to be able to measure the distance of the
sun, or the diameters and orbits of its planets, in

inches and barleycorns. His sublime language, at the
dedication of the temple, " the heaven, and heaven
of heavens," as has been justly said, carries the devout mind as far into immensity as the billions and
trillions by which we labour to express the distances
of the stars. When he described the apparent motion
of the sun, from east to west, and his course through
the signs of the zodiac, his mind rose as fully to the
grandeur of the subject, as could that of a Newton or
a Herschell. He could feel the sublime force of the
language of Job, describing the earth " self-balanced,"
and the constellations which hang, beyond the northern
pole, over empty space. " Thou stretchest out the
north high over emptiness, and hangest the earth upon
nothing." I am mainly solicitous to show that the
author of Ecclesiastes, as it is impossible now to estimate accurately the amount or correctness of his
astronomical knowledge, did not take a narrow or contracted view of the universe. It is probable that his
conceptions of the vastness and grandeur of the universe were equal, in their strength and range, to those
produced by the greatest discoveries of modern astronomy. " True it is, we have gone far beyond the old
astronomy in reducing the distances of the nearest
parts of our visible universe to numerical estimates,
on whose accuracy we may rely with a good degree of
confidence. But we may rationally doubt, whether, as
far as the effort of conception or imagination is concerned, any great advantage comes from this to the con-
templator of the universe, or any greater aid to devout
and adoring thought, than the heavens presented to
pious souls before these numerical estimates were
made. In some cases the very minuteness and accu-

racy of the measurement may detract from the emotional effect. Great as the number is, still, when we regard it as expressive of terrestrial distances, and know precisely by how many involutions, it has been raised from miles, and feet, and barleycorns there is somehow a lessening of that sense of grandeur and vastness which accompanies more indefinite computations. The wandering Greek, or the mystical-minded Egyptian priest, or the devout Jew, or the rapt, stargazing Chaldean, believed as well as we do, that these bodies were at a vast distance ; but with them, thousands of thousands, and myriads of myriads, or ten thousand times ten thousand, may have expressed conceptions in reality as great as our own, and sometimes vastly greater or more powerful."*

We are now prepared, in part, at least, to appreciate the impressiveness and weight of Solomon's words, which we have under consideration. He surveyed the universe in its vastness, by the light of all the science of his day; and pronounces it utterly vain, unless we are to consider it, in respect to its intelligent creatures, as having relation to a spiritual, future state of existence. What was it made for ? What is it continued in existence for ? Does the Creator thus divert himself with trifles ? Answer, skeptic ! You have said or opined that man, so far as a future existence is concerned, is no better than a brute ; that the same thing happens to one as the other ; that death is the end of both. Then, tell me, why did an all-wise, Almighty Creator build this goodly frame of things ? Men are the only visible, rational beings, inhabiting this planet. If you say it was built for im-

* Prof. T. Lewis, LL. D., Bib. Repos., April and July, 1849.

mortals who preceded them on its surface, or who are
to come after them, or for the gratification and improvement of intelligent immortals who view it from
some distant point of the universe, then you, in effect,
disclaim your skepticism, and admit the existence of
a spiritual world, and the doctrine of immortality;
and then, why may not man, why may not you yourself, skeptic, be immortal? Your denial of a future
life makes the universe an enigma which the ingenuity of man can never solve.

But in his survey of the universe, the penitent monarch did not confine himself to its grander and more
sublime features—to the wonders of astronomy; his
commercial enterprises in conjunction with the Tyrians, whose flag is said to have floated simultaneously
in the British and Indian Seas; the voyages of his
ships to the gold lands of Ophir, situated either on the
western coasts of the Indian Peninsula, or the eastern
shores of Africa, must have tended to extend his geographical knowledge much beyond that of the learned
of his own, or any previous age. His commercial al-
lies, in addition to their explorations to the north,
made voyages of four thousand geographical miles to
the south, far within the tropics, to the Indian Seas.
He had a most extensive and accurate acquaintance
with almost every branch of natural history. He
could study and admire nature, in its minuter forms
and processes, as well as in those grander aspects presented in the sun, and moon, and planets—in mount-
ains, oceans, and rivers. He could study and admire
the wayside floweret, although he possessed not the
nomenclature of the modern botanist; the wonders of
the insect world excited his curiosity, although he pos-

sessed not the microscope to reveal the infusoria of the waters, and the organized forms with which the very dust is thick ; " he spake of trees, from the cedar-tree which is in Lebanon, even unto the hyssop that springeth out of the wall ; he spake also of beasts, and of fowls, and of creeping things, and of fishes ;" he was able more perfectly than any preceding naturalist to explain the laws and processes " which govern and distinguish the tribes, classes, families and habits of the vegetable and animal creation." He was no mere sciolist : he did not undervalue learning ; he did not look out upon nature with a purblind vision ; he did not take the narrow, contracted views of an uncultivated, prejudiced mind ; but, with the most comprehensive knowledge, and exalted conceptions, he looked up and around him—at the broad, glittering heavens, at Lebanon, waving with its cedars—at the sea, tossing with its billows, and at the flower which bloomed, and the worm which crawled at his feet. He looked at the heavens and the earth, at the calm and toilsome labour of man, and the moving life of the elements of nature, and he pronounced it all a VANITY, such as no superlative, in human speech, can fully express, if the intelligent inhabitants, and contemplators of this scene are only so many successive generations of beings who cease forever to exist when they die.

If the conclusion of the penitent preacher was sound, by the light of the science of his day, it is certainly no less so in ours, when the discovery of telescopic vision has conferred on us a power immeasurably greater, and whose limits are as yet unattained. While we may be said to stand with a universe on either hand, one concealed by its distance, and the other shrouded by its minuteness from the unaided, or even aided sense, we have by the assistance of modern invention and discovery, a much more perfect knowledge of the vastness and extent of the universe, than was possessed by the philosophers, who held their nightly vigils on the plains of Shinar, or turned their patient gaze toward the heavens from the towers of Thebes and Memphis. Looking through Lord Rosse's leviathan telescope, celestial objects would be revealed to us which are " at such bewildering and inconceivable distances, that light would be nearly twenty thousand years traveling from them to the earth, though constantly speeding at the known rate of one hundred and ninety-two thousand miles in a second of time." It would resolve many of those dim and misty-looking objects, known as *nebulæ*, which are scattered over the heavens, into a blaze of stars. Directed toward the fixed stars, their number and brilliancy would fairly bewilder the beholder. Directed toward the comparatively proximate region of the planets, and especially to the moon, it is said to be difficult to describe what is brought to view, without being suspected of exaggeration.* Lay aside the telescope, and go with the geographer over the continents, islands, and oceans, into which the earth's surface is divided. With the geologist, explore the internal structure of the earth, and mark the various changes which it appears to have undergone. With the chemist, trace the diversified and complicated phenomena of the substances of the external world, and from their analogies, deduce general laws. Take up the microscope, and with the minute philos-

* See Article in Fraser's Magazine.

opher, examine the tiny dew-drop, which trembles on the extremity of a spear of grass—it will present an ocean of life ; or the delicate flower-cup, and you will behold fragrant pastures, replenished with living tribes. Thus from " the remotest *nebulæ,* and from the revolving double stars, we may descend to the minutest organisms of animal creation, whether manifested in the depths of the ocean, or on the surface of our globe, and to the delicate vegetable germs which clothe the naked declivity of the ice-crowned mountain."

Such is the physical universe. Is it all physical and visible ? If there be no spiritual world, who can explain its final cause ? Who is not ready to exclaim with the contrite monarch of old, " Vanity of vanities ; all is vanity. What profit hath a man of all his labour which he taketh under the sun ?" What is the meaning of this long-continued farce, one generation of short-lived beings swept away merely to make room for another just as evanescent ; and the same thing over and over again, from age to age ? What is the whole scene of human affairs to the rational observer, but an empty show, or a tragical pageant ? and what is the creation of the world, and of man himself, so far as he can understand the enigma, but a piece of magnificent folly ?

For sixty centuries men have been making trial of this world to find out, if possible, whether it can yield them solid, lasting happiness. Solomon, even in his day, was constrained to exclaim, when contemplating the world under this aspect, " All is vanity," and to use the strongest kind of affirmation as to the unprofitableness of human striving after the long-sought prize. As he looked back he saw a long succession of generations passing through substantially the same experience. The men who were cotemporary with Abraham, and the men who were cotemporary with Moses, had the same fears and hopes, the same trials and disappointments, as the men of his own generation. He saw that it afforded no greater satisfaction to one generation, than it did to another. If any one was tempted, for a moment, to think that he had discovered some new form in which the trial might be made—some new source of happiness—it was only because he was ignorant of, or had forgotten, what had happened to men in former times. There had been time enough—a sufficient number of generations—for the experiment to be fairly made, and Solomon could not understand how the men of his time could rationally expect that a world which had failed to afford real happiness to others, constituted precisely as they were, could afford it to them.

Nearly three thousand years have passed away since Solomon lived, and pronounced that verdict, which is contained in Ecclesiastes, on this world, considered under the aspect that man must find his whole happiness, and the end of his existence, in it. And during these thousands of years, has there been any thing in men's experience of this world, " concerning which one may say, See, this is new ?" To this question, Solomon furnishes the true answer : " It hath been long ago, in ancient times which were before us." There can never be any other result of this experiment than that which has been produced already a thousand times. If Solomon, viewing the present world under this aspect, had occasion to write on it, " Vanity of vanities," have we discovered any reason for effacing the inscription ?   Have we, in contemplating the material creation, and human striving, discovered any sufficient, final end of either ?

Let the skeptic, who rejects the light of revelation, and denies the existence of a future state, answer.

The material universe stands as a great transparency, not only having the inscription, " There is a God, the Maker and Governor of heaven and earth ;" but having also, this seal, MAN CAN NEVER DIE.

THE VANITY OF LEARNING.

(12.) *I, the Preacher, was king over Israel in Jerusalem.*

The author of Ecclesiastes again announces himself as a king in Jerusalem, adding that he filled this office " over Israel," *i. e*, over the whole Jewish nation, before the separation of the ten tribes ; which, together with the expression that he was king in Jerusalem, unmistakably points to Solomon as the author of the book. In maintaining the theory that Solomon was not the real author, but is only personated in this book, which was written long after his day, it has been said that the emphasis laid on *was* shows that the day had passed by when Koheleth was king ; but this emphasis is employed because Solomon wishes to draw attention to the fact that he was king, or it was after he became a king, that he had that experience, to which he is now about to appeal, in further confirmation, of what he had said (v. 2–11) respecting the vanity of the world and all it contains, as the means of promoting solid happiness. He was a king, and had power and riches, and not a man in the ordinary walks of life ; and therefore possessed all the facilities which any mortal could have, for making a fair experiment.

(13.) *And I gave my heart to seek and search out, by wisdom, concerning all things which are done under heaven, this difficult employment which God hath given to the sons of men, that they may exercise themselves therein.*

The *all things*, to the investigation of which he so earnestly applied his mind, refer to the nature of things, as well as the actions of men ; for viewed under the aspect under which he was considering them, the objects of nature were as great a vanity as the actions of men. The words rendered *difficult employment*, refer to the study to which he had devoted his mind, which he elsewhere styles a weariness of the flesh, xii. 12. He puts the highest honour upon the zealous pursuit of knowledge, by declaring that God has assigned this very employment to his intelligent creatures, diligently to exercise themselves therein. Hence it is not his object to undervalue study, or that knowledge which is the result of study. He exalts it as man's noble, because divinely appointed, work ; but, at the same time, he is about to show its utter vanity as the means of securing and rendering stable our present happiness.

(14.) *I surveyed all things which are done under the sun ; and, behold, all are vanity, and a fruitless striving after wind.*

I *surveyed*, refers to his studious search into all things. After having given his mind to a most careful investigation of human affairs, and the material works of nature, he pronounces the effort to discover a resting-place of the mind, and the final cause of the creation, a striving after the wind, *i. e., studium inane.*

(15.) *That which is crooked can not be made straight; and that which is wanting can not be numbered.*

There are imperfections and deficiencies in human affairs which no study or wisdom can remove, or can reconcile to the complete happiness of man, in the present state. There are problems in nature, and in human lot, which no philosophy can solve, when we circumscribe our view to the present as the only state of existence. It seems to be the object of the proverb contained in this verse to show why all things, even those which are made the special objects of investigation by scholars, when contemplated in that aspect under which Solomon was considering them, should be incapable of yielding satisfaction. Knowledge, under such circumstances, could only make men more keenly sensible to their misery.

(16.) *I communed with my own heart, saying, Lo, I have increased and added to wisdom more than all who have been before me in Jerusalem; yea, my heart has much considered wisdom and knowledge.*

The author represents himself as in the attitude of reflection, and self-communing, and as coming to the conclusion that in the matter of learning, all that goes to make up theoretical knowledge, or practical wisdom, he excelled all, whether rulers or others, who had preceded him at Jerusalem. As it was his object to show the inefficacy of mere learning to solve the mysteries around him, and afford satisfaction, the pertinency of this reference to his own attainments is at once obvious. That he did not over estimate them is clear from inspired history. (1 Kings iv. 29–34.)

(17.) *And I gave my heart to know wisdom, and to know madness and folly : I perceived that this also is striving after wind.*

In his philosophical inquiries, he left no experiment untried ; he even observed senseless and foolish conduct, and its consequences. He turned in every direction, in his search after the means of lasting happiness, as men in pursuit of a treasure will look for it in the most unlikely, unpromising places ; he looked downward as well as upward ; he grovelled as well as soared. No one should accuse him of having made a too partial investigation. He had surveyed the whole field from the loftiest heights to which science can climb, to childish ignorance, and even the levities and incoherencies of insanity. And he asserts that all this search had proved an empty, fruitless striving.

(18.) *For in much wisdom is much dissatisfaction ; and he that increaseth knowledge increaseth sorrow.*

Solomon does not, by these expressions, as in verse 13, refer to study as a difficult or laborious employment, or as a weariness (as in xii. 12) to the flesh. He does not refer to that mental depression which often follows intense study, or to the bodily indisposition which it may occasion. He does not mean to say that the science of his day was so meager, and all was so quickly learned, which it was possible to learn, that the pursuit of it was very unsatisfactory and vexatious. He did not mean to question "the pleasure or good that towers high above all other mere worldly enjoyments and pursuits, and ranks as inferior only to true piety—the pursuit of knowledge." Had he been in the position of a Newton or a Laplace, of a Davy or a Humboldt, his verdict would have been the same. He was looking for peace and happiness ; he felt that he had a soul ; he was speaking as a religious being ; and he declares that if we are to look no higher than those things of which science takes cognizance in the material universe, or which are forced upon our attention in the experience of men, then to increase knowledge is to increase sorrow ; for the more men cultivate their faculties and enlarge their knowledge, the more strong and vivid becomes the conviction, that this search for happiness and the great end of the Creator, in the kingdoms of nature and providence, is a fruitless striving after the wind. The more an intelligent being is elevated and refined by knowledge, the more keenly will he feel the sadness of his condition, if he must put up with the belief that life, in the present state, is the whole of existence.

The purport of the entire passage is clearly this, that science in its inquiries, whether directed to physics or morals, can not of itself alone solve the problem of human existence, nor discover the purpose of the creation.

SCOPE OF ARGUMENT IN § II.

Solomon commences by again alluding to his kingly office. He was king over Israel in Jerusalem. As every thing he attempted was on a magnificent and royal scale, so it was on this same scale he cultivated science. His civil cares must have been many ; but he lived in a time of profound peace, and after his empire had been firmly established by the military prowess and wise statemanship of David. He, moreover, lessened the cares of government, by dividing his kingdom into provinces, over which he placed as many governors. Thus he secured leisure for those learned inquiries, to which, as he informs us, he applied his mind with so much zeal and diligence. He had ever before him the inspiring influence of the example of the most illustrious of fathers. He had been treated as a pupil, as well as a son. He could never forget the earnest words of his parental teacher. " Get wisdom, get understanding ; forget it not." Such a teacher, who had a sense of the importance of knowledge, and who had royal treasures at his command, who was fully able to appreciate the intellectual endowments of a son who was to support the honour of his name and throne, would not fail to open to him all the avenues to learning. He employed not only the first of Israelitish scholars, such as Heman and Ethan, but there can be no doubt he gave to the heir-apparent access to all the stores of knowledge to be found in Chaldea and Egypt. It is most rational to suppose that he resided in this latter country, to prosecute his studies, and then formed that matrimo-

nial alliance with one of its princesses, which was con-
summated soon after he ascended the throne. A
man of fewer intellectual gifts than Solomon would
not have been slow to catch the spirit of a people
who neglected nothing which could accomplish the
mind, and aspired to the honour of being inventors of
the arts and sciences. The first libraries were collected in Egypt, and there he must have had access
to these infant repositories of the knowledge of the
world, which they styled the "remedy for the diseases
of the soul." The astronomy of his teachers was not
mere astrology. So accurate were their observations
of the celestial motions that they could calculate
eclipses, and were the first to regulate the years from
the course of the sun. They were not ignorant that
to three hundred and sixty-five days some hours must
be added to keep pace with the sun ; their only error
lay in supposing that but six hours were wanting ;
that is, in their intercalation, they lacked only a few
minutes of that perfect accuracy to which modern
science has attained. It was in Egypt that geometry
had its birth. The obelisks, pyramids, and temples,
attest the perfection to which the arts, at a very early
day, were carried in that country. "It is a wonderful
fact," says one of the most distinguished investigators
of Egyptian antiquity, "that the first information
which we have with regard to the history and manners
of the Egyptians, shows us a nation which is far advanced in civilized life. The same customs and inventions which prevailed in the Augustan era of this
people, are also found even in the far distant age of
the cotemporary of Joseph."*

* See Hengstenberg's "Egypt and the Books of Moses."

But Solomon was not satisfied with acquiring all the learning of Egypt. He did not, when he graduated at his university, consider his education completed. He went on with his inquiries; he pursued other branches, until he won the reputation of excelling the wisdom of all the children of the east country, and all the wisdom of Egypt. He therefore speaks not only as a king, but as a prince among scholars. He did not undervalue learning; he did not despise it because he was destitute of it. But what does this man, who had sunk his line as far into the depths of science as any philosopher of his own, or any preceding age, who had transferred the seat of science and literature from the Egyptian capital to his own, and made his court the resort of all the most learned men of the surrounding nations, what does this man say?

He says that learning can not solve its own problems, and the further its investigations are carried only increases the difficulty. What is the great object of science? It is to ascertain and explain what are called the laws of nature. It makes no progress, except as it determines these, and is able to point out their harmonious operation in producing the various phenomena of the physical world. One science concerns itself with the elements and properties of air, of water, and of all bodies, and will tell you the exact proportion in which they are combined; it will even demonstrate the disastrous consequences, if that proportion, in atmospheric air, for example, were destroyed. The minute philosopher discovers a perfect geometrical regularity in the smallest snow-flake, its concentric circles, its diverging radii, its equidistant points, and its exact angles. The astronomer lifts his tubes to the heavens, and in the nice and exact movements of its orbs, discovers the traces not only of omnipotence, but of infinite skill. And so in every department of scientific inquiry, the discoveries exhibit an affluence, a wisdom, and a power, on the part of the Creator, which justly excite our amazement. These discoveries, moreover, hold out the assurance that those parts of nature which have as yet defied all attempts at exploration, or are beyond the reach of the explorer, are governed by the same harmonious and beautiful laws.

Now, how is it possible for a philosopher to be so unreflecting as never to ask the question, what a world, which exhibits so much skill in its construction, and is governed by a mechanism and laws so admirably adjusted throughout, was made for ? How can he be a philosopher and not ask it ? It would seem that it would be constantly pressing upon him ; that it would be with him the question of all questions, in comparison with which the laws that govern electrical phenomena, or the affinity that gives its exact form to the crystal, or the forces which control planets and comets, would be pronounced as altogether subordinate. These very laws dictate the inquiry, what was this world made for ?

The hypothesis that it was made for the habitation of generations of men, living for a few scores of years, and that it is to be the only theatre of their existence, is altogether unsatisfactory. Such a purpose seems to be too trivial for the mighty outlay in the universe. It represents Jehovah as creating a world which has not an end corresponding with the vastness of the work, or those evidences of perfect adaptation and design which may be discovered in its minutest parts. Shall we discover adaptation to an end in the organism of an insect, in the leaves, and the capsule of a plant, and so in every part of the creation, from the least to the greatest, and not discover an adaptation as perfect in the complex whole ? To the philosopher who refuses to admit the existence of another state of being, we put the question whether in his inquiries he has discovered any thing, or has the prospect of discovering any thing which can throw light on this question. Have you succeeded any better than Solomon, and the skeptics of his day, in searching out the reason of all the things which are done under heaven ? If we are not to look for the great purpose of the creation beyond what we see in the universe itself, or beyond what is addressed immediately to our senses, then, is not the study of it, since it makes us acquainted with the greatest absurdity imaginable, mere vanity and striving after the wind. It only serves to convince us that the whole scene of human affairs is but a paltry pageant, rendered gorgeous and imposing, by the sublime works and magnificent arrangements of an almighty architect. Well might a philosopher weep, and aver that in much wisdom is much disappointment, if death be the end of man ; if the result of all his studies be that the world is but a great charnel-house, and the business of scholars only to interpret its curious devices and decorations. Would not ignorance be better ? It is emphatically true, and every discovery in science is making it more plain that, if we are not to look for the end of creation beyond what is addressed immediately to our senses, then in much wisdom there is much dissatisfaction, and an increase of knowledge is an increase of disappointment, for the chemist, the geologist, the botanist, the astronomer, in unfolding the curious and exact laws which pervade every part, are only accumulating evidence that it has no end worthy of its creation, and is no better than a magnificent absurdity. We look at the springs and wheels of a watch, and discover that the parts are not only suited to each other, but that the purpose of the definite and uniform motion which is thus obtained, is to furnish us with an accurate measure of time. We look at a steam-engine, and we discover that its great purpose is to propel our ships and carriages, or to drive our looms and spindles. We discover the evidence of intelligence and skill in the parts, by their fitness to promote the great end. It is this which excites our admiration. It would matter not how intricate were the parts, how admirably wrought and polished they might be, or what mechanical forces might be involved in their construction or action, if, when the whole was completed, and put together, it failed to act with the required motion or power. Not only our admiration of the whole, but our admiration of the parts, depends upon the useful purpose which the machine is seen to answer. How then can the philosopher admire the parts of the created universe, however perfect their adaptation, in their subordinate, and related places, when it is impossible for him to read the purpose of that whole, which they constitute ? Must not his admiration, in this case as well as the other, depend upon his being able to discover this purpose, and the suitableness of the parts thereto ? If Solomon had occasion to say that, " in much wisdom is much dissatisfaction, and he that increases knowledge, increases sorrow," then those who have carried, and are carrying their investigations much further, and at every step are discovering evidence of the highest art and skill, but refuse to look for the great purpose of the creation in a state beyond the present, may well adopt the same language ; and in their mouths it will have an intensity of meaning which it never possessed in that of the royal sage of Jerusalem. They contemplate that which is most admirably finished in all its parts, but which is unfinished, broken and dismembered, considered as a whole. They may find that science has many knotty points—that there are some doors at which human curiosity knocks in vain—but the hardest problem of all is that which is the greatest, and lies back of all—nay, is that which, considered in a large view, makes others worthy the attention of the scientific inquirer—" What was the world made for ?" As that which is not can not be numbered, so this question can not be answered, unless we are to look for the finishing of that plan, a part of which we now see, in an invisible, future state. Suppose that some skeptical philosopher has been able, as was expressively said of one,* " to drive all the sciences abreast ;" that with a prodigious power of memory, and a peculiar mode of classifying and retaining knowledge, he has been able to form the most extensive acquaintance with every branch of learning, so that his knowledge bears " something like an appreciable ratio to the sum total of literature and science"—what an enigma must the universe be to such a philosopher ! how his brain must be racked, and his mind puzzled and baffled in

* Leibnitz.

7

his attempts to find out the final cause of that universe which he has made his study ! He has thrown away or refuses to accept the key which will unlock the mystery. He tries to discredit the truth, that there is a spiritual world, and that man has an immortal soul. Pitiable condition ! in his great learning, he has much dissatisfaction. Is not the simple-minded peasant, who dwells in his mountain home, who knows not what it is to speculate on the phenomena of nature, who " just knows, and knows no more, his Bible true," happier far ? is he not wiser too ?

And if science is nonplussed, when it leaves immortality out of view, in accounting for the purpose or ultimate end of the physical universe, what can it do, when it leaves the region of physics, and attempts to unravel the mysteries of Divine providence ? The philosopher, to be worthy of the name, must believe that there is a God, and that the world was made, and is governed by him. But how can he interpret the events of Divine providence, so far as individuals and communities are concerned, if he deny the reality of a state to which this is but preparatory ? What mean our disappointments, and the defeat of our plans and enterprises ? Why do the most virtuous often suffer most, and the basest of men seem frequently to be the most prospered ? Are these events left to accident or chance ? Does a righteous God, whose superintending care extends to sparrows, to motes, and to animalcules, thus disregard his moral creation ? The denial of a future life turns, if possible, the moral into a greater enigma, than it does the physical creation.

Does it not then follow that great learning, considered as the means of obtaining true satisfaction and repose of mind, is utterly vain, a mere feeding on the wind ?

But perhaps it may be said that man discovers an end worthy of his creation in the pleasure to be derived from the acquisition of knowledge, and the cultivation of his intellect, during his brief existence in this world. That there is such a pleasure, I do not of course feel disposed to deny—one of the noblest and purest that do not spring directly from the enjoyment of God. Nor does this admission impair in the least the strength of the argument ; rightly viewed, it will be seen rather to enhance its force. For how the reflection, that reason is so soon to be quenched in the grave, must tend to impair the happiness derived from this source, and even weaken the motive to mental improvement ! Why should we enter upon a course of intellectual cultivation—why should we attend to the arts and sciences—why store our minds with knowledge, if, in the midst of this glorious pursuit, with new fields opening before us, rich in mines of wealth, and the thirst of acquisition ungratified, we are to be struck down, and the intellectual light forever quenched within us ? Why should a career be opened before us that we may fall midway, or stumble at the first step ? Why should we be brought to the door of a temple, to catch a glimpse of the grandeur within, yet to perish in attempting to cross the threshold ? Can such short-sightedness, think ye, be discovered in the plans of an all-wise providence ? Does the work of God, in the noblest part of his noblest creature, display such a defect ? And has man been endowed with mind only to meet, as soon as he has learned the use of its powers, with disappointment? Who can believe that the mind of a Milton, when the body it had occupied ceased to live, perished, and is never again to be active? Who can believe that he does not now, in a more glorious song, celebrate the wonders of redemption, and the bliss of "Paradise Regained?" And who would not dread to be endowed with powers capable of such vast compass— with an imagination that takes a universe for its field, or can find a world in an atom—at home both in the past and in the future, and making both equally subservient to its purposes—if, in their full and vigorous exercise, they are to be brought to a sudden and everlasting close? Who can bear to believe that thought will ever cease? that memory will ever perish? that mind, filled with such aspirations after immortal existence, and to extend the limits of its knowledge, and capable of such anticipations of glory and expansion, is destined to a term of existence, reaching so little beyond that of the merest insect? If the greatest of modern philosophers could liken his acquisitions to the amusements of a child with pebbles on the seashore, in comparison with what remained to be learned, and possessed such conceptions of the progressive improvement of which his powers were capable, who can believe that, having been permitted to enter the outer court of the temple of knowledge, and the desire thus awakened within him of penetrating its inner recesses, death quenched his hopes, and defeated his aspirations? I ask again, would not ignorance be better? If the only end to be reached by study is the grief of having the objects of knowledge multiply around us, and the despair of ever knowing as much as we are ignorant of, the savage or the idiot may well be congratulated on their happiness.

Finally, will it be said that great learning yields a sufficient reward, even on the supposition of there being no hereafter, by gratifying the ambition of leaving a name and a memorial among succeeding generations on the earth ? But a literary immortality is not so easily gained, and is, after all, even in the case of the most successful devotees of science and literature, no immortality. What a lesson is read to us on the vanity of literary fame, when we enter the great libraries of the world ! How comparatively little is known of the men who contributed to fill these crowded alcoves, beyond their names and the titles of their works, in catalogues so voluminous that they may themselves almost be styled libraries. The mere catalogue of the immense library of the British Museum is contained in two hundred folio volumes. In a remote antiquity, we read of a library which at last contained seven hundred thousand volumes. But never was the accumulation of books more rapid than it is in our day ; and the art of printing has put it beyond the torch of war, or of the incendiary, ever to rob science or literature of any truly valuable contribution. In Germany alone, it is estimated that there are about fifty thousand men who have written one or more books. The catalogue of every Leipzig half-yearly book-fair contains the names of more than a thousand German authors. " According to a moderate calculation," says Menzel, " ten millions of volumes are annually printed. Should the number increase at the rate it has hitherto done, the time will soon come, when a catalogue of ancient and modern

German authors will contain more names than there are living readers. In the year 1816, there were published, for the first time, more than three thousand books ; in 1822, for the first time, above four thousand ; in 1827, for the first time, above five thousand ; in 1832, for the first time, above six thousand ; and in 1837, nearly eight thousand." In 1854, the number of books printed exceeded ten thousand.* A catalogue of the books published in Great Britain from 1814 to 1846, which contains only the titles of the new works, and new editions of old ones, makes a closely-printed volume of five hundred and forty-two pages.

From the accumulations of these huge masses of literature, two reflections arise, which serve at once to illustrate its vanity, if there be no higher immortality than that which is conferred by literary fame on earth. The first refers to the great and constantly increasing difficulty (arising from the vastness of the materials) of becoming truly learned. What can the scholars of coming ages do, " as the domain of human knowledge indefinitely widens, and the creations of human genius indefinitely multiply ? They may know more, and with greater accuracy than their less favoured predecessors ; nevertheless, their knowledge must bear a continually diminishing ratio to the sum of human science and literature ; they must traverse a smaller and smaller segment of the ever widening circle. Nay, it may well be that the accumulations of even one science (chemistry or astronomy, for instance) may be too vast for one brief life to master."

But supposing this difficulty overcome, and that

* Gordon's Translation of Munzel's "German Literature."

one has won the reputation, among his cotemporaries, of being a profound scholar, yet let him read in the fate of others, as great or greater, the vanity of hoping for a literary immortality. It has been truly said to be probable, that nine tenths of those who are familiar with the doctrines of Newton, have never studied him, except at second hand. And "if comparative neglect be the lot of the writings even of Newton, what must be naturally and universally the fate of inferior men? Of that treatise of Descartes, in which he lays the foundations of analytical geometry, how few of those who have pursued that science to heights and depths of which Descartes never dreamed, ever perused a syllable! The case of the cultivators of chemistry, and of many other modern sciences, is still more desperate. A few years will obliterate all traces of their works ; their names will soon be known only in the page of the historian of science, who will duly record in a few brief lines the discoveries their authors made, and the still greater blunders they committed." " The empty titles of their books will be recorded in catalogues ; and a few lines be granted to them in biographical dictionaries, with what may be truly called a *post mortem* examination of criticism ; a space which, as those church-yards of intellect become more and more crowded, necessarily also becomes smaller and smaller, till for thousands, not even room for a sepulchral stone will be found." " Of the literature," I quote from an article in a late number of the *Edinburg Review*, " which chiefly occupies each generation, the bulk, even of its treasures, perishes ; and as time makes fresh accumulations, those of preceding ages pass for the most part into quiet oblivion. The process which has taken effect on the past will be repeated on the present age, and on every subsequent one ; so that the period will assuredly come when even the great writers of our days, who seem to have such enduring claims on our gratitude and admiration, will be as little remembered as others of equal genius who have gone before them ; when, if not wholly forgotten or superseded, they will exist only in fragments or specimens—these fragments and specimens shrinking into narrower compass as time advances. In this way time is perpetually compiling a vast *index expurgatorius.* Probably scarcely a day now passes but sees the last leaf, the last tattered remnant of the last copy of some work (great or small), of some author, perish by violence or accident—by fire, flood, or the crumbling of mere decay. It is surely an impressive thought—this silent, unnoticed extinction of another product of some once busy and aspiring mind ! Paradoxical as it may seem, the chief cause of the virtual oblivion of books is no longer their extinction, but the fond care with which they are preserved. The press is more than a match for the moth and the worm, or the mouldering hand of time ; yet the great destroyer equally fulfills his commission by burying books under the pyramid which is formed by their accumulation. It is a striking example of the impotence with which man struggles against the destiny which awaits him and his works, that the very means he takes to insure immortality, destroy it ; that the very activity of the press—of the instrument by which he seemed to have taken pledges against time and fortune—is that which will make him the spoil of both. The books themselves may no longer die, but their spirit does ; and they become like old men whose bodies have outlived their minds—a spectacle more piteous than death itself. The great bulk of writers must be content, after having shone for a while, to be wholly or nearly lost to the world. Thus does the fame which looks most like immortality resemble every other form of that painted shadow ; in most instances it dwindles into a name, and that name not always legible. *Vanity of vanities ; all is vanity."*

7*

§ III. Chap. ii. 1–17.

THE MOCKERY OF MIRTH, LUXURY, AND WORLDLY SPLENDOUR.

(1.) *I said in my heart, Come now, I will try thee with mirth, and do thou enjoy good: and, behold, this also was vanity.*

Solomon here describes himself as making a new experiment. He had tried great learning and discovered that he could not find solid and lasting happiness, in its pursuit and acquisition ; he now proposes to make trial of sensual pleasure. The *good* which he bids his soul enjoy is the pleasure of sense— the gratification of appetite, of refined tastes, and the love of earthly grandeur. But this attempt proved as vain, or more vain, than the former one.

(2.) *Of laughter I said, It is mad : and of pleasure, What avails it?*

Turning to boisterous mirth or rioting, he was constrained to say that it was more becoming a maniac than a rational being ; and in respect to pleasure, worldly pleasure of every kind, he asks, what good does it do, or what does it avail in yielding real happiness ?

He means to sweep the whole field, from laughter, or silly, boisterous mirth and rioting, to the most refined pleasures of sense.

(3.) *I resolved to stimulate my body with wine, and to lay hold on folly, while my mind should still continue to guide with wisdom; until I should see whether this is the good for the sons of men, which they should pursue under heaven all the days of their life.*

The word which is translated *to stimulate*, Gesenius renders by *firmare*, to strengthen. It literally means *to draw, to draw out*, in the sense of extracting. By means of wine, Solomon determined to extract from his flesh, *i. e.*, excite, all its dormant sensibilities to pleasure, to put a keener edge upon its lusts and passions. Hitzig, whom Stuart follows, singularly translates, *to draw or drag along my body by wine*, as a man is borne in a chariot. In correspondence with this, as the steed is often furious, they represent Koheleth as employing discretion or wisdom as a charioteer. It is no wonder that the latter writer, although he adopted it, thought that such a symbolical representation seemed strange and far-fetched.

Solomon was not so unwise as to seek happiness in beastly drunkenness. He knew full well that such intoxication only fills a man with greater misery. He resolved to go no further than that pleasurable excitement which a limited use of wine would produce— that his *mind should still continue to guide with reason*. He would not drink to insensibility, or to the loss of self-control. He must not lose, but use his intelligence, in watching the experiment, the hazardous experiment he was trying. *Wine* may be used here, by synecdoche, for delicious meats, or luxurious living. It was his object to make trial of such a style of life that he might learn whether there could be found in it that *good for the sons of men which they should pursue* during their mortal life. This singular attempt to unite folly and wisdom that, if possible, he might extract from the strange compound some elixir for the miseries of existence, while it proves the exhaustive character of Solomon's experiments in search of some solid happiness in the world, also illustrates the desperate state to which ignorance of revelation, or its willful neglect or rejection, may drive the mind of a thinking man.

(4.) *I made me great works; I builded me houses; I planted me vineyards.*

From a general, he descends to a more particular account of that earthly good (v. 1.) in which he had sought happiness ; and in this and some of the following verses presents a somewhat formal enumeration. And first he refers to the great works and buildings he constructed for the purpose of surrounding himself with objects of splendour and luxury. He built not only palaces for himself and his Egyptian wife, which occupied years in building, but cities even—such as Tadmour of the desert, and Baalath, known in modern times as Palmyra, and Baalbec, 1 Kings ix. 15–19. Burger says it is wonderful, that in this enumeration of Solomon's great works, no mention should be made of the temple he built at Jerusalem, and adds that the author seems to have omitted it, influenced by reverence.*   But the true reason of its being omitted is plainly because Solomon was enumerating only those great works by which he sought to contribute to his grandeur, and furnish the means of sensual pleasure. The temple was built during the years of his early piety, for the worship of God.   Burger includes this omission among the reasons he assigns for not attributing the authorship of Ecclesiastes to Solomon. (See the *Prolegomena* of the same work, p. 12.)

(5.) *I made me gardens, and pleasure-grounds, in which I planted fruit-trees of every kind.*

He sought to make nature, as well as art, contribute to the formation of that paradise with which he had resolved to surround himself.   He sought pleasure from horticulture, and the beauties of nature—from flowers and tempting fruits.

(6.) *I made me reservoirs from which to water the grove, producing trees.*

There are reservoirs in the vicinity of Jerusalem which are still known as Solomon's pools.   Richardson thinks that the antiquity of their appearance entitles them to be considered as his work.   They are lined with solid masonry, and one of them is more than six hundred feet long.   If the pools of Solomon were similar in extent and solidity of construction to these, they might well be included in his great works. The object he had in view in constructing them is stated ; it was the multiplication of those most beautiful objects in nature, trees, to add further adornment and variety to the paradise he was constructing.

* Comm. in Ecc. p. 27.

(7.) *I purchased servants and maidens, and had servants born in my house ; and much wealth in herds and cattle belonged to me, more than all who were before me in Jerusalem.*

These slaves were the children of the Amorites, Hittites, Perizzites, Hivites, and Jebusites, who were left in the land, and not destroyed when the children of Israel took possession of it. (1 Kings, ix. 21.) The extent of his household, and his great wealth in herds and flocks may be judged of by the daily provision which was made for their sustenance. The " provision for one day was thirty measures of fine flour, and threescore measures of meal, ten fat oxen, and twenty oxen out of the pastures, and a hundred sheep, besides harts and roebucks, and fallow deer, and fatted fowl." " And Solomon had forty thousand stalls of horses, for his chariots, and twelve thousand horsemen. And those officers provided victuals for king Solomon, and for all that came unto king Solomon's table, every man in his month ; they lacked nothing. Barley also, and straw for the horses, and dromedaries, brought they unto the place where the officers were, every man according to his charge." 1 Kings, iv. 22–28. No ruler, and no man of his nation, had ever equaled Solomon in the abundance of his wealth of every kind.

(8.) *I amassed for myself also silver and gold, and the treasures of kings, and the provinces : I procured for myself men-singers and women-singers, and the delights of the sons of men—musical instruments, and that of all sorts.*

He kept constantly at sea a navy, bringing gold and silver, and ivory, and apes, and peacocks. The princes of neighbouring nations sent him presents of vessels of silver and gold ; he made silver so plenty that "it was nothing accounted of in the days of Solomon."

He filled his palaces and pleasure-grounds with the sweetest strains of music, both vocal and instrumental. He gathered all those singers who excelled, both male and female ; and to these he added players on instruments of all sorts which had then been invented. In rendering, in conformity with the received version, the Hebrew *shidah ve-shidoth* musical instruments of all sorts, I have been governed by the consideration, that this meaning, on the whole, seems best suited to the passage. Other meanings have been suggested, such as *female captives, fields, cup-bearers, wife and wives.* This last is the meaning preferred by Gesenius, making the singular refer to the queen, the king's proper wife, and the plural to his concubines. It may seem singular that such a variety of meanings should be given to these words, but they do not elsewhere occur, and their derivation is doubtful. Musical instruments agree well with gardens and groves, and choirs of singers, and that scene of elegant and refined voluptuousness which Solomon was describing. These instruments were cymbals, and psalteries, and harps, and trumpets, and were used as accompaniments of the voice. 2 Chron. v. 12, 13.

(9.) *So I waxed great, and increased more than all that were before me in Jerusalem ; my wisdom also remained with me.*

Solomon again calls attention to the fact that in trying the experiment as to what sensual pleasure can do for the happiness of man, he had excelled, in the riches and facilities at his command, all who had preceded him at Jerusalem. Not Absalom, nor Adonijah—not even David, had equaled him in splendour and magnificence. But he retained his wisdom, or discretion. In all these appliances of luxury and earthly grandeur, he was on his guard ; he did not become a besotted sensualist or debauchee. He was bringing hilarity and the most elegant and refined pleasures of sense to the test of philosophy, to see if he could find in them the secret of true happiness.

(10.) *And whatever my eyes desired I kept not from them, I withheld not my heart from any joy ; for my heart rejoiced in all my labour, and this was my portiom from all my labour.*

He thus concludes his account of this costly and grand experiment, by including in the inventory of his sensual pleasures, all that could please his eyes, or could give the least joy to his heart. Not one of these things were beyond his reach. He had as much delight from them as mortal could derive. If any other man had experienced any worldly pleasure, of which he could boast, Solomon more. But this fleeting enjoyment was all the portion or reward which he received from his labour in providing all these vast and expensive means of pleasure. A momentary joy was all he could expect or receive. There was no lasting happiness to be had as the reward or portion for all this outlay and toil.

(11.) *Then I surveyed all my works which my hands had wrought, and the labour which I had toiled in performing : and behold, it was all vanity and striving after wind, and there was no profit under the sun.*

Standing amid his gardens and groves, redolent with perfumes, or vocal with music, or wandering through his gorgeous palaces, and surveying the costly means which his skill had invented, and his regal wealth supplied, for the indulgence of voluptuousness, and the discovery of something more satisfactory than the short-lived pleasures of the hour, we have here the result of the wise man's experiment ; this is his conclusion : " All is vanity and striving after wind ; substantial happiness can never be found in this way under the sun."

(12.) *Then I turned myself to consider wisdom, and madness, and folly ; for what can the man do that cometh after the king ? even that which has been already done.*

Having considered what satisfaction can be derived from knowledge (i. 12–18), and what from the pleasures of sense (ii. 1–11), he now proceeds to compare these two sources of happiness, and to pass judgment on their relative value. That judgment is stated in the verses immediately following. Again he alludes to the peculiar advantages under which he had made these experiments. " What can the man do who shall attempt after me to repeat these experiments ? Can any one expect to try them on a scale equally

grand, or one more favourable to extracting from learning and pleasure all they can minister to the abiding
happiness of man ?" He can only do over again precisely what I have done, or fall short of what I have
done on so royal a scale.

(13.) *And I saw that wisdom excelleth folly
as far as light excelleth darkness.*

This is that judgment which he passes on the relative value of knowledge and the pleasures of sense,
when compared as sources of true happiness. They
differ as widely as light and darkness.

(14.) *The wise man's eyes are in his head,
but the fool walketh in darkness ; yet still I myself perceived also that one event happeneth
to all.*

" Knowledge is power ;" this is the great advantage
which the instructed man has over the ignorant. It
is this which makes him acquainted with many advantages and ways of being happy which are concealed
from the ignorant.

Yet notwithstanding the advantages of knowledge
over ignorance, he still clings to the conclusion, to
which he had before arrived, that there is but little
satisfaction if all the knowledge which a man can
gain must be gained in this world, and end when he
leaves it. If death be the end of both the scholar and
the clown, the former has but little advantage over
the latter. Its continuance is limited to a few
fleeting days. The grave reduces them to the same
level.

(15.) *Then I said in my heart, As it happeneth to the fool, so it happeneth to me ; then why was I more wise ? Then I said in my heart that this also is vanity.*

The idea in the close of the preceding verse is stated more at large. If death is the end of man, what motive, what sufficient motive, have we for cultivating our minds, and extending our knowledge ?

(16.) *For there is no remembrance of the wise man more than of the fool forever ; seeing that in the days to come shall all that now is be forgotten. And how dieth the wise man ? as the fool.*

The works, the learning, the discoveries of scholars, can not ensure them a remembrance among succeeding generations. What a significant monument of disappointed hopes is a great library even, where, under piles of books, lie entombed the offspring of so many once teeming, active brains. And in the article of death itself, what advantage does philosophy give the philosopher over the simplest swain, or cottager ? Can it pluck away the sting of death ?

(17.) *Therefore I hated life, because what is done under the sun appeared evil unto me ; for all is vanity and striving after wind.*

This was Solomon's experience, when he was seeking satisfaction from the world, or when he banished from his mind, or ignored for a season, a future world. He felt how empty, and unsatisfying is this world.

His whole nature revolted at what he saw and felt. Every thing looked dark, evil, and mysterious. And to the same state must every reflecting man be brought who rejects the doctrine of immortality. O wretched condition ! for a man to hate his own existence.

SCOPE OF ARGUMENT IN § III.

The author of the book of Ecclesiastes discovered that the fame which a man may attain from the cultivation of letters is evanescent, and even that the pleasure which is derived from the acquisition of knowledge would be greatly diminished, and the motive to self-culture weakened, by the reflection that the soul exists only in the present state. While an earthly immortality is a painted shadow, a cultivated mind must feel more keenly than an unreflecting one, the sad destiny of speedy annihilation. Hence in much wisdom is much dissatisfaction, and he that increaseth knowledge increaseth sorrow.

He enters upon another experiment. He leaves the study for the gay world. " He adjourns," as Henry observes, " out of the library, the laboratory, the council-chamber, into the park and the play-house, his garden and summer-house ; exchanges the company of the philosophers and grave senators for that of the wits and gallants and the *beaux esprits* of his court, to try if he could find true satisfaction among them." He pushes the experiment, not satisfied with an half-way attempt and to the pleasures of fancy adds those of luxury. He tries the exhilaration of the wine-cup, and has his table loaded with the luxuries of all climes, still acquainting his heart with wisdom, or comparing philosophically these sensual gratifications with the more refined pleasures of a cultivated intellect. In the indulgence of the lower appetites, he sought for a solution of that problem which he had failed of finding in the cultivation of the higher faculties. We may well pronounce it a marvelous attempt ; but he meant with his experiments to cover the whole ground ; and we shall see, when we have gone through them all, that it is difficult to conceive of any experiment which he did not try.

Behold now, Solomon, in the midst of the gay, the voluptuous, and the profligate ! He fills his court with buffoons and clowns, and those who with their witticisms and jests could excite merriment, and laugh away preciseness and melancholy. His palaces and pleasure-grounds resounded with boisterous mirth and revelry. Methinks I hear him say, " Come, now, O my soul, rejoice ; give a free rein to every desire ; throw care to the winds. I will see whether, in the noise of song and laughter, I can drown the voice that echoes in my ears, or lose the bitterness of the reflections which my study of the universe has awakened." Perhaps he went, with his gay and frivolous retinue, from one royal residence to another, from his own sumptuous palace to that built for his queen, from Jerusalem to Baaleth, or to his city in the desert, hoping to find, in change of scene, the long-sought prize. But in vain ; when the laugh was loudest, and merriment was carried to its highest pitch, the sickening sensation would return upon him, that eternal oblivion awaited him in the grave. Had he left his reason behind him, given it a final adieu, when he plunged into these gay and frivolous scenes, it might have been different ; but he resolved to carry his habits of reflection with him, and to sit in judgment on a life of amusement and merriment, whether it was a becoming way to spend an existence which must so soon terminate forever. And when he looked at the whole subject in the light of reason, laughter sounded in his ears like the ravings of insanity. "I said of laughter, It is mad." How unseemly in a creature who is so soon to perish forever ! And how can mirth put any different aspect on human life ? Does it not rather aggravate its mockery ? Is it not like dressing a corpse with garlands and bridal ornaments ? If death be an eternal sleep, or but a leap into the dark, does it become those who may at any moment feel the lethargy creeping over them, to be merry ? does it become those who are hastening toward the precipice from which they are to make their final plunge, to dance and sing on the way ? A philosopher, distinguished by his writings on political economy, has recorded of a no less celebrated cotemporary, that when he was drawing near to death, he cheerfully amused himself with Lucian, a game of whist, and some good-humored drollery about Charon and his boat. The man who sought thus to amuse himself, in his dying moments, has been styled the great " master of negations." He denied every thing, not only revelation, but the very existence of the external world. He maintained that we have no knowledge of any thing beyond death—that, at the best, it is but a leap into the dark. Did he then act in the character of a philosopher, when he gave himself up to amusements so trifling, at the very moment he was expecting to sink into nothingness, or take this fearful leap ? If he was sincere in his opinions, are we not compelled to the belief that he was acting an assumed and most unnatural part, in his drollery about Charon and his boat, and his laughs over the jokes of Lucian ? Well has Bishop Horne* remarked that the man who could meet death in such a frame of mind, "might smile over Babylon in ruins, esteem the earthquake, which destroyed Lisbon, an agreeable occurrence, and congratulate the hardened Pharaoh on his overthrow in the Red Sea." What ! laugh and be merry when just poising upon the awful precipice of annihilation or oblivion ! Shall this be called heroic firmness in death ? It is only the ma-niac who would do it. Compare the modern philoso-pher with the ancient philosopher of Jerusalem. One says it is becoming the philosopher to jest and smile as death—that death which may terminate existence for ever—approaches. The other says of laughter, " It is mad ; and of mirth, What can it do ?" Which de-serves the name of a philosopher ? †

He next proceeds to give an account of his great works, and his luxurious style of life. He would try

* In his letters to Dr. Adam Smith.

† Lines written by the Princess Amelia, a little before her death :

Unthinking, idle, wild, and young,
I laughed, and danced, and talked, and sung ;
And proud of health, of freedom vain,
Dreamed not of sorrow, care, or pain ;
Concluding in those hours of glee,
That all the world was made for me.
But when the hour of trial came,
When sickness shook this trembling frame,
When folly's gay pursuits were o'er,
And I could dance and sing no more,
It then occurred how sad 'twould be,
Were this THE ONLY WORLD FOR ME.

something more dignified than jests and laughter—splendour and luxury. He erected palaces ; he laid out gardens, parks, and vineyards ; he dug artificial lakes, and built superb reservoirs ; he increased his retinue, his flocks and herds; he amassed imperial treasures of silver and gold ; and employed bands of musicians and choirs of singers. None of our modern epicureans can ever hope to equal that princely style of life which Solomon adopted. Not even the richest princes and nobles of Europe could vie with the splendour and luxury of his court. He equalled, or went beyond, all that we have ever read of oriental luxury, in ancient or modern times. He may well claim to have made him great works, for he built cities—among others Tadmour of the Desert, and Baalath, known in modern times as Palmyra, and Baalbec—which are among the most celebrated of the ancient cities of the east. Tadmour was situated nearly midway between the rivers Orontes and the Euphrates, in the great Syrian desert, and at length became one of the great emporiums of trade between India and Rome. The traveler sees in its ruins—which lie scattered over the sand for the space of a mile or two around—the evidences of its former strength, grandeur, and importance. Baalbec lies at the base of Mount Lebanon, about forty miles from Beyrout, and was a city of even greater magnificence than Tadmour. It was nearer Jerusalem, and being much more attractively situated in respect to natural scenery, than the former city, was undoubtedly one of the court residences. It is said that its ruins strike the mind of the beholder with an air of greatness beyond those of the ancient cities in Greece and Egypt, and afford evidence of the boldest plan ever attempted in architecture. It is by no means improbable that some of the enormous stones—stated to be so massive that the ordinary mechanical contrivances now in use would be inadequate to move them—which are still to be seen in the foundations of the walls and monuments which mark the sites of those ancient cities, were wrought by the masons whom Solomon employed. It was in these magnificent cities, as well as at Jerusalem, that he carried out the experiment of testing whether the supreme good which men ought to propose to themselves, was to be found in sensual pleasure or luxurious living—whether in them was to be found a sufficient end for an existence which must cease at death. Here was ample scope for an inventive genius, for architectural taste, for the employment of the most skillful artizans and workmen, and for occupation and entertainment in watching the progress of the mighty enterprise.

But it was doubtless in his palace at Jerusalem that the display of art, of wealth, and luxury, was the most vast and imposing. It is not improbable that " the king's palace"—" the house for his kingdom"—" the king's house," " the house of the forest of Lebanon," and " the house where he dwelt," which he was employed thirteen years in building, were together one vast pile so arranged as to accommodate the several divisions of the royal household. We may suppose that this imposing structure was situated in the vicinity of the temple, in a large oblong inclosure, with ample apartments for the officers of the court, foreign embassadors, and distinguished visitors. " The chief buildings occupy the centre of an area, and appear in three sections or divisions. The middle section is a spacious portico, or hall, forty-five feet high, and one hundred and fifty feet in length, by seventy-five in breadth." The ceiling of this magnificent hall is of cedar, and supported by forty-five cedar columns, fifteen in a row. The abundant use of cedar in the construction of this section of the palace, may have given it the name of " the house of the forest of Lebanon." It contained, in addition to the great hall or reception-room, a throne-room, or judgment-hall, where the king appeared with his crown and regal robes on occasions of state. On each side of this central division was an open square, appropriated, perhaps, to fruits and flowers, and filled with arbours, fountains, and statuary, and whatever a refined taste might suggest or luxury crave. The gardens on the right would separate the block in which were the king's private apartments from the middle division, containing the great hall and throne-room, and those on the left would serve the same purpose for the apartments of the queen. Thus we have a range of palaces, each distinct in itself, but probably connected by various passages. They were built of the most massive and beautiful materials ; even the foundations were of " costly stones," and the walls within were wainscoted with slabs of great value. The throne, although large in its dimensions, was built of solid ivory, and overlaid with the purest gold. Two carved lions stood on each side of the seat of the throne, and twelve lions stood, six on each side, on the steps leading up to the throne. He had two hundred targets, and three hundred shields, all of wrought gold, which were deposited in " the house of the forest of Lebanon," and probably were worn by his body-guard on great occasions of state. The vessels and dishes of his table were of solid gold, silver being considered too cheap a material for such a purpose. The nobles of his court, his attendants, and pages, appeared in a costume becoming the splendour which surrounded them. He had almost inexhaustible treasures in silver and gold, in oxen, horses, asses, and camels. His vineyards produced him wine, his gardens and orchards the most delicious fruits ; the daily supply for his table, for all attached to or visiting the royal household, was not less than two hundred and fifty bushels of fine flour, five hundred bushels of common meal, ten stall-fed and twenty grass-fed beeves, one hundred sheep, and an indefinite quantity of poultry and wild game. A host of servants surrounded him to anticipate every want ; the most skillful players upon the psaltery, the harp, and other instruments, were in constant attendance. He had whatever his eyes desired ; he withheld not his heart from any joy which his imagination could conceive. When he rode he was attended with an armed guard of sixty chosen men, with drawn swords. His chariot was made of the wood of Lebanon, the bottom of it was of gold, its canopy or covering was of richly embroidered purple, supported by pillars encased with silver. One of his visitors, although accustomed to royal magnificence and splendour, when she had seen his palace, the meat of his tables, the attendance of his ministers and servants in their rich apparel, his cup-bearers, and his ascent by which he went up to the house of the Lord, was overwhelmed with amazement, and exclaimed, " the half was not told me.'

It has been asked how such a king as Solomon could

expend so much time, labour, and money, for the purpose of magnificence and display. We have the answer in this book. He was putting it to test on a scale such as only the richest of earthly monarchs could try, whether this world, when you deny to man the privilege of looking beyond it, for his highest happiness and exaltation, can redeem his existence from the veriest mockery. He excelled all who were before him in Jerusalem ; and what can the man do, whether king or subject, in any age or country, who cometh after this king ? who ever did or can excel, or even equal him in earthly parade and grandeur ? The display of wealth by the nobles and merchant princes of London and Paris, in our day, is no more than as the amusements of children, in comparison with the splendour that surrounded the king of Israel. And the same would doubtless hold true at an earlier period in modern history, when to affect earthly grandeur was more in vogue than in our day. Wallenstein, with his vast estates and revenues, his immense household and retinue of retainers and nobles ; the Duke of Sully, possessed of all that the most aspiring mind could aim at—the confidence of his royal master, accumulated wealth, great honours, and power by his offices to do almost what he pleased ; Cardinal Wolsey, rivaling the pomp of royalty itself, sitting in a golden chair, sleeping in a golden bed, dining from a table covered with cloth of gold, his garments shining with gold and silk, even his horse-cloths and harnesses of the same costly materials, and surrounding himself with a household of barons, knights, and sons of the first families, looking for preferment, to the number of eight hundred persons—none of these, not even Henry

VIII., whose servant that ambitious ecclesiastic was, and whose wealth may well entitle him to be styled the modern Crœsus, equaled, or had it in their power to excel the royal magnificence of that monarch whose confessions we have in Ecclesiastes. If they had possessed wisdom like that of Solomon, and their wisdom had remained with them as it did with him ; if they had made the same experiment, with the same enlightened views, *viz.*, whether a sufficient end for human existence can be found in earthly grandeur alone, would they not have come to the same conclusion, that all is vanity, and striving after the wind ? Would they not have adopted the mournful soliloquy which the great English dramatist has put into the mouth of Wolsey ?

> "Farewell, a long farewell, to all my greatness!
> This is the state of man; to-day he puts forth
> The tender leaves of hope, to-morrow blossoms,
> And bears his blushing honours thick upon him:
> The third day comes a frost, a killing frost:
> And—when he thinks * * * full surely
> His greatness is a ripening—nips his root,
> And then he falls, as I do. I have ventured,
> Like wanton boys that swim on bladders,
> These many summers in a sea of glory ;
> But far beyond my depth; my high-blown pride
> At length broke under me ; and now has left me,
> Weary and old with service, to the mercy
> Of a rude stream that must forever hide me.
> Vain pomp and glory of this world, I hate ye!"

What a mockery there is in all the pomp and glory of this world, if there be another for which we can be prepared only by the mortification of pride and sensual lusts ! And may it not with equal truth be said, what a mockery there is in it all, if there be no other,

and man reaches the goal of his being at the grave?
What does it amount to? Is it not as if a man were
to put on ornaments, and dress himself in gay apparel,
and ride in state to his execution. He hastens to oblivion; the rude Lethean stream will soon sweep over
him. He may live ten, twenty, or forty years, but he
will soon lie beneath the cold, dull marble, and be
forgotten. What avails it that he lived in a palace
for this brief season, and surrounded himself with all
the splendours and luxuries that earth can yield?
Can it alleviate the poignancy of the thought, that he
is soon to bid an eternal farewell to existence? The
martyr, conscious of innocence, might go to the stake
with smiles, because he expects to live forever in the
presence of that Saviour to whom he is faithful to the
end. But how can one who does not thus expect to
live, unless he bids adieu to all reflection (as Solomon
did not) when he plunges into scenes of splendid luxury and dissipation, avoid feeling that every cup of
joy is drugged with bitterness, or avoid seeing the
ghastly skeleton seated at every feast? for he must
leave these scenes, and there is nothing better beyond
—there is NOTHING beyond. Perhaps it may be
said, that as oblivion so soon awaits us, it is better to
be happy while we may; we may as well sing and
dance, as mourn and lament on our way to our doom.
But will the man, the wise man, whose eyes are in his
head, who has learned to use, and loves to use, his reasoning faculty, say so? Will the man who searches
into the final cause of human existence say so? Is a
satisfactory answer thus obtained to the question, What
was man made for? Ah! how sickening is the thought
that all that wealth and the honours of the world can

do is to furnish him with adornments and gay trappings on his way to nothingness. But who can be possessed of such folly as to regard the full gratification of every sensual appetite as commensurate with his intellectual and moral endowments, or the great purpose of his being ? Thought, understanding, volition, as they appear in man, are not requisite for beings created merely to eat and drink, and after a few days, go down to the place of silence. The dullest animals may gorge themselves, and have sense to search out their food, and some of them even to make provision for the future. But man is not like the beasts that perish ; he is filled with aspirations after eternal existence, and he is endowed with powers fitting him for this noble end. With no higher aim than mere sensual pleasure, man would be an anomaly in the universe, with useless endowments ; or, if employed, necessarily perverted and misapplied. We might well ask, " Wherefore hast Thou made all men in vain ?" To say that with such an intellectual and moral nature as man possesses, he was created merely for the enjoyment of carnal pleasures—to " walk in honour's gaudy show," or repose amid the luxuries of wealth, is to impeach the wisdom of the great Creator ; it is to assert a failure in respect to the chief of his works, while we admit that even in inanimate matter may be traced the evidence of perfect design.

Solomon, in conclusion, is led to compare earthly splendour and luxury with learning, as independent sources of happiness, and to give the preference to the latter. He concludes that a man who has knowledge and a cultivated intellect is better off than one who has palaces and pleasure-grounds, and all the luxuries of wealth at his command, who is at the same time destitute of knowledge. But although knowledge is better than something else, it is not the chief good ; he still adheres to his former conclusion, that if there be no future state, learning is a most vain thing, and tends to increase man's dissatisfaction. There is but little difference between a wise man and a fool, if death be the end of both ; and he might well be sick of life, if its highest aim be to increase that knowledge which can only serve to make the conviction stronger and more painful, that he must shortly sink into the same oblivion as the ignorant slave, or an infant which knows not its right hand from its left.

§ IV. Chap. II. 18–26.

(18.) *Yea, I hated all my labour which I had performed under the sun ; which I should leave to the man who shall be after me.*

Solomon had been speaking of his great works, and lest any should think that he might have found solid happiness in the pleasures of business or successful enterprises, he proceeds to point out the fatal defects which attended this kind of gratification. His dissatisfaction arose, in the first instance, from the reflection, that he must leave all these things. He could live only a short time to superintend and enjoy them. Others would soon come into possession of them. But his grief was not merely because he must leave them ; it was enhanced by another consideration stated in the next verse.

(19.) *And who knoweth whether he shall be a wise man, or a fool? And yet shall he have dominion over all my work in which I have toiled, and which I have wisely performed under the sun. This also is vanity.*

If the heir-apparent, Rehoboam, of whom perhaps he had some distrust, should not turn out to be a wise man, how soon would the glory of the kingdom wane ! And how little could these magnificent works, on which Solomon had expended so much thought and treasure, do to save it and the reigning prince from contempt ! How hard it is for those who have made an idol of the world, and have seldom permitted their thoughts to extend beyond it, to leave it, and especially to give up their adored possessions to heirs in whose sagacity and economy they have little confidence ! What a poor insignificant end of life it is, for men to give themselves up to the accumulation of a great estate in so changing a world as is this, where their possessions are liable so soon to pass into the hands of others, the children of strangers, or enemies, even ! (Ps. xlix. 10–14.) Did Solomon have some forebodings of the disasters that were to attend his successor's reign ? Did he see through the vista of coming years, and gaze on the ruins of Tadmour and Baaleth ?

(20.) *Then I came even to give up my heart to despair, in respect to all my work in which I had toiled under the sun.*

He speaks just as every thinking man who has fixed all his hopes on things below, must speak—I say just as every man who gives himself to serious, calm reflection, however successful he may have been in his enterprises, must speak. If death is to end all—if he has no treasures laid up in heaven—if there be no heaven in which to lay up treasures—well may he give up his heart to despair, in respect to the work to which his strength and life have been devoted. He must leave his wealth to others. His inward thought may have been that his houses should continue forever, and his dwelling-places to all generations ; and he may have called his lands after his own name, but a moment's calm thought teaches him that if death be the end of man, he is at last no better than the brutes that perish.

(21.) *For there is a man whose labour hath been with wisdom, and knowledge, and gratifying success ; but to a man who hath bestowed no labour on it, he must leave it as his portion. This also is vanity, and a great evil.*

The man who had managed his kingdom with so much wisdom, and his worldly affairs with so much sagacity, here referred to, is Solomon himself. His commercial enterprises, carried on in conjunction with the Tyrians, had been crowned with success ; his architectural labours had proved equally successful ; but his kingdom, his wealth, and his great works, and perhaps greater plans, must soon be left to one who had had no experience, and in whom perhaps he had discovered but little proof of an industrious, enterprising, or sagacious spirit. The reflection that it was his own son to whom his kingdom and fortune were to be left, did not prevent him, when considering them under the aspect of a man's finding his whole happiness in them, from crying out again, " Vanity."

(22.) *For what hath man of all his labour, and the chafing of his spirit, with which he wearies himself under the sun ?*

This question is designed to give greater emphasis to that sentence of " Vanity" which he had pronounced on his glorious reign, and his successful enterprises. And considering men generally, what adequate reward do they receive from the things of this world, for all their toil and that chafing of the spirit incident to business ? What have they ? Nothing that deserves to be named, or compared with the necessary toil and vexation.

(23.) *For all his days are sorrows, and his business a vexation ; yea, his heart findeth not rest in the night. This also is vanity.*

His days are only so many sorrows ; one care presses on another ; no sooner is one dispatched than another comes. He must encounter the selfishness, the faithlessness, and the stupidity of men. His nights are sleepless ; the mishaps of the past day, and the perplexities which await him on the morrow, hold his eyes waking, and keep him tossing through the long and dreary watches. Solomon is describing one who is governed by worldly views alone, by ambition and avarice, who is not satisfied with ordinary gains, but who is determined to test, to the utmost, what boundless wealth, and the highest style of splendour can do, to make men truly happy. He does not mean to deny that active employment is a source of happiness to men ; but he is describing those who are so intent upon the world, that they multiply their business engagements, and load themselves with so many cares, that life is one perpetual bustle—the mind in a state of continual excitement—filling the day with perplexity, and the night with disturbing visions. Overwork, overtasking the faculties, is as much opposed to the laws of our being as neglect of occupation.

(24.) *There is no good for a man unless he should eat and drink, and let his soul enjoy good in his labour. Even this, I have seen, comes from the hand of God.*

This sentiment naturally follows what goes before respecting the unhappiness of a life too full of the cares and perplexities of business. There is no good or advantage to man from any worldly success, unless he is in a frame of mind to enjoy the fruits of it. It is the will of God, and by his blessing, that such advantage should come to those who apply themselves to worldly business with proper aims. Solomon does not condemn an active, enterprising spirit, in the things of this world, even as he does not condemn study ; it is the too ardent pursuit of the world, or it is the pursuit of it with erroneous expectations, which he condemns. Nor is it mere Epicurean indulgence, or addiction to the pleasures of sense, which he pronounces to be *the good* which a man should seek, in giving himself to the business of the world. On those who are good in the sight of God (ver. 26), He bestows the gift of a tranquil, contented, cheerful spirit —a temper which can not be had, except from the hand of God, or without virtue and religion. " This is an important sentiment of this book," remarks Dr. Noyes, of Harvard University,* " and recurs repeatedly as the result of the author's meditations upon life. See ch. iii. 12, 13, 22 ; v. 18–20 ; vii. 14 ; viii. 15 ; ix. 7–10 ; xi. 9. From a comparison of these passages together with ch. v. 1–7, and the whole of ch. xii., it is manifest that it is not sensual indulgence which

* Notes on Prov., Ecc., and Cant., p. 229.

the author commends as the best thing a man can attain in a world of vanity, but only such a cheerful,
joyful participation of present blessings as is consistent
with the thought of God and retribution, or with
obedience to the commands of the Creator."

(25.) *For who can feast, and who else can enjoy himself more than I?*

The rendering *more than I,* is in strict conformity
with the Hebrew text, as it stands. Solomon seems
again to refer to his peculiar advantages, by reason of
his eminent station, and eminent success in amassing
wealth, for making the experiment as to whether the
means of gratifying every sensual appetite, can of
themselves afford true happiness, every thought of
God and a future retribution being put out of the
mind. No one could tell better than Solomon, from
his extensive experience, whether true happiness could
be found in this way. But the Septuagint adopts a
reading which would make the sense of the verse,
Who can eat, and who can rejoice, without him, i. e.,
without God, or without the Divine blessing. This
makes it a mere repetition of what is said in the preceding verse, that the spirit by which we may enjoy
the good things of the world can come only from God,
that it is his blessing alone by which we can have any
real satisfaction from the world.

(26.) *For to the man who is well-pleasing in
his sight, God giveth wisdom, and knowledge
and joy : but to the sinner he giveth the unsatisfying toil of gathering and amassing, that he
may give it to him who is well-pleasing in the*

sight of God.   This also is vanity and grasping at wind.

God reserves the blessing of enjoying the things of this world, for those who love him, and are well-pleasing in his sight.   He gives them wisdom, that they may use these things in such a manner, that they may be real blessings, and not snares and curses ; he gives them a thankful, contented mind.   But the transgressor is given up to a discontented mind, to unsatisfied desires, to wearisome labours, that he may increase wealth which must afterwards fall into the possession of others, unlike him in character, the virtuous, who will devote it to good and charitable uses.

That, therefore, of which vanity is predicated is the attempt to find happiness in the bustle of prosperous enterprises ; the greatest success is of short continuance, and the fruits of the most successful labour must soon be left forever—perhaps left to the unworthy the inefficient, the ungrateful.   But even that cheerful, thankful participation of temporal blessings, which God grants to those who are well-pleasing in his sight, and which is consistent with thoughts of him, and of eternity—even this enjoyment, like that which springs from the pursuit and acquisition of knowledge, when " compared with good which is great, and true, and lasting, is little less than vanity and a fruitless affair. *Absolute vanity* the enjoyment of the fruit of one's labour, is not ; but in comparison with the enjoyment which a rational and immortal being is capable of, in comparison with a happiness uninterrupted, solid, and lasting, all this is vanity."*

* Stuart *in loc.*

SCOPE OF ARGUMENT IN § IV.

Solomon led a life of remarkable activity ; he was engaged in vast enterprises, which must have fully occupied his thoughts and time. His reign, unlike that of his father, was distinguished for its undisturbed peace, enabling him to devote his undivided attention to those arts and pursuits which flourish best in a season of public repose. Commerce and architecture, as well as study and pleasure, were prosecuted by him on a scale of royal magnificence ; so that in respect to them, too, he might well ask, " What can the man do that cometh after the king ?" What pleasure or satisfaction, of a solid and lasting kind, can any man find out from the most successful enterprises of an active business life, which has not been within my own reach and possession ?

At his first entrance on the stage of public life, he was charged with a work which required the highest architectural skill, and involved a vast amount of labour and expense. David had made most extensive preparations, for the erection of a magnificent temple for the worship of the Most High ; and when denied the honour to which he had aspired he did not relax his efforts to accumulate the materials that would be necessary for so vast a work. The total value of the gold and silver which he amassed, according to one table of ancient currency, amounted to £800,000,000. The standard of value among oriental nations, is, however, too uncertain, and has too much changed, to justify the assurance of any great degree of certainty as to this amount. We know that immense treasures, from the commerce established with Tyre, and the spoil and tribute of conquered nations, must have been accumulated. He laid aside, from the public coffers, and his own private income not only an immense mass of the precious metals, but he collected iron, brass, stone, and timber, the value of which it would be futile to attempt to estimate.

These treasures, and collected materials, met the young king at the threshold of his reign ; and he very soon entered on the great work of building the temple. It occupied seven years ; and the labours of a quarter of a million of men were at different times employed on it. The temple itself—the temple proper —was comparatively a small building, only twice as large as the tabernacle. It was not designed, like Christian churches, to contain a great number of worshipers within it ; their homage was to be paid in the courts, or enclosed spaces, in front of the sacred house. It was seventy cubits long, and but twenty wide. " The floor of the temple was formed of planks of fir, covered with gold. The inside walls and the flat ceiling were lined with cedar beautifully carved, representing cherubim and palm-trees, clusters of foliage and open flowers, among which, as in Egypt, the lotus was conspicuous ; and the whole interior was so overlaid with gold, that neither wood nor stone was anywhere to be seen, and nothing met the eye but pure gold either plain, as in the floor, or richly chased, as on the walls, and as some think with precious stones in the representations of flowers, and other enrichments. Even the inside of the porch was lined with gold." Over the ark, which was the same as that made in the wilderness, Solomon constructed two colossal cherubim of gold, whose inner wings outspread, touched each other, while the outer wings touched the opposite walls of the sacred chamber. In the outer chamber there were also seven golden candelabra instead of one ; and besides the table of shew-bread, which was the only table in the tabernacle, there were here ten golden tables, and others of silver, on which were laid out above a hundred golden vases of various patterns, with the different utensils—the censers, spoons, snuffers, etc.—all of gold, used in the service of the temple. " From this it will be seen that the importance of the temple of Solomon, which we have been led to regard as one of the wonders of the ancient world, consisted not in its size, which, as regards the principal building, has been greatly exceeded in every civilized country ; but from the elaborate, costly, and highly decorative character of its whole interior and furniture, and also in the number, extent, grandeur, and substantial masonry of its surrounding courts, chambers, walls, and towers. Indeed, it is not too much to presume that these outer constructions forming the massive ring in which the costly gem of the temple was set, cost as much as the building itself, immense as was the quantity of gold bestowed upon it." [Kitto.]

But the temple can not, perhaps, properly be included in those great works in which Solomon made trial of occupation and business to discover if possible the secret of true happiness. It was built at the command of God ; the labour was greatly lightened by the immense preparations which had been made for it by David ; and it was built before Solomon had been led into idolatry. It illustrates, however, the activity

which marked his capital, the stirring life which filled
its streets from the beginning of his reign.

He built great palaces for himself and for his queen.
He was thirteen years building his own palace. " He
built also the house of the forest of Lebanon ; the
length thereof was a hundred cubits, and the breadth
thereof fifty cubits, and the height thereof thirty
cubits, upon four rows of cedar pillars," etc. 1 Kings
vii. 2–12. It was composed of stones, massive and
beautiful beyond precedent. They were " hewed
stones, sawed with saws within and without." Josephus informs us that the walls of the palace were
wainscoted with sawn stones, or slabs of great value,
such as are dug out of the earth for the ornaments of
temples, or to make fine prospects in royal palaces ;
and so beautiful and curious are they as to make the
mines whence they are dug famous. Had we entered
that palace in the retinue of the queen of Sheba, who
came in great state to Jerusalem to visit Solomon, we
should have beheld a scene of splendour, which perhaps has had no parallel in any age or country. In
the centre of the vast pile, we should have entered a
spacious portico, forty-five feet high, one hundred and
fifty feet long, and seventy-five wide, the ceiling supported by forty-five cedar columns, fifteen in a row.
From it we should have passed into the judgment-hall,
containing that most wonderful and imposing of all
the structures connected with the palace, the THRONE,
on which the king sat to give audience to the ambassadors, philosophers, and royal visitors of other nations.
It was carved out of ivory and overlaid with the
purest gold. On either side of this great central
block were the private palaces of the king and queen ;

the whole ornamented with trees, lawns, fruits, and flowers, with fountains and bowers, and connected by a vast bridge, resting on arches over the Tyropœon, with a gallery or porch, which Solomon had constructed along the whole southern wall of the buildings of the temple.

But the king not only fortified Jerusalem and adorned it with splendid palaces, he built several strong frontier towns, Hazor, Megiddo, Beth-horon, Gezer, Baalath, Tadmour. The two latter were the most celebrated. Baalath or Baalbec was situated in the north of Palestine, in the valley between Lebanon and Anti-Lebanon. The ruins which may still be seen there astonish every beholder. They are said to exhibit a bolder plan in architecture than any ancient cities in Italy, Greece, and Egypt. In the sub-basement of the great temple, which there is reason to believe is much more ancient than the ruined Roman structure that now rests upon it, there is a stone sixty-nine feet in length, thirteen in depth, and eighteen in breadth, affording altogether a block of raised rock of sixteen thousand one hundred and forty-six cubic feet; while in a neighbouring quarry, which tradition declares to be that from which Solomon obtained his great stones, may be seen the fellow of this enormous rock, cut and ready for use, as if to challenge posterity to come up to the deeds of antiquity, by removing it from its position.

Tadmour is the same as Palmyra, the city of Palms, and is situated in the midst of the Syrian desert, between Damascus and the Euphrates, about four days' journey east of Baalbec. It stands in a vast desert, in solitary and gloomy magnificence, and even in its ruins, presents an appearance singularly impressive. Splendid colonnades of white marble, many of which are still standing, surround the remains of ancient temples and palaces, and thousands of prostrate pillars attest a magnificence surpassing that of the renowned cities of Greece and Rome. Most of these ruins doubtless belong to an age subsequent to that of Solomon. His object in building this city was to secure the advantages of the caravan trade across the great Syrian desert. He swayed the sceptre over all the territory to the Euphrates ; and possessing the strongholds which commanded the places of passage over that river, Tadmour, as a place of rest and refreshment in the midst of an arid, sandy desert, and becoming also a place of sale and exchange of commodities, gave Solomon control of the great trade which existed between the countries east of the Euphrates, and the markets of Syria and Egypt.

This leads us to notice as another feature in the stirring life of the author of Ecclesiastes, his commercial enterprises. As has been already suggested, Tadmour became a place of traffic and exchange. Here the great caravans from the East halted, unladed their camels, and made sale of their commodities to the agents of Solomon, who dispatched them to the markets of the Mediterranean, or made sale of them to the dealers from the West, who visited this famous mart for the purposes of trade. The sagacious monarch had foreseen that the construction of this fortified city would afford such security to the caravans, against the predatory Arab tribes, as would secure to him the monopoly of the India trade. He already, by the favour of Pharaoh, his father-in-law,

had to the exclusion of the commercial princes, the
advantages of the lucrative trade with Egypt; and
by way of the Red Sea he had access to the precious metals and rare productions of the east African
coast.

But it was a treaty of commerce with the Phenicians which opened new and distant fields to this
royal, sagacious merchant. This active, adventurous
race maintained intercourse between the nations from
the Indian Ocean to the west and north of the old
continent, and by the colonies which they planted, exerted a greater influence on the course of ideas, and
the world's civilization than their more highly-gifted
neighbours, the inhabitants of the valley of the Nile.
It was the special mission of this ancient commercial people to give a general spread to alphabetical
writing, and to convey into Greece the means of per-
petuating to the latest posterity the imperishable
treasures of the cultivated intellects of the people of
that country. The amber trade took them into the
Baltic, and the trade in tin to the British seas; and
they had settlements near the tropics on the west
coast of Africa. One of the smallest nations, commerce had given them great influence and wealth.
Solomon was not slow to perceive this; but his own
people had no knowledge of the sea, or of ship-build-
ing; and the commercial jealousy of the Phenicians
would not lead them to extend him any assistance, unless he could propose to them some reciprocal
advantages. With their amber and tin trade, with
their traffic to the west and the north, he did not propose to interfere; but he had ports at the head of the
Red Sea, by which these bold mariners could gain

access to regions lying east and south, never visited by them before. Suddenly the port of Ezion-geber wore an appearance of unusual activity, and re-sounded with the busy toil of the Phenician ship-wrights, preparing such ships as were suitable for the long voyages they were accustomed to make. The fleet at length set sail, and passed through the straits of Babel-Mandel to Ophir, and was gone three years. The articles which were brought back were gold, silver, sandal-wood, precious stones, ivory, apes, and peacocks. It would appear highly probable that the Phenicians must have visited the western coasts of the Indian peninsula. We know they proceeded four thousand geographical miles to the south—far within the tropics. But as it appears difficult to form an idea of western India as a fruitful source of gold, it is probable that these expeditions also visited south-ern Arabia, and the auriferous coast of Sofala in east-ern Africa.*

Solomon's surely was a most busy life. In addition to the cares of office, he entered on the execution of architectural schemes which occupied years, and em-ployed hundreds of thousands of men. Besides pal-aces, he built cities. In addition " to land traffic which controlled the trade of both India and Egypt," he sent his ships on long voyages, far within the tropics, to the Indian seas. He was thus thrown in contact with men of different races, and almost every variety of character ; and to have all these different schemes and enterprises carried on with success ; to attend to all this variety of business, in all its ramifications, must have given him the fullest occupation. No wonder

* Humboldt's Cosmos, pp. 137, 138.

his days were often only so many sorrows ; and that his heart found no rest in the night. He was over-burdened with cares ; his agents and workmen often, by reason of inefficiency, or carelessness, or indolence, failed to discharge their duties aright. His ministers of state, his superintendents and officers, could not relieve him of the chief care of planning and giving direction to these mighty enterprises. The wisdom with which they were managed, and the success which attended them, could not relieve him of the thought that he must soon leave them forever—a thought which showed how vain was all this extended business—whatever the interest and exhilaration with which its successful progress might be watched—how incapable it was of yielding solid happiness to an immortal being. And he must leave these fruits of toil and successful enterprise, perhaps to an heir entirely incompetent to take charge of them. A much less measure of the things of this world, requiring far less toil to amass them, would have amply furnished all the means requisite for that grateful participation of temporal blessings, consistent with the thought of God, and the judgment, which God bestows as a reward on all who are well-pleasing in his sight. No wonder he exclaims all is vanity and grasping at wind.

" If a man's reason," says John Howe, " guide him to an active negotiating life, rather than that of contemplation ; and determine him to the endeavour to serve mankind, or the community to which he belongs ; by how much the worthier actions he performs, and by how much more he hath perfected and accomplished himself with parts and promptitude for such

actions ; the loss and vanity is but the greater thereby, since he, and those he affected to serve, are all
going down to the silent grave. What matter were
it what became of the world, whether it be wise or
foolish, rich or poor, quiet or unquiet, governed or un-
governed, if the thoughts of its benefactors are all ere
long to perish forever in the grave ? Who would not
rather bless himself in a more rational neglect and re-
gardlessness of all human affairs ; and account an un-
concerned indifferency the highest wisdom."*   If there
be no eternity, what need is there of a high civlization,
or of civilization at all secured by education, good government, commerce, and the cultivation of art, mainly
valuable for the help they extend to prosecuting the
great designs which belong to an immortal state ?

There is unquestionably much happiness to be found
in proper action. Occupation, right employment, is
the true philosopher's stone. The drone can be happy
only as the Cappadocian slave, or the brute that dozes
in the stall is happy; " Should you distill the aggre-
gate of insignificant incidents that compose the whole
tenor of their feeble lives, not a drop perhaps would ascend in the alembic."   But our action must, as I have
said, be proper ; our employment must be right employment ; it must be governed by virtuous ends and
aims, and with a wise reference to our accountability,
and not that which ambition, avarice, the love of sensual indulgence, or of worldly display dictates. It is
such action alone that will

> "Sweep distemper from the busy day,
> And make the chalice of the big round year
> Run o'er with gladness."†

* " Vanity of Man as mortal."   † Wordsworth.

It will turn our days into blessings, and give to the heart of him who performs it rest in the night.

It would be difficult to conceive of a more active and eventful life than that of Napoleon Bonaparte. It was passed in camps, in courts, and in exiles. He was not only one of the most consummate generals, he was possessed of splendid and varied talents ; he did much for the improvement of France, and to adorn her gay metropolis. He was constantly busy. But O how far from being happy ! That abstracted, sad, and melancholy look which distinguishes the pictures which may everywhere be seen of him, tell the tale. His restless ambition would never permit him to be happy. When at the height of his power and glory, his mind was disturbed, so disturbed in respect to who should be his heir, that he scrupled not to commit one of his greatest wrongs. In his last exile, how remorse and vain regrets must have preyed, like the cancer which was so rapidly eating away his life, upon his spirit ! With all his ready determination, his promptitude of execution, his indomitable perseverance, and inexhaustible resources, could he have been enlisted in philanthropic enterprises, his tomb, although permitted to remain on a desolate rock in the midst of the ocean, would have been a "Mecca" for all mankind.

Another example of lofty but misdirected powers we have in Lord Byron. Had his genius been consecrated to virtue—had his talents been devoted to the interests of humanity—gardens of fruitfulness might now have bloomed, where only frightful deserts have been created. The fatal poison of his productions is the more insidious because "it lurks among the gorgeous beauties of poetry."

In the efforts of Byron to improve the political condition of Greece, we discover the inefficacy of every such attempt, based upon no better principles. It was a good cause ; he was a distinguished, energetic man ; and yet he served it ineffectually. His religious sentiments and habits were at war with his enterprise. He could not hasten the liberties of Greece by appealing to the valour of the heroes of Thermopylæ and Marathon. Her classic antiquities, and even her history, glowing with chivalric patriotism, touched no chord in the breasts of her degenerate sons.

The melancholy, or rather the misanthropy of Byron, was a prominent feature in his character, and its exhibitions filled up a large space in his life. Noble birth, luxury, literary fame, battle in behalf of liberty for an oppressed people, failed to make him a happy man. The "mysteries of horror" were often his theme ; and though to escape them he submitted to a voluntary exile from his native country, and became a self-devoted martyr to Grecian liberty, he could never escape from that enemy to his peace, which he carried about in his own bosom, which converted his days into sorrows, and robbed him of rest at night, and caused him to hate his own life. With our knowledge of his character, principles, and manner of life, we are not surprised at the confession which is attributed to him : " Were I offered the choice," said he, " either to live over again, or to live so many more years onward, I should certainly prefer the first ; and yet my young days were vastly more unhappy than I believe those of other men commonly are. I once attempted to

enumerate the days which might, according to the
common use of language, be called happy. I could
never make them amount to more than *eleven ;* and I
believe I have a very distinct remembrance of every
one. I often ask myself whether between the present
time and the day of my death, I shall be able to make
up the round dozen." The fabled notion of the *sep-
tem placidi dies,* the brief tranquillity, the halcyon
days of human life, seem in his case to have been
almost literally verified. It is doubtless in reference
to this painful experience, that he inquires in one of
his poems,

> " Did man compute
> Existence by enjoyments, and count over
> Such hours 'gainst years of life—say would he name
> Threescore ?"

THE BEAUTY OF DIVINE PROVIDENCE SEEN ONLY IN THE
LIGHT OF A FUTURE STATE.

———————

(1.) *To every thing there is a fixed season, and an appointed time to every event under heaven.*

Solomon is here speaking not of suitable opportunities for the performance of our duties, or for engaging in certain business, which when once lost, are lost forever, but of that fixed and necessary order, which God has established in the events and circumstances of our lives. He is not saying that there is a proper time for men to do all these things which he proceeds to specify, in the following verses ; but he paints human life in its necessary lights and shades, and shows that the shades are as necessary as the lights to the perfection of the picture.

(2.) *There is a time of being born, and a time of dying ; a time of planting, and a time of plucking up that which is planted.*

Solomon mingles events which depend entirely on the will of God, with those which seem to depend more upon the will of men—the time of birth and of

death, with the time of planting and gathering the
fruits of the earth—to teach us that the latter class
of events is as much subject to his controlling providence as the former.

(3.) *A time of killing, and a time of healing ;
a time of demolishing, and a time of building.*

Men corne to a violent death by accident, by the
hands of murderers, by the sentence of the law, or die
from wounds received in war. Others are healed of
their wounds. While some solid structures of cities
and houses are demolished, others are built up.

(4.) *A time of weeping, and a time of laughing ; a time of mourning, and a time of dancing.*

Our friends die, or they prove faithless, and we
weep ; but the affliction passes by, and we rejoice
again. A time of public sorrow is succeeded by one
of rejoicing.

(5.) *A time of casting abroad stones, and a
time of collecting them together ; a time of embracing, and a time of abstaining from embracing.*

Hitzig supposes that the first part of this refers to
the scattering of stones, by an invading army, over
cultivated fields, and to the gathering of them together again for the purpose of restoring the land to a
state fit for cultivation ; and in support of this ingenious and plausible interpretation cites 2 Kings, iii.
19, 25, which passages prove that it was one of the
customs of ancient warfare, not only to fill up the
wells, but to cover the arable land of an enemy with

stones—and Is. v. 2, which describes the gathering out of stones in preparing for a vineyard. Or the reference may be to the gathering of stones for the purpose of building walls and houses, and their being thrown down again, in the sack of cities.

There is even a time when it is proper that the dearest relatives and friends should refrain from any outward signs of affection. To exhibit such signs is not commonly suitable in public places, and may well be omitted in times of grievous calamities which call to fasting and prayer.

(6.) *A time of seeking, and a time of losing; a time of keeping, and a time of casting away.*

There is a time when men not only seek and find property, but when they lose it ; then there is a time when they may properly keep it ; and the time is almost certain to come when it is their duty to distribute it for the good of others.

(7.) *A time of rending, and a time of sewing; a time of keeping silence, and a time of speaking.*

The Jews rent their garments as a sign of grief (Gen. xxxvii. 34) ; the time of sewing, therefore, or the mending of such rents, figuratively expresses the end of grief. As to the proper time for keeping silence, it perhaps occurs oftener than even wise men are disposed to think.

(8.) *A time of loving, and a time of hating; a time of war, and a time of peace.*

Hatred often succeeds to love ; the strongest aversion may be conceived to the very objects and persons once fondly loved. There are times when nations seem to be under the sad necessity of waging war, but peace will at length return.

Such are the changes which enter into human experience, under the wise orderings of Divine Providence ; such the fluctuations from joy to sorrow, from light to darkness, which checker human life. How can man expect stable happiness from so unstable a world ?

(9.) *What profit hath the toiler, from that in which he toils?*

In this question we have the beginning of that conclusion which may be deduced from verses 2–8, or rather from verse 1, of which the other preceding verses are only an amplification. Its purport is, What can man do, what avail all his efforts to escape evil, and obtain substantial happiness in a world subject, by a fixed law of Providence, to such changes and vicissitudes ?

(10.) *I have surveyed the allotment which God hath assigned to the sons of men to be exercised therewith.*

Here it is most distinctly asserted that all the vicissitudes of life are Divinely appointed, and are not left to fate or accident, and that Solomon viewed them as all under the direction of God, for the discipline of his creature, man. But this he makes more clear in the next verse.

(11.) *He hath made every thing beautiful in its time; also he hath put eternity in their heart, without which no man can find out the work which God doeth from the beginning to the end.*

He asserts that there is a beauty over all the works and ways of Divine Providence. *Beautiful,* as in our version, rather than *good,* expresses the true meaning. He is describing how these works and ways strike the mind of a beholder, who surveys them from the true stand-point. He sees how every event takes place at the proper time, and fits, like the successive cogs of a wheel, each into its proper groove, carrying forward, with a steady movement, the great plan of Divine wisdom ; and all this vast machinery moving with as much silence, as precision and order. He listens, and hears no jar, no grating. " Beautiful !" he exclaims.

He next tells us what that true stand-point is, or how it is that man, amid the seeming defeats, disasters, and cross-purposes, which surround him, can discover beauty in the mysteries of Divine Providence. God hath placed eternity in his heart, without which he could not understand the work which God doeth from beginning to end ; *i. e.,* he hath planted the idea or conviction of immortality in every human heart ; and it is in the light of that duration that he sees, or is willing to wait until he shall see, the perfection and consummate beauty of all God's works and ways, without any exception, from the beginning to the end. Some idea of a future life—call it, if you please, an intrinsic sentiment, or primitive judgment—seems to be inherent in the very nature of man. As no tribe of men, however barbarous, have yet been discovered, who appeared to be wholly destitute of some idea of God, so no tribes have yet been found among whom may not also be discovered some traces of a belief in a future state. Man's moral nature points to the continuance of his conscious personal existence hereafter. And it seems one of the most marvelous of all strange theories, which denies any knowledge of a future state to the Jews, a people comparatively so cultivated ; and even, as has been done, to their inspired teachers.

It needs to be stated, however, that the word translated *eternity,* in the version given above, has occasioned great disparity of views among interpreters. It is not, however, an uncommon word, and is admitted, in every other instance in which it occurs, to mean *hidden, indefinite time or age,* eternity. The LXX. translated it by αιών ; the Vulgate by *mundum,* which our translators followed, rendering it *world.* Gesenius, in his Thesaurus, renders it *the desire of worldly things.* Hitzig, whom Stuart follows, renders it, resorting to the Arabic for analogy, *intelligence.* But Heiligstedt and Gesenius have shown that the word never has this sense anywhere in the Hebrew Scriptures. Bauer, Rosenmüller, Michaelis, Des Vœux, Adam Clarke, and others, adhere to the uniform sense of the word in the other places in which it occurs in the Scriptures, and translate it as above, by *eternity.* And why should we hesitate to translate it by a word which agrees so perfectly with the sense, and makes it perfectly plain how the ways of Providence may be made to wear the aspect of infinite wisdom and love ? Shall we hesitate because some of our modern wise men are disposed to maintain that Solomon had a less distinct conception of a future state than Socrates, or than can be found among almost any race of ignorant barbarians ?

(12.) *I know that there is no good in them, but for a man to rejoice, and enjoy good during his life.*

With the idea of eternity before his mind, and referring all the operations of God to that endless duration, he can, notwithstanding the present mystery which often shrouds them, even rejoice, and enjoy the good things of this life. And in no other way, can any considerate man, in view of the present darkness of Providence, be happy.

(13.) *And moreover, (I know) that as often as any man eats and drinks, and enjoys the good of all his labour, it is the gift of God.*

By revealing in the heart of man a future state, and thus reconciling him to his present allotment, so that he can cheerfully partake of the fruits of the Divine bounty—such cheerful participation, or the capacity for it, under such circumstances, is the special gift of God.

(14.) *I know that all which God doeth shall be for eternity ; nothing can be added to it, nor any thing taken from it ; and God doeth it that men may fear before him.*

The word translated *eternity,* or forever, is the same which was so rendered in the 11th verse. But here there has been no dispute.

God has made every thing with reference to eternity—all his operations have reference to that state—point to eternal retributions, an unchangeable destiny. And he has done this to awaken salutary fear in the hearts of men.

(15.) *That which hath been, is now ; and that which is to be, hath already been ; and God seeketh out that which is past.*

God's providence will continue the same from age to age. As human nature is the same in every age, it needs the same discipline ; and therefore we need not expect any material departure from that general course which Divine Providence has pursued toward men in former times. God will renew, or reproduce the past, even some of the darkest features in human experience ; but we shall see the beauty of the whole in the light of eternity.

SCOPE OF ARGUMENT IN § V.

The appointed vicissitudes of Divine Providence, in the government of the world, are inexplicably mysterious, unless we are to look for the light which can clear them up in some other state than the present. To the men who reject Divine revelation, or who live in blind disregard of that argument for another life which springs up in the heart of every man, the course of Providence must be an enigma. They can not understand the work which God does. It is only in the light of that future existence, which shines in every human breast, but is revealed with unclouded splendour in the holy Scriptures, that the mysteries of Providence are cleared up, or we can read the purpose of that discipline to which men are now subjected.

The expression, "to every thing there is a season," is not to be understood as meaning that there is a fit or appropriate time, when man may or ought to do the things that are mentioned ; the meaning is, that the changes referred to are fixed and unavoidable, and controlled by a power higher than man's. There is a certain time appointed by God for the birth and the death of every individual, and all the intermediate changes between these events. Men do not regulate the time of their entering on existence ; they do not regulate the time of their departure from this world. The time which they may select for planting may be the time for plucking up—their time for building may be the time for demolishing—their time of rejoicing may be the time for weeping—their time of amassing may be a time of losing—their time to love may be a time of hatred—their time of peace a time of war. The changes and events of the world are out of man's power ; he can not interrupt or alter their course. To the man who contemplates the wide scene of human affairs, the conviction is not only forced home that there is a God, but the question will arise, in view of the order and regularity which prevail under his providence, What is the great end or purpose which the infinitely great and wise Jehovah seeks in respect to his creatures ? As the perfection and order which mark the material world, lead to the inevitable conclusion that it was not created merely to be the abode of creatures who are to live a few years, and then cease wholly from existence, so the beauty and order of Divine Providence, the wisdom and the power displayed therein, pre-assure us of another state of existence to which the present is but probationary and preparatory. The analogy between this part of the subject and another which has been before considered, is close and striking. When we look out upon nature in its widest extent, and take not the narrow, contracted views of uncultivated, prejudiced minds ;—when, with comprehensive knowledge, we look at the heavens and the earth, and the moving life of the elements of nature, we are ready at once to pronounce it all the vainest of vanities, if the intelligent observers of this scene are to be regarded as ceasing to exist when they die ; because we thus put it beyond our power to assign any adequate end to the creation. Precisely so with respect to the wonders of Divine Providence ; like the wonders of the material universe they syllable forth some great purpose with respect to intelligent creatures which can not be understood if we deny to man a future existence. The enigma can not be solved unless we are to regard the discipline to which men are now subject as having reference to another state.

We may first contemplate Providence in its widest range—in the broad sweep of centuries. As we have the most exalted conceptions of the power and wisdom of the Deity when we attempt to follow the astronomer in his survey of the heavens, we shall find them hardly less so when we trace his adorable providence in the universal history of mankind. Some great writers have sought to make the philosophy of history consist in an application of rhetorical rules to the description of its events. Others have sought to elicit from their narratives moral lessons, or to connect with them political and philosophical reflections. But one of the most distinguished of modern historians[*] has said that Christianity "is the fulfillment of all hopes, the perfection of all philosophy, the interpreter of all revolutions, the key to all the seeming contradictions of the physical and moral world—it is life—it is immortality." The events of this world are not left then to mere accident ; but he who reads them intelligently will discover in them a great moral purpose. We may go back to the beginning of history—to the very origin of our race—and trace the stream from the spot where it took its rise, through all its branchings and meanderings, to the present time, and we shall have accumulating evidence that it has been directed by a Divine hand. It has not flowed, for the shortest distance, in a given course, fortuitously. Great conquerors and rulers have arisen ; God raised them up as instruments to carry out his purposes, in his most holy and wise governing of his creatures, and all their actions. Great nations have appeared, and when the Divine purposes, in respect to them, have been answered, have disappeared again. "Those revolutions," asks a celebrated writer,[†] "which, in their progress, precipitate dynasties and nations to the dust, those heaps of ruin which we meet with in the sands of the desert, those majestic remains which the field of human history offers to our reflection, do they not testify aloud to the truth that God is in history ? Gibbon, seated on the ancient capitol, and contemplating its noble ruins, acknowledged the intervention of a superior destiny. He saw—he felt its presence ; wherever his eye turned, it met him ; that shadow of a mysterious power reappeared from behind every ruin ;

[*] J. Von Müller.   [†] Merle D'Aubigné.

and he conceived the project of depicting its operation in the disorganization, the decline, and the corruption of that power of Rome which had enslaved the
nations. Shall not that mighty hand, which this man
of admirable genius discovered among the scattered
monuments of Romulus and of Marcus Aurelius, the
busts of Cicero and Virgil, Trajan's trophies and
Pompey's horses, be confessed by us as the hand of
our God ?"

There has been not only a time to plant mighty
empires, but a time to pluck them up—a time to
build great cities, and a time to break them down.
Even war and carnage have been permitted, and over-
ruled to the accomplishment of God's great purpose.
There have been times to slay, as well as times to heal
—times of war, as well as times of peace—times of
losing, as well as times of getting—times of weeping
and lamentation, as well as times of rejoicing. Such
is the vivid and impressive comment of the inspired
penman on the phases of human history. And if it
be true that they have their interpretation in the revelations of Christianity ; if the philosophic historian
is able more perfectly to comprehend his subject, and
reconcile its seeming contradictions in their light, then,
surely, we may, or rather must infer from that Divine
control which is exercised over human affairs in their
greater and more protracted events, that there is a
purpose in respect to the human agents concerned,
which is defeated, unless their existence is to be extended beyond the present state. The less is certainly
comprehended by the greater. If history necessarily
appears to be a confused and disconnected medley of
events, except as they are made to centre around the

disclosures of the Bible, and are interpreted by the light which streams forth from it, then, it certainly follows that the overruling hand of God in these events, leads us to presuppose a future state of existence for man. Immortality, a distinguishing doctrine of Christianity, is but one of those revelations which serve to interpret the revolutions and changes recorded by the pen of history.

I would further add, that if when we surveyed the material universe—descending from the remotest nebulæ, or the revolving double stars, to the minutest organisms of animal life, or those delicate tissues of vegetable matter which cover the surface of rocks—we were constrained to feel that the outlay was too vast merely to deck a theatre for the existence of generations which perish forever, when they leave it, are we not compelled to a similar conclusion, when we study the history of Divine Providence toward the children of men? The doctrine of a particular providence being established—which no one who takes even a cursory view of the current of human affairs, can well deny—would not the outlay here also be too vast, in other words, would it not be derogatory to the Divine Being, to suppose that he would thus interest himself about human affairs, if human beings are destined to a term of existence reaching so little beyond that of the merest insect? Are human affairs of sufficient importance thus to attract the Divine regard, and call into exercise so much foresight and skill, if the actors themselves are of so little consequence?

What is the doctrine of a particular providence? It is that God not only exercises a general superintendence of the affairs of the universe, but that his care extends to every individual, and to every part. That Jehovah exercises such a superintendence over all his creatures, and all their actions follows directly from the acknowledged perfections of his character. Being such a God as he is, he is not only qualified for such a management of his creatures, but his benevolence must prompt him to it. Moreover, all his creatures are dependent on him for continued existence ; they are just as dependent for the continuance of it, as for the commencement of it ; one is as much an act of his will as the other. Look now at the perfect order and system which reign throughout the universe. Look at the revolution of the heavenly bodies, and the regular recurrence of the seasons, and the unfailing productive powers of the earth, in illustration of this point ; but look rather at the laws which govern human society, and human events. Are they not the same from age to age ? If we confine ourselves to limited periods, small isolated bodies of men, we may fail to descry regularity and order ; but when we extend our view, do we not see that Providence is pursuing one steady course of discipline toward the successive generations ? Just, as was noticed, when we were considering the material works of God, " the thing which hath been, it is that which shall be ; and that which is done is that which shall be done, and there is no new thing under the sun"—so in the works of Providence, " that which has been is now ; and that which is to be hath already been ; and God reneweth that which is past." That discipline of his Providence, which consists in changes, trials and disappointments, upon which God entered with his creatures six thousand years ago, that he might train them for a better world than this, he still pursues ; for the principles of fallen human nature are the same and the snares of the world are the same. The same discipline which was necessary to fit Abel, and Enoch, and Abraham for heaven, is just as necessary to prepare men in our day for that world ; therefore God reneweth that which is past. But if there be no future state, what means this particular watchful providence, which every thoughtful man must perceive in human events, and of which almost every man is sooner or later made conscious, in his own experience ? Why should the great God thus concern himself about beings so evanescent and of so little importance ? And if there be no better world for which the present is preparatory, who can explain the meaning of that wonderful uniformity in variety which has marked God's providential dealings with men through so many ages ? But when we admit that there is a world of future blessedness for which men need preparation, and consider that men are the same, and that the world, in its power of fascination and delusion, is the same to them from age to age, all is clear.

But we have an equally impressive view of this subject when we confine our attention to events which refer to ourselves, or take place under our immediate observation, and which will never become matter of historical record. Events are constantly taking place which are entirely incomprehensible by us, and which might furnish ground to question the benevolence and justice of the Supreme Being, did we not expect the mystery to be solved in the light of another world. How often do we see the fondest hopes disappointed, and the fairest plans crossed ! Sometimes the health or even reason, of some faithful servant of God, or useful citizen, in the prime of life, fails. Sometimes the man of liberal soul, whose deeds of charity have made the widow's heart sing for joy, is stripped of his possessions. Sometimes we see the parent on whom a numerous family depend for support, suddenly laid low ; and sometimes the only child of a widowed mother, or of some aged venerable father, is carried to the grave.

Where, I ask, shall we look to have the mystery of such providences as these cleared up, if not to a future life ? To those who are full of this world's cares, are governed by its principles alone, who love it supremely, whose vision is bounded by it, such providences are an inexplicable mystery. But blessed be God ! he has planted the idea of immortality in our minds ; we know that there is another state of being ; that death does not interrupt the progress of a soul which had begun to glorify God in the present, by the cultivation and proper application of its spiritual faculties. In the broken column or shaft of polished marble, sometimes seen over the grave of a young man, the moral is touching and striking, and in one respect conveys a true impression. His virtuous aspirations and purposes, so far as this life is concerned, are broken off. But in another respect, the impression is untrue ; for there can be no defeat or failure, no rupture of the lofty purposes of a soul consecrated to virtue and to God through the blood of the Redeemer. The lines, unbroken, stretch on beyond the grave. The mortal sinks out of sight, but the immortal enters on a scene more favourable to its upward and onward progress.

The trials and disappointments of this life are not

the result of mere accident, or because the Governor of the universe has left the world to itself. They constitute the allotment which God has given to the sons of men to be exercised therewith. This is the moral discipline which he has instituted. So religion teaches. But if we despise its light, whither shall we look for comfort, tossed to and fro as we are upon this unquiet and often tempestuous sea ? What madness there is in scepticism and irreligion ! O tell me not that we are adrift like floating sea-weed, or sailors on the splintered spars of a wreck, without helm, compass, or chart. God reigns. His hand is in our very reverses. " He hath made every thing beautiful in its time." Trials do not mar the Divine picture ; they constitute its darker shades, and are not only essential to its perfection, but to the picture itself. The painter must make as much use of shadow as of light, in his wonderful art ; it is the shadow by which he brings out the light, and gives outline and proportion to the objects on which his pencil is employed. If every part of some admired painting were concealed from our view but the background, or certain dark clouds belonging to it, or the deep shadow, cast by some mountain or temple, we should certainly discover no beauty in it ; so if we see not the complete beauty of Providence, by reason of the vicissitudes and sorrows to which we are at present subject, it is because " we see but parts of one extended whole." We see not the whole of the picture. Events must be contemplated in their relations, tendencies, and seasons, and by the light of Divine revelation, in order to understand how God hath made every thing beautiful in its time. " Set down a man ignorant of mechanics in the midst of a system of extensive and complicated machinery, and he will gaze about him in vacant wonder, all appearing, to his dizzy and stupefied sight, involved and intricate perplexity. But introduce an experienced machinist, and by the hasty glances of a few moments, he discerns the proportions and relations, and the mutual dependences of all the parts—the connection of the whole with the great moving power, and its perfect adaptation to a proposed end—and his mind is delighted with the admirable display of contrivance and skill. Creatures like us, in contemplating the Divine procedure, are in the situation of the former. The scheme of providence may appear to us a maze of endless confusion, and even at times, of jarring inconsistency—one part frequently crossing and conteracting another. But the sole cause of this is our ignorance ; the very limited and partial views which we are able to take of it. Had we powers that enabled us to take a full and comprehensive, and connected view of the whole, from the originally proposed design, through all the successive steps of its progressive development, to its final and entire completion, we should see " every thing beautiful in its season"—a perfect and delightful harmony, complicated indeed, but in proportion as it is complicated, the more astonishing, in all the affairs of worlds, and kingdoms, and families, and individuals. All is beautiful harmony,"*

"All chance direction which we can not see."

The believer to whom the course of Providence, by reason of present ignorance, is an enigma, has learned

* Dr. Wardlaw's Lect. on Ecc.

to refer all to the Divine hand, to acquiesce in the Divine will, and to wait until the mystery is cleared up in the light of eternity. He has learned not only to be satisfied with his lot, but to rejoice in it ; amid this scene of uncertainty to maintain his cheerfulness, to " eat and drink, and enjoy the good of all his labour," assured that all the allotments of Divine Providence have reference to a future immortal state, where, to all who have learned in the present to fear the Lord, all enigmas will be solved, and all knots untied.

§ VI. Chap. III. 16–22.

THE INEFFICACY OF HUMAN LAWS, OR OF JUSTICE AS AD-
MINISTERED AMONG MEN, TO REDEEM THE WORLD FROM
THE REPROACH OF VANITY; OR THE NECESSITY OF A
FUTURE JUDGMENT.

(16.) *Moreover, I saw under the sun that in
the place of judgment iniquity was there; and in
the place of justice, injustice was there.*

Solomon here introduces another fact as a new evidence of the insufficiency of the world to impart real
happiness, and of the necessity of a life beyond the
present: it is the injustice which is so often shown
between man and man not only, but which is sometimes experienced before the appointed tribunals of
justice, or from the hands of magistrates and rulers.
The injustice which is permitted in the earth had
been the occasion of equal perplexity to some before
him, when reflecting on the providence of God : see,
e. g., Ps. xxxvii. and Ps. lxxiii.   This perplexity could
be solved by them only in the light of a future state of
retributions ; and in the same manner it was solved by
the writer of Ecclesiastes.   Professor Stuart, referring
to the wisdom which was conferred, in so remarkable

a degree on Solomon, for the administration of justice among his people, argues that this book could not have been written in his time, as if his knowledge of, or his observations in respect to, the injustice which exists among men, and is often inflicted by the very tribunals which have been set up to prevent it, were confined to his own kingdom, his own acts, or to his own times. And who can say that during the years when he fell into such great sins, he himself retained that singular integrity and wisdom which marked his decisions in the earlier part of his reign ? In looking back, who can say that in the place of judgment, where he himself had presided, he could not see iniquity there ?

(17.) *I said in my heart, God will judge the righteous and the wicked ; since there is a time appointed for every purpose, and for every work.*

The word which the authorized version translates by the adverb *then*, by a slight change in the pointing means *appointed* [*constituit*] *;* and this is the sense given to it in the version above. Van der Palm and other eminent critics favour this pointing. He had before said (v. 1.), that to every thing there is an appointed time ; he now says that there is an appointed time, when God will judge the righteous and the wicked, and rectify all those mistakes, which, as stated in the preceding verse, are permitted in consequence either of the ignorance or the injustice of men, to exist in this world. He saw, in the light of a future judgment day, how the providence of God might be cleared of every reproach, and those who are now suffering from the wrongs which men are permitted to inflict, might learn to wait for the disclosures and awards of that day. The neological writers of Germany, it is true, say, that we are not to suppose that the last judgment is here referred to at all, but only that retribution which may be expected in this world. Dr. Noyes, the Hancock Professor of Hebrew, in Harvard University, also thinks it most probable that the present life was exclusively in view; yet he explains the phrase, *will judge the righteous and the wicked* to mean that he will acquit and deliver the righteous, and condemn and punish the wicked. But when has such retribution been meted out to the righteous and the wicked in this life? Nay, it is because it is not seen to be thus meted out (as stated in the 16th verse) that Solomon now declares that God has appointed a day when he will render equal and impartial justice to both these classes of men. He here anticipates the conclusion which is brought out with so much emphasis in the final words of the book, " For God shall bring every work into judgment, with every secret thing, whether it be good, or whether it be evil." The German neologists do not admit that any of the Old Testament writers speak of a judgment after this life. The surrounding heathen nations knew more respecting a future state of existence than they are willing to admit was known by such men as Moses, David, Solomon and Isaiah. Because other Old Testament writers (as they say) did not reveal a future judgment, then this revelation is not to be looked for in Ecclesiastes. Even if their premises (which are inadmissible and incredible) had good foundation, their conclusion is a *non sequitur.*

Knobel is constrained to admit that the concluding words of the book (quoted above) refer to a judgment after death ; and, on this account, he contends.that they must have been interpolated by some other hand than that which wrote the body of the work. By such criticism as this, how easy it would be to rob the Bible of all its distinctive teachings. Professor Stuart in commenting on this verse, has well said, " I see no way of consistency, but that of supposing a future judgment and retribution. The motives to piety without this are inert and powerless. If you say that the prospect of a judgment during the present life is sufficient, we may well ask how that can be, when Koheleth tells us, that " there be wicked men to whom it happeneth according to the work of the righteous (viii. 14) ; and that all things come alike to all, (ix. 22) ? What retribution is there in all this ? " " A more inconsistent man than Koheleth, it would be difficult to find, putting all his views side by side, provided he has abjured all *futurity*, and yet insists on retribution to the righteous and the wicked ?" &c.

(18.) *I said in my heart (this happens) on account of the sons of men, that God might search them, and make them see that, left to themselves, they are beasts.*

I concur with Dr. Scott, that to make it out that these verses (18–22) contain the objections of infidels to Solomon's doctrine of a future existence and judgment is an interpretation wholly unsatisfactory. They stand related to v. 16, which declares that injustice is often inflicted on men, even by the authorized ministers of justice. This is permitted that it might be made manifest that men "left to themselves,"—in which translation I have followed D. Burger, Jr.,—and to disregard that higher tribunal to which they are accountable are little better than brute beasts. Oppressive rulers, and corrupt judges, reduce themselves to a level with the beasts that perish—they act as if they were to perish too at death—and will not be judged by him who is higher than the highest. It is man's immortality and accountability alone which elevate him above the brutes. In translating, *on account of the sons of men*, I have again followed Burger, who says "per *propter* reddidi; pendere autem censeo a sub-nellecto *hoc fit*, quod facile suppletur si reputemus, auctorem hic cogitare de ratione cur injustitiam in terris fieri patiatur Deus, huic autem quæstioni colo nostro responderi."[*]

(19.) *For as to the lot of men, and the lot of beasts, one and the same lot befalls them : as the one dieth, so dieth the other, and there is one breath to all; and there is no pre-eminence of man above a beast ; for all is vanity.*

Solomon here declares that the same death awaits the bodies of both men and animals. The same phenomena precisely, mark the physical effects of death in the case of the latter, as in the case of the former. The blood ceases to flow, and the heart to beat—the body becomes cold, and the limbs are rigid. They all depend on the same vital air for breath. In respect to his dependence on air for the breath of life, and his ultimate exposure to death, the death of the body,

* *Comm. in Ecc. in loc.*

man has not the least pre-eminence above the beasts. He is just as evanescent as they.

(20.) *All go unto one place; all are of the dust, and all return to dust again.*

He follows this parallel further. The bodies of men after death have no higher honour than that of beasts. They undergo a similar decomposition, and return to that dust in which they had a common origin. We must not fail to connect these two verses (20 and 19) as we did the preceding one, with the 16th and 17th to which they have a similar relation. Unjust judges, and all wicked men, left by their Creator, without immortality, and future accountability, would really have no elevation, worth boasting of, above the brutes that perish ; and they might, like the wild beasts of the desert, act toward the weak and defenceless, as if strength and power always imparted right. It is the great doctrine of immortality, more than the gift of reason, which confers on man his pre-eminence over the animals of the field and savage beasts of prey. Life is of no value ; nay, it becomes a curse, if men may be the sport of oppressors and atrocious judges, and can not look forward to a righteous tribunal beyond this life.

(21.) *Who knoweth whether the spirit of the sons of men, goeth upward (to God), and the spirit of beasts, whether it goeth downward to the earth ?*

It is not doubt which the author here expresses, as to the destiny of the human spirit, for he has already told us that God has appointed a day when he will judge the righteous and the wicked, and he afterwards expressly tells us that " the Spirit shall return to God who gave it." (xii. 7). This verse is closely related not only to the preceding, but to that which immediately follows it ; it would have been well if the two had been included in one. The question is not (as I have said) one of doubt ; but the interrogative form of expression appears to be substituted for the direct to give it greater strength and emphasis, meaning that *if we fail to know or consider that man has this pre-eminence above the beasts, that at death his spirit returns to God*, then follows the conclusion stated in the next verse. A question may be one of astonishment, or challenge ; and instead of implying doubt may contain the most emphatic answer, as when we say, " Who knows that George Washington ever betrayed his country ?" that is, Who does not know that he never betrayed his country ? While the same lot befalls the bodies of beasts and men at death, and in the grave, who knows that the spirit of a man at death will have any pre-eminence over that of a beast ? that is, Who does not know that this great difference exists, that the spirit of man returns to God who gave it, to be judged, and the spirit of a beast goes downward to the earth ; has no account to give up ?

(22.) *Then I saw that there is nothing better than that a man should rejoice in such actions as please him ; for that is his inheritance : for who shall bring him to see what shall be after him ?*

This, as I have said, is the conclusion, or the inference drawn from the interrogative, or rather the hypothetical manner of stating the subject in the preceding verse. If we fail to consider that man is exalted above the rest of the animal creation at death, by the return of his immortal spirit to God, then we can see that it is best for a man to rejoice in whatever course of life most pleases him ; this is all his portion. If he is to perish like the brutes, then let him, though he be a ruler or a judge, imitate the brutes in their ferocity and cruelty, and in the gratification of his animal appetites ; for he has nothing to fear in the future—no righteous retribution. The whole passage, instead of showing that the writer was in a perplexed state of mind, that his mind was darkened with the mists of doubt and skepticism, proves that he had the fullest confidence in a future state and retribution. Instead of there being no trace of the doctrine, that man shall live after death, in Ecclesiastes, its author asks a question which implies that every one knew, or might know, that the spirit is independent of the body, dies not with it, but returns to God who gave it, to be judged, and live in another state.

SCOPE OF ARGUMENT IN § VI.

Those are mere dreamers, who expect literature, the fine arts, a luxurious style of life, or polite manners, can remove the reproach of utter vanity that rests upon this world, when its connection with another is denied. Ages have passed, and not even the stringent arm of courts or parliaments has been able to correct or forestall those social evils under which the whole creation groaneth. In addition to the imperfections which attach to all human institutions and laws, men are often the victims of deliberate injustice. Corruption has been found in the place of righteousness, and iniquity has coiled itself up in the very seat of judgment. With all the wisdom and study of those who devote themselves to improve governments and laws, and with the best intentions on the part of the administrators of them, the innocent are often made to suffer, while the guilty escape—the industrious and deserving pine in neglect and poverty, and the dishonest and dissolute roll in affluence and luxury. Men who have betaken themselves to courts of justice for redress, have often received only the greater wrong. The author of this book, by his own observation and experience (he was himself both a king and a judge, and in this latter capacity was greatly distinguished), was constrained to look forward to a future state, and one too of righteous retribution. "Then said I in my heart, God will judge the righteous and the wicked : for a time is appointed for every purpose, and for every work."

At its commencement, he seemed to assume the stand-point of the mere speculatist. He looked out on the material universe, and then on man in his busy cares and toils, or his delirious joys ; but he could discover no sufficient reason for their creation and continued existence, unless it is to be discovered in the future existence of man. All was unmeaning, aimless, and absurd. At length he brings out, as in the 11th verse of this chapter, the great truth that God putteth eternity in the hearts of men, i. e., plants the idea of immortality in their very souls, without which no man can understand the meaning of what he doeth from the beginning to the end. He proceeds next to state distinctly, that God has appointed a day in which he will judge the world ; and from this point we shall find him continuing to speak in the same decisive tone until he winds up with these solemn words as the conclusion of the whole matter : "Fear God, and keep his commandments ; for this is the whole duty of man. For God shall bring every work into judgment, with every secret thing, whether it be good, or whether it be evil." Solomon's belief in a future state, and a state of retribution, can be doubted by those only who explain away the plainest declarations to this effect in Ecclesiastes, and who do not perceive that it is this belief which underlies and gives character to this entire book. They must explain away the language, now under consideration, "God shall judge the righteous and the wicked, for there is a time for every purpose and for every work." They must deal in like manner with the passage : "Rejoice, O young man, in thy youth ; and let thy heart cheer thee in the days of thy youth, and walk in the ways of thy heart, and in the sight of thine eyes ; but know thou that for all these things God will bring thee into judgment ;" and with the passage, "Then shall the dust return to the earth as it was ; and the spirit shall return to God who gave it ;" and with the last words of the book, "God shall bring every work into judgment with every secret thing, whether it be good, or whether it be evil." I can not think that it is a question whether the judgment or retribution here spoken of was to take place in the present or the future world. An existence and retribution after death was the very solution which the writer of this book employed to remove the doubts and difficulties, which otherwise must perplex the minds of men, in regard to the course of human things. There is a time appointed in the eternal world, or at the judgment-seat of Christ, for every purpose, and for every work. There the injustice done to men in this world by civil rulers or judges, whether deliberate or unintentional, will be made to appear, and the wrong will be repaired.

Neologists deny that there is any allusion to futurity, or a state of retribution after death, in the book of Ecclesiastes. Indeed, they deny that the Jewish Scriptures do in any place teach any thing respecting the future destiny of our race. All those plain declarations respecting judgment and futurity, are made to refer to this world and the doings of men. They argue that because a future state is not taught (as they affirm) in the other Jewish Scriptures, therefore, it can not be, whatever expressions to the contrary may be found, in Ecclesiastes. Even were their premises correct, it does not appear how their conclusion would certainly follow; but we deny the correctness of both the premises and the conclusion.

The celebrated author of the Divine Legation of Moses asserts, and argues at length, that the Mosaic covenant contains no promises directly relating to a future state, because Moses was secure of an *equal providence*, and therefore needed not subsidiary sanctions, taken from a future state, without the belief of which the doctrine of an universal providence can not ordinarily be vindicated, nor the general sanctions of religion secured. But this appears a very insufficient reason for withholding from God's ancient servants the comfort and support to be derived from the direct revelation of a future state. The patriarchs, even before the time of Moses, were inspired with the hope of a future state of blessedness, sweetly expressed in the language descriptive of their death, which speaks of them as being gathered to their fathers. This hope, in their case, was perhaps clearer than at some subsequent periods in the history of God's ancient people. One of their number, the seventh from Adam, having walked with God was translated, without seeing death, into the presence of God. This was more than a promise or prediction ; it was demonstration. A spiritual invisible world was palpably opened, and men saw one of their number, in body and soul, disappear within its mysterious portals. And does not an inspired apostle teach us that when Abraham went out from his own country, at the command of God, by faith he looked for a city that hath foundations, whose builder and maker is God ? And does he not describe him as dying in faith, embracing the promises which he had seen afar off, and confessing that he was a stranger and pilgrim on earth, and desiring a better country, that is an heavenly ? He further intimates that the doctrine of the resurrection of the body had been made known to him, for in recounting the triumphs of his faith, in offering up Isaac, he said that he accounted that God was able to raise him up even from the dead. With Christians at least, an inspired apostle will be regarded as a competent interpreter of the full purport of the patriarch's faith. And what could the patriarch Jacob have referred to, when on his dying bed, as his sons were gathered around him to receive his parting blessing, he exclaimed, " I have waited for thy salvation, O Lord," but to the eternal felicity of God's people in heaven? And that Moses was not ignorant of a future state appears from the fact that he had the revelation which had been made of such a state through the translation of Enoch, and the same revelation which had been given to the father of the faithful—the same promises of heavenly felicity comprehended in the Abrahamic covenant— all recorded by his own pen; and it appears also from the account which Paul gives of the victory of his faith, whose authority in this, as well as in the former case, must be conclusive. Why did he, when he was come to years, refuse to be called the son of Pharaoh's daughter? Why did he choose rather to suffer affliction with the people of God than to enjoy the pleasures of sin for a season; esteeming the reproach of the cross greater riches than the treasures in Egypt? The apostle answers, "because he had respect to the recompense of reward"—language which must be understood as referring to future reward, not only because analogy requires such an interpretation, but because the whole passage is otherwise rendered barren, and stripped of all point and energy. It was the confidence that in his flesh he should see God, which sustained the patriarch Job under his complicated trials. Hear David sing, in the confidence of a good hope, " My heart is glad, and my glory rejoiceth : my flesh also shall rest in hope. For Thou will not leave my soul in hell; neither wilt thou suffer thine holy one to see corruption. Thou wilt show me the path of life ; in thy presence is fullness of joy ; at thy right hand there are pleasures forevermore." " As for me, I will behold thy face in righteousness ; I shall be satisfied,

when I awake, with thy likeness." In the writings of
the prophets we find many strong expressions of hope
of a future state of reward. " Say ye to the righteous," saith Isaiah, " that it shall be well with them ;
for they shall eat of the fruit of their doings." That
this promise refers to future and eternal good is evident, because in this world we do not see it fulfilled ;
the righteous are often much more afflicted than the
wicked. The same prophet calls on those who dwell
in the dust, the pious dead, to " awake, and sing,"
" for thy dew is as the dew of herbs, and the earth
shall cast out her dead." [See this question fully discussed in the Introduction.]

I deemed it important to show, as I think has been
clearly done, that the doctrine of a future state is no
such exotic in the Jewish Scriptures as to warrant the
rejection of this doctrine as having no place in Ecclesiastes. It is taking too much for granted—far more
than can be proved—that immortality can not be
made out from the writings of Moses and the prophets.
Patriarchs and prophets inquired and searched diligently, as men in earnest ; they strained their eyes
for some light to relieve the midnight gloom which
hung over the prospects of the race. Nor did they
seek in vain. Their eyes, it is true, were not glad-
dened by that full-orbed light which has burst upon
the world since the doctrine, the resurrection, and
ascension of Christ into heaven, but they caught with
joy the dawn of this bright day. Solomon stood in
the twilight of the morning, which fact it becomes us
on whom shines the effulgence of the noon, to bear
in mind. He might have had doubts, during the
period of his sad decline in piety, but he quickly dis-

covered that the denial of a future state involved such absurdities as required a far greater degree of credulity than its admission. It is this expectation, therefore, as I have already said, which pervades and gives character to this book. Instead of there being no allusions to this subject in Ecclesiastes, it is replete with them ; it is the key to its right interpretation. Instead of its containing declarations inconsistent with a belief in this doctrine, or passages which can be interpreted only as the words or arguments of an objector, this feature of the book arises from the very nature of Solomon's argument to meet doubts respecting, or the positive denial of, a future state. He shows that on the supposition of there being no hereafter, the whole creation, including man at his best estate, whatever experiments he may try in his search after the chief good, is utterly vain, and without any suitable end or purpose ; man has no pre-eminence over a beast.

But to show that the doctrine of a future state, independently of express texts, underlies this whole portion of God's word, look at its teachings respecting the providence of God. It shows that the only way by which we can reconcile the inequalities of Providence, under which the good man suffers in common with the bad, and often suffers much more in the present world, is to suppose the existence of a future state, in which God will reward every man according to his deeds. We are told there are just men to whom it happeneth according to the work of the wicked, and wicked men to whom it happeneth according to the work of the righteous. And again we are told that all things happen alike to all ; there is one event to the righteous and the wicked, to the clean and the unclean. How can these inequalities of Divine Providence be reconciled with the justice and benevolence of the Divine character ? We are told in answer, that he that feareth God shall be delivered ; we are told that when the body returns to the dust, the soul returns to God, *i. e.*, to be judged, a passage which discriminates between the soul and the body, and asserts the independent existence of the former, as clearly as any other in the whole Scriptures. Finally, we are told that God will bring every work into judgment, with every secret thing, whether it be good, or whether it be evil, words which so clearly refer to a future judgment, that those who deny to the author of this book any expectation of another life are driven to the miserable subterfuge of maintaining that they were written by another hand.

But it is time to recur to the particular topic which is brought to our notice by the passage under examination, and to consider the manner in which the inspired penman infers from the imperfection which cleaves to human governments and tribunals of justice, a future state of retribution. It was true in his day, and it is equally true now that thousands of more years have passed away, that governments and laws, however wisely framed, or faithfully administered, often operate to the great and irreparable injury of individuals. The Law and the Tribunal are unquestionably the great friends and conservators of society at large ; but this has not prevented untold sufferings in many particular cases. I refer not now to the numerous instances in which civil rulers and judges have perverted their power into an engine of oppres-

sion, or have set themselves to defeat the ends of justice. With the most enlightened minds, and the
best intentions, great errors have been committed.
Solomon himself, although he acquired great reputation for superior wisdom and sound judgment, by his
decision in the case of the two women who appeared
before his tribunal, each claiming the same child as
her own, was fully conscious that he might, in other
cases, have signally failed in distributing equal justice.
Nay, conscience may have pointed him back to some
period when iniquity was seated on his own judgment-
seat. So too, in later times, a Mansfield, the great
ornament of English jurisprudence, " whose services
to a distant posterity will be rewarded by his name
being held in honoured remembrance," allowed his
noble ambition for power and fame to be mixed with
humbler impulses. The excellent Sir Matthew Hale
presided at the trial of two persons, who were condemned to death, charged, as we now know they must
have been, wrongfully, with the sin of witchcraft. And
how many innocent of all crime, have pined away their
days in gloomy prisons ! How many have been sacrificed on the scaffold or the gallows for crimes which
they never committed ! We have only to turn to the
history of English jurisprudence, in the seventeenth
century, for a humiliating illustration of the abuse
and perversion of justice. The notorious and infamous
Jeffreys, a debauchee, and common drunkard, whose
hands were polluted with gold, sat as Lord Chief Justice of the King's Bench. He condemned the illustrious patriot, Algernon Sidney, to mutilation and
death, for alleged treason, on no better evidence than
certain speculations on different forms of government ;

contained too, in an unpublished manuscript never shown to any one, and containing nothing beyond the constitutional principles of Locke and Paley. He caused Richard Baxter, who had been offered a bishopric in the Church of England, to be convicted and heavily fined, because in a book on church government, he had reflected on the Church of Rome in words which might possibly be applied to the bishops of the Church of England. Baxter pleaded *not guilty*, and prayed, on account of ill health, that his trial might be postponed. To which Jeffreys exclaimed, " Yonder stands Oates [Titus Oates was at that moment suffering part of his sentence in Palace Yard], and he says he suffers for the truth ; but if Baxter did but stand on the outside of the pillory with him, I would say two of the greatest rogues and rascals in the kingdom stood there together." And then his lordship turned up his eyes, clasped his hands, and began to sing through his nose, in imitation of what he supposed was Baxter's style of praying. When the sick and aged minister essayed to speak a word for himself, Jeffreys " bellowed (to use the language of Macauley), Richard, Richard, dost thou think we will let thee poison the court ? Richard, thou art an old knave. Thou hast written books enough to load a cart, and every book is full of sedition as an egg is full of meat. By the grace of God I will look after thee. And there," fixing his eyes on Dr. William Bates, one of the most eminent Nonconformist divines, who stood by Baxter's side, " there is a doctor of the party at your elbow. But * * * I will crush you all." And in the same century figured such judges in the

English courts, as Brampton, Heath, Foster, Scroggs, and Wright.

And for things like these, incident to our present state of imperfection, is there no remedy ? Is there no higher tribunal before which these errors will be corrected, these judges shall appear, and the wronged shall be righted ? Would a righteous God permit such things, and make no provision for the clearing of injured innocence ? Solomon meets these difficulties with the doctrine that there will be a time when "ONE higher than the highest" will vindicate the cause of the injured, and rescue blasted names from the infamy of the felon's death and grave. " God will judge the righteous and the wicked ; for a time is appointed for every purpose, and for every work."

Yes ; there will be a judgment-day ; a day of righteous, and of final award. Then those who have lived under unjust suspicions, in the present world ; who have been accused, and pronounced guilty, by men, of crimes which they never committed, will be vindicated ; and those who, although guilty, eluded the hand of justice, and even maintained a fair reputation to the day of death, will be condemned. In that day deeds done in darkness and closets will be made known on the house-tops, and " published to more worlds than this." Then the tyrant and the oppressor will be called to give up their account ; then the unjust judge will stand before an impartial tribunal ; then the master who was cruel to his slave, or who defrauded the hireling of his wages, and he who defrauded the widow and the orphan of their rights, will be confronted with the victims of their cruelty, and with HIM who is the avenger of the oppressed, and of the widow and the fatherless.

Such a judgment is necessary. It may be terrible to contemplate; but it is a merciful arrangement. It harmonizes even with our imperfect sense of what a righteous Governor must do, in vindication of that righteousness which he loves, and for the punishment of that iniquity which he hates.

§ VII. Chap. IV. 1--12.

(1.) *Then I turned and surveyed all the op-pressions which are done under the sun ; and be-hold, the tears of the oppressed ! and they had no avenger ; and from the hand of their oppressors, there was violence, but to them no avenger.*

From considering the injustice which is often di-rectly perpetrated by judges and governors, he turned and considered the oppression which prevails even in the best state of society, in which the sufferers appear to have no relief—no one to take their part. Many wrongs have existed hitherto in the purest states of society, for which there appears to be no remedy, no present relief, so far as man is concerned. Leave God and a future state of retribution (which the author of this book has so clearly announced in ch. iii. 17), out of view, and where is the defender of the oppressed ? who can espouse their cause, and bring relief. If you say that civilization in its progress will bring about a better state of things, still we ask, who will avenge the millions of oppressed who have lived and died, or are

still alive, on the earth, and must die, before civilization can bring the promised relief ?

(2.) *Therefore I pronounced the dead happy,
who have been long since dead, more than the living, who are yet alive.*

That is, if there be no avenger of the wrongs of the
oppressed, no time appointed when God will judge
the righteous and the wicked, then those who have
got through with the miseries of this life are better
off than those who are still enduring them. If death
be an eternal sleep, they have no more unavenged
wrongs to endure ; but those who are alive will be exposed to such wrongs, until they too enter upon the
same sleep.

(3.) *Yea, better off than both of them is he
who doth not yet exist, who hath not seen the evil
work which is done under the sun.*

The dead have suffered from oppressions, the living
are suffering ; but the man not yet born, is not yet a
sufferer, and until he is born, must be better off than
they. The amount of what the writer of Ecclesiastes
here says is, that it would be better not to enter upon
such an existence as ours, if there be no time appointed
when God will judge the righteous and the wicked.
" What he says here," Professor Stuart strangely remarks, " is surely no pattern for us. He only tells us
ingenuously, how he felt and acted under the gloomy
state of his fretted mind. Thousands every day, now,
sympathize with him. The only mystery about the
matter is, that he does not here say one word about a

future world." On the contrary, he had, as Professor
Stuart himself shows, in the immediate context, revealed a future judgment, and is here stating, according to his plan in this book, the utter vanity of the
present world as a source of solid happiness, when that
doctrine of a future judgment is ignored.

(4.) *Again I saw that for all toil, and every*
successful enterprise, a man is envied by his fel-
lows. This also is vanity and striving after
wind.

The meaning is, that when a man, instead of resorting to oppression or injustice to build up an earthly
estate, relies upon his prudence and skill in business,
if successful, instead of gaining credit by it, he is envied, or perhaps disparaged and traduced; and this
disposition on the part of his fellow-men renders his
success utterly vain as a means of happiness. It is
not merely the wrongs of the powerful and great, but
that imperfection in men which leads them to envy
others, who, by a legitimate and honest industry, have
gained some advantages above them, which shows that
the pursuit of worldly good, as a means of solid happiness, is vanity, and a mere striving after wind.

(5.) *The fool foldeth his hands together, and*
eateth his own flesh; (saying,)

If envy and obloquy be the reward of activity and
success, perhaps some might conclude that the *sum-*
mum bonum was to be found in idleness. But no, says
Solomon, he is a fool; he gains not the coveted prize;
he destroys himself.

(6.) *Better is a handful with quietness, than both the hands full of toil and striving after wind.*

The best explanation of this verse is that of Desvœux, who makes it contain the words of the fool, who folds his hands together, and resolves because the prosperous are envied that he will do nothing. " Better," he says, " is a handful, or the merest pittance, with freedom from envy and jealousy, than such toil and striving after the wind as fall to the lot of successful men."

(7.) *Then I turned and saw another vanity under the sun.*

(8.) *There is one alone, and no one with him; yea, he hath neither son nor brother; yet there is no end to all his toil; neither are his eyes satisfied with riches; neither saith he, For whom do I toil, and bereave my soul of good. This also is vanity; yea, it is an evil thing.*

Solomon sketches another picture, in contrast with that of the idle and thriftless man ; it is that of the busy miser ; and viewing human nature and the world under this aspect, again discovers its vanity as a source of real happiness. If there be no hereafter, all is vanity and striving after wind.

(9.) *Two are better than one, because they have a good reward for their labour.*

They may not only assist each other, but their enjoyment of the fruits of their labour will be enhanced by the pleasures of society.

(10.) *For if they fall, the one shall lift up his fellow ; but woe to him who is alone, when he falls, and hath not another to lift him up !*

The falling here may be understood figuratively, as well as literally, and may apply to all those cases in which one man stands in need of the kind and friendly offices of another.

(11.) *Again, if two lie together then they have warmth ; but how can one be warm alone ?*

Solomon employs a very familiar illustration to show the advantage of friendship and society, in contrast with the loneliness and wretchedness of the miser.

(12.) *And if one prevail against one, two shall withstand him ; and a threefold cord is not quickly broken.*

Another advantage of society, in illustration of the same thing, the vanity of wealth, used as it is by the miser, exclusively for private gratification, whose voluntary isolation excludes him not only from sympathy, but exposes him the more to unavenged wrongs, and robberies from violent men. He closes with what has become, and was perhaps even then, a familiar proverb.

SCOPE OF ARGUMENT IN § VII.

Mark the oppressions which, from time immemorial, have filled the world ! The bitter cup of slavery has been pressed to the lips of millions by those on whose side was power. Behold the tears which have moistened the soil in which they have digged, or the pillow where they have sought a momentary forgetfulness of their sorrows. Poor wretches! they have had no comforter—no avenger—none among men, none whose hand is yet visible. In many countries the mass of the people have been held in a state of servile dependence, bought and sold, like sheep and oxen, with the very acres which their own toil had purchased. In the colliery districts in England it was ascertained, by a parliamentary investigation made a few years ago, that men and even women were harnessed like beasts of burden to cars, which they were required to drag through dark underground passages, and that some of these poor creatures spent their whole lives, under the ground, seldom or never coming to the light of day. In the manufacturing districts what hardships have been inflicted upon young children, required to toil from early morning till night, robbing them of the rosy hue and buoyancy of youth, deforming their bodies ; and upon poor seamstresses in the cities employed, for the merest pittance, from sixteen to eighteen hours out of the twenty-four, with an intermission only sufficient for swallowing a scanty meal. See the injustice, which is often perpetrated in the most civilized countries, where the government is administered by rulers as wise, and as just as Solomon ; the strong taking advantage of the necessities of the weak, so weak that they must accept the terms which are proposed or perish ;—see widows and orphans despoiled of their homes, and of the very bread they were about to put into their mouths. Such is the selfishness—such the cruelty of man. Now if there be no God, who is the Patron of the oppressed and needy,

11

the husband of the widow, and the father of the fatherless—no hereafter, no day of judgment—well might the royal preacher of Jerusalem, and the preachers of Europe and America too, praise the dead, or rather the unborn, who have not yet seen the evil work that is done under the sun. Yea, if death be an eternal sleep, happy are they who are done with life's " few pleasures, and its many pains." Happy are the dead, who have been long since dead, more than the living who are yet alive. Yea, better off than both of them is he who doth not yet exist, who hath not seen the evil work which is done under the sun. Better not to be born then to be born to such an existence as ours, if there be no judgment, no time appointed for reckoning with men, and rectifying the wrongs and abuses of the present life.

" Very ghastly is the picture," exclaims Dr. Hamilton of London, in the ninth of his series of lectures on the Book of Ecclesiastes, " which our world presents when we look at it as the scene of injustice and cruelty ; and very painful is the view it gives us of our arbitrary and oppressive human nature. Could we only see what God is daily seeing, and hear what God is daily hearing, we would be apt to join with Solomon (and I would add, that without the hope of future adjudication, we should certainly join with him) in praising the dead, who are already dead, and who are past our pain or danger. For even now in this noon of the nineteenth century, which in the ear Eternal, is the loudest of earth's voices ?—which is the loudest in the ear of History ? Is it the psalm of thanksgiving ? Is it the harvest hymn of ripe fruition and cheerful prospects ? Is it the new

song of redeemed, and regenerate adoration ? —
What is the speech which day utters unto day—the
watchword which one terrestrial night passes on unto
another ?   Alas ! it is lamentation and mourning.   It
is the music of breaking hearts ; it is the noise of the
oppressor's millstone, whose grinding never waxes low.
It is the sighing of the prisoner whom the despot has
doomed ; the groaning of the victim whom lucre has
enslaved, or whom superstition means to immolate.
The heavy plunge far out on the moonlit Bosphorus is
the close of one household tragedy ; in that sudden
shriek and weltering fall on the Venetian pavement
ends another.   These cries of horror announce the funeral of some Ashantee prince, and the wholesale
slaughter which soaks his tomb ; while from Austrian
dungeons and Ural mines, the groans of patriots confess the power of tyrants.   And even if the modern
surface were silent, history can not be deaf to the
voices underneath.   For wheresoever she sets her foot
there is a stifled sob—that cry which nothing can
deaden or keep down—the quenchless cry of blood—
blood like Abel's, blood like Stephen's, blood like the
Saviour's own ; and as if the turf were all one altar,
and every pore a several tongue, she hears the slain
of centuries invoking heaven's pity—Bethlehem's inno-
cents—Roman martyrs—Bartholomew's victims ; and
the ground begins to quake as the muffled chorus
waxes louder : 'How long, O Lord, holy and true,
dost thou not avenge our blood on them that dwell on
the earth ?'

" There are few deeds of kindness which are not sufficiently notorious, few acts of munificence or mercy
which the world's right hand has not hinted to its

left. But when history begins her sterner survey—when from popedoms and dynasties, and republics even, she lifts the gilt and purple canopy—what sights of paltry vengeance or ingenious cruelty offend the reluctant gaze! What secrets of the prison-house do Bastiles and Inquisitions, San Angelos and London Towers disclose, as the daylight of inquiry breaks in, and the earthern floor gives up its slain, and the stone wall gives out its skeletons! There are depths of the ocean to which the plummet of the mariner, and the dredge of the naturalist, and the exploring foot of the diver have never traveled down; but even there as she takes her telescope, history sees the bones thick strewn of the hapless men whom the buccaneer, and the pirate, and the flying slaver have flung quick into the deep; and there are dim recesses of old story from which no gleams of humanity or tenderness beam forth; but even thence, by the light of Egyptian brick-kilns, and Druid bale-fires, and Assyrian conflagrations, we are reminded that the anguish of his fellow has always been the amusement of the warrior and the solace of the priest. So that, morally regarded, and taking in the continuous survey of all places and all time, green may be the colour of the globe, but red is the livery of man. Babel may have split the dialects of earth into a thousand tongues, but amid them all, the old vernacular of anguish still survives. And in the music of the spheres, its Maker may have given to our world its proper note; but it is a minor tune which is ever sung by its inhabitants, by neighbour nations, and by the several classes of society, evermore to one another crying, ' Woe, woe, woe.'

" Such oppressions Solomon beheld, and more especially judicial oppressions—cruelty under the cloak of law (iii. 16)—and from the contemplation his mind sought refuge in the supreme tribunal. " I said in my heart God shall judge the righteous and the wicked." * * * This is a great principle, and not to be lost sight of—the weakness of oppression, the terrible strength of the oppressed. I do not allude to the elasticity of the human heart, though that is very great, and is apt, sooner or later, to heave off despotisms and every sort of incubus. I do not so much allude to that, for, elastic though it is, it sometimes has been crushed. But I allude to that all-inspecting and all-adjusting power which controls the affairs of men. "God shall judge the righteous and the wicked" (iii. 17), or as the close of the book more amply declares it, " God shall bring every work into judgment with every secret thing, whether it be good or whether it be evil." And with two worlds in which to outwork the retribution, and with a whole eternity to overtake the arrears of time, Oh ! how tyrants should fear for God's judgments ; and that match which themselves have kindled, and which is slowly creeping round to explode their own subjacent mine, in what floods of repentance, if wise, would they drench it ! Had they been wise enough to remember that on the side of the oppressed there is always infinite power, Pharoah would have dreaded the Hebrew infants more than the Hebrew soldiery, and Herod would have been more frightened for the babes of Bethlehem than for the legions of Rome. To David the most dreadful of foes would have been the murdered Uriah, and to Ahab the hosts of Syria, compared with the corpse of Naboth, need have given no uneasiness.   More than all the might of Britain, had Napoleon cause to dread the blood of D'Enghien ; and beyond all foreign enemies, should modern nations tremble for their slaves : FOR ON THE SIDE OF THE OPPRESSED IS OMNIPOTENCE, AND THE MOST DEATHLESS OF FOES IS A VICTIM."

But look again : those who are above oppression are not beyond the reach of another form of evil passion—the envy of their fellow-men.   While the down-trodden escape this, none can be exalted above it.   Thus it appears, that not only are the weak and friendless examples of that vanity which is stamped on every thing below, but those whom (to speak after the manner of men), fortune favours, find the happiness which they have so zealously coveted in a worldly portion, greatly impaired by the imperfection which exists in their fellowmen.   This imperfection is sufficient to spoil the enjoyment which they hoped to secure in an exalted station, or by the possession of a great estate.   Let a man be enterprising and shrewd in a legitimate business ; let him by his talents and merit raise himself to distinction among his fellow-men ; let him be successful in amassing a princely fortune, he will be envied by his neighbours ; he may even be disliked and hated on account of his success.   Such is the uncharitableness of human nature, such its weakness, that a severe penalty attaches to a successful career, however virtuous.   Men come to look upon those who are above them as in some way their enemies, and to attribute their own low estate to the success which has crowned the enterprise and industry of others. The successful man is even liable to be traduced, accused of peculation and crime.   Poverty without special grace is exceedingly apt to embitter the spirit, and to foster jealous and unkind feelings toward the prosperous. So that whether a man be classed among those who are stripped of liberty and property, or those who have the power and luxuries of wealth at command, in either condition he will be constrained to bewail the vanity and vexation of spirit to which he is exposed. Even in his acts of charity, the public-spirited and generous citizen is liable to be accused of some selfish or sinister design. If, in the prosecution of his enterprises to success, he looked forward to the day when he might become a public benefactor, he finds that his most generous acts are disparaged by his motives being impeached. Ingratitude in the very objects upon whom his generosity is bestowed, or an obvious feeling on their part that he is but giving them that to which they have a rightful claim, will so sicken and sadden his mind, that he, too, will need special grace in order to persevere in his labour of love. This imperfection in men themselves, stains and poisons the most attractive and purest form of earthly good, and proves that such good can not constitute a sufficient and satisfying portion for the soul. An all-wise and benevolent Father must have provided some better thing for that soul which sprung from him. He has appointed a day when he will disperse all the mists which prejudice and envy have caused to gather around the character and name of the truly virtuous, and will say to all those who have given no more than a cup of cold water to one of his disciples, " Come, ye blessed, inherit my kingdom forever."

With the thrifty man of business, Solomon next contrasts the idle man, who foldeth his hands together, and because he sees his industrious and successful neighbour envied, refuses to work ; languidly exclaiming, " Better is a handful with quietness, than both the hands full of toil and striving after wind." But want is too real an evil for a man to deceive himself long in this way. He may escape the cares of business, and the vexations which arise from the suspicion and envy of his fellow-men, but hunger will bring him to his senses, and convince him that the chief good, the το καλον, is not to be found in idleness.

He changes the scene, and sketches another portrait ; it is that of the *miser*. He is alone in the world. He is as completely bound up in himself as if he were the solitary inhabitant of the earth. He acknowledges no kindred ; he has neither son nor brother. All the finer sensibilities of his soul have been blunted ; the love of gold has produced a complete apathy in regard to the wants and sufferings of others. Yet there is no end of his labour to gain that which does him or others so little good ! and his eye is never satisfied with counting over his hoarded gold ; he never asks himself, For whom do I labour and deprive myself of the comforts, and even the necessaries of life ?

Near the close of last year (1855) there died at Upper Sandusky, Ohio, a well known miser, named John Herryman. He was a German who, by some means, had amassed a fortune, variously estimated at $25,000 to $50,000. Of his history, place of nativity, or friends, nothing is known ; and any allusion to these matters, even by his most intimate friends, always exasperated him. He leaves, so far as at present is known, no one to inherit his estate, which will, in all probability, escheat to the State. No will has yet been discovered, and it is not likely that he left any. The manner of life and parsimonious habits of the deceased are almost incredible. For the last sixteen years, he has constantly worn the same clothes, carefully run or darned all over with strong thread, so as to prevent the possibility of wearing out. He contracted the disease of which he died, by walking over bad roads, during the most inclement weather of the season, all the way to distant counties, to pay his taxes on the land he owned there, without sufficient clothing to protect him from the cold. It is related of him that a short time since, notwithstanding the piles of gold and silver he had hoarded away, he actually carried an old horse-shoe he had picked up, about to the shops till he succeeded in selling it for half a dime. For these facts I am indebted to the newspaper published in the place of his residence. He seems to have been an almost exact counterpart of the original of that portrait which Solomon sketches.

In Topham's "Life of John Elwes, Esq.," who was for some time a member of the British Parliament, we have another melancholy example of the same kind. After inheriting a large estate from his father, at about the age of forty he succeeded to the property of his uncle, which amounted to no less than £250,000. Yet this wretched man, notwithstanding his immense wealth, denied himself of almost every comfort in order to increase his store. He would sit in wet clothes sooner than have a fire to dry them ; he would eat his provisions in the last stage of putrefaction sooner than have a fresh joint from the butcher's. When he rode out of London, he would select that road where turn-

11*

pikes were fewest, and to save the expense of shoes upon his horse, he would ride upon the soft turf adjoining the road. To save fire, he would walk about the remains of an old green house, or sit with the servant in the kitchen. One of his morning employments was to pick up any stray chips, bones, or other things, to carry to the fire in his pocket. His shoes he would never suffer to be cleaned, lest they should be worn out the sooner. As he drew near the close of life, money was his only thought. He would be frequently heard at midnight as if struggling with some one in his chamber, and crying out, " I will keep my money : I will ; nobody shall rob me of my property." On the 26th November, 1789, he died ; his property amounted to above eight hundred thousand pounds, which was soon dispersed throughout all parts of England.

> " Oh, cursed lust of gold ! when for thy sake
> The fool throws up his interest in both worlds ;
> First *starved* in this, then *damned* in that to come."

Surely, then, the world, concentrated in the form of gold and silver, and loved for its own sake, is just as ineffectual to satisfy the soul, and just as unworthy of its immortal nature, as any other form in which it can be presented and loved ; and well did Solomon say of it, " Vanity ; yea, it is an evil thing." The soul was not made for such an idolatry as that into which these poor men fell. They perverted and abused their affections ; "they dug for dross with mattocks made of gold." Solomon was determined to exhaust all the expedients to which men can turn in their search after some solid ground of happiness in this world, and to show them that the true end of their existence can not be found below. Hence he takes the miser, and the idle man, as well as the lordly oppressor, and the upright, enterprising, and successful man of business, and from them he establishes the great doctrine of this book ; viz., that when we consider things under a certain aspect—that man must find his whole happiness, and the great end of his existence in the present world—then they are all the merest vanity.

(13.) *Better is a youth, poor and wise, than a king old and foolish, who will not any more be counseled.*

In the remaining verses of this chapter, Solomon points out the insufficiency of the world, even to those who have risen to the highest places of authority and honour, to yield unalloyed and lasting happiness, by reason of the uncertainty and inconstancy of popular favour. He makes allusion to certain events which he sagaciously foresees, or which had been revealed to him, as an inspired man, in illustration of the subject. But the history of almost every king, and great ruler, would furnish facts corroborative of the same inconstancy.

The young man "poor and wise" is undoubtedly Jeroboam, whose father, Nebat, was a servant of Solomon, but who was early left to the care of a widowed mother. Kings xi. 26–28. Although his origin was so humble he was "wise;" that is, possessed of fine talents; or the allusion may rather be to the arts of intrigue and cunning, in which he proved himself to be an adept. The "old and foolish king" is, un-

doubtedly Solomon himself. He does not mean, however, to acknowledge that he was silly, or that his
mental faculties had been weakened by age ; nor that
Jeroboam was better qualified to be the king ; but
this he foresaw, or it had been revealed to him, was
what the people would be ready to say, whenever an
occasion presented, or as soon as they dared. " Better," say they, " is the youthful Jeroboam, who has
already won the title of a mighty man of valour, and
who is possessed of qualities so engaging, sprightly,
and active, than an old king, whose mind age has begun to impair, and who will no longer listen to counsels which point to any change in his long established
policy."

(14.) *For from the house of captives he comes
forth to reign ; whereas, even in his own kingdom, he was born a poor man.*

" The house of captives" well describes Egypt,
where the children of Israel were in captivity. Moreover, that country seems to have been " the common
asylum of fugitives from Judea." It was here that
Urijah took refuge when Jehoiakim sought to put
him to death. (Jer. xxxi. 21). And it was to Egypt
that Jeroboam fled, when Solomon discovered his ambition to ascend the throne, and sought to bring him
to punishment for his treason. He took refuge in the
court of Shishak (Sesouchis), where he remained until
the death of Solomon. He had not the least claim,
by descent, to the crown. He was the son of a servant ; was born poor. But Solomon discovering his
abilities had appointed him to an honourable and lucrative office, in one of the principal tribes of Israel.

The young man, possessed as he was of a pleasing address, took advantage of his position to intrigue against his royal master. He instilled into the minds of the people the idea that the government was oppressive ; he secretly aspired to the throne. The discovery of his treason, necessitated his flight from his country ; but it is not improbable that during his absence he kept up a secret, and traitorous correspondence with those whom he had already disaffected toward the government. And no sooner did the tidings of Solomon's death reach him than he returned, and became a rival of Rehoboam, the rightful heir to the crown, and drew away ten tribes from their allegiance, and became their king. He ruled over a kingdom in which he was born a poor man.

(15.) *I saw all the living, who walk under the sun, with the young man, the second who stood up in his stead.*

Solomon had perhaps seen in other kingdoms examples of what he here describes—a propensity to prefer a young and popular ruler to an old monarch. But we may rather understand him as recording what he had foreseen, in respect to his own kingdom ; *viz.,* that there would be a defection of the great majority of the people, in favour of the young man who was to come forth out of the house of captives. The expression, *all the living who walk under the sun* is hyperbolical, and refers to the overwhelming majority of the Hebrew people, who would espouse the cause of Jeroboam. *The second* designates Jeroboam ; and as the number implies *a first*, it is well suggested by Professor Stuart, that it brings to view Rehoboam, whose birth gave him the lawful title to the entire kingdom. In vision, Solomon saw the great mass of the nation siding with Jeroboam, instead of his own son, who had the *first* and rightful claim to the crown. He saw not only in his own case, but in that of his son, a signal instance of popular inconstancy toward kings.

(16.) *There was no end to all the people before whom he went forth ; yet they that come afterward shall not rejoice in him.   Yea, this also is vanity, and striving after wind.*

Solomon describes his vision further. He continues the hyperbole in speaking of the popularity of Jeroboam ; there was no end to all the people that made him their leader. But he saw even in his case, popular as he at first was destined to be, another instance of the uncertainty which attends the toils of ambition. How the message of the good prophet Ahijah must have caused his ears to tingle, and his heart to quail ! Only one of his family, and he a mere infant, should come to his grave, and be mourned ; "him that dieth of Jeroboam in the city shall the dogs eat ; and him that dieth in the fields shall the fowls of the air eat," and none shall be "so poor as to do them reverence." His family should be utterly extirpated. (1 Kings xiv. 7–14). His name would be infamous with posterity. How vain then, is ambition, even when its most aspiring hopes are all gratified ! How can it be better described than to say, it is a mere fruitless striving after wind !

SCOPE OF ARGUMENT IN § VIII.

Men are prone to look to a crown, a throne, a scepter, as the insignia not only of power and wealth, but of happiness. The inmates of a palace they imagine have access to sources of pleasure from which the majority of the race are debarred. They are treated with deference, they are courted and flattered; they are surrounded by an obsequious retinue; the luxuries of all climes are provided to regale their taste; they can command whatever may contribute to the magnificence of their residences, the most exquisite works of art, paintings, and statuary, fountains, and gardens, and parks. Whenever they appear in public, it is in a dazzling equipage, in costly robes, surrounded with lords and officers, and soldiers arrayed in showy uniforms. They have offices, sinecures, estates, and benefices to confer. They have only to nod and their slightest wishes or commands are instantly obeyed. They have only to say to one of the highest officers of the land, "Go," and he goeth; or to another, "Come," and he cometh. Neglects and slights never can occasion them a moment's uneasiness, for they are never exposed to them. To want, or to the apprehension of it, they are utter strangers; the very superfluities of their tables would feed famishing crowds. They have but to show themselves to the people, to be cheered by their acclamations, "Hail!" "Long live!" "*Vive!*" Heads are uncovered, and the crowd opens, as by enchantment, to let the cavalcade sweep by. If some discontented or insane man, some hired miscreant, or some foreign foe should aim a blow at the royal personage, a thousand hands would be instantly stretched out for his protection. If he feels pain, men most distinguished for science and skill are in a moment at his side, to do all in their power to give him ease. "Ah!" say the unthinking multitude, "now we have found the long-sought prize," or "we have discovered where it may be found; we have learned its hiding-place. That happiness which flies from the great mass of men must make its home in the palace; the king must be happy; the royal family must be happy. They wrong this world who say that there is nowhere to be found in it true, real happiness. The powerful, popular ruler of a great nation must be excepted from the application of that sentence, which seems to have been passed upon the rest of the race, and which so effectually excludes them from any thing like solid, lasting happiness. Aye, we have found out the secret, now; it is power, civil power and station, which can redeem the world from the charge of being utterly insufficient to render any man truly happy."

But let us not too hastily settle upon this conclusion, and pay a compliment to the world which we shall only too quickly be constrained to take back. Let us summon our witnesses—as we have, and can expect to have, no experience ourselves in this matter—and learn from them, from the inmates of the palace, from kings and princes, whether their couches of down are always couches of rest, whether the rich and tempting viands on their tables are always successful in provoking a lost appetite, whether no chill ever finds its way through the walls to smite their frames, whether no fever ever burns in its coolest

recesses, whether the gilded ceilings always ward off
pain from the heads and care from the hearts of those
who dwell below.   And whose testimony ought to be
more highly prized than that of Solomon himself ?
He was a king, one of the most renowned kings of any
age or nation.   We have the facts of his history in an
inspired record, and we have his own testimony on the
very point now under consideration.

At the beginning of his reign he was received with
the highest favour by the people.   David, before his
death, to defeat the machinations of Adonijah, with
whom the famous captain Joab, and the priest Abiathar had joined, secured to him the throne ; and there
was no one to question his right to the succession.
The favour of the people was manifested toward him
at that time by their rejoicings.   " They blew the
trumpet, and all the people said, *God save king Solomon.*   And all the people came up after him, and the
people piped with pipes, and rejoiced with great joy,
so that the earth rent with the sound of them."
1 Kings i. 39, 40.   David was not yet dead, and
might have made the same pathetic allusion to that
propensity which has been said to prevail in monarchical countries, " to prefer the heir apparent to the
reigning prince," which Solomon had occasion to make
in his old age : " Better," say the people, "is a young
prince, than an old, foolish king, who will not listen
to counsel."   All Israel obeyed him.   "And all the
princes, and the mighty men, and all the sons likewise of king David, submitted themselves unto Solomon the king.   And the Lord magnified Solomon
exceedingly in the sight of all Israel, and bestowed
upon him such royal majesty as had not been on any

king before him in Israel." 1 Chron. xxix. 23–25. He succeeded to a kingdom, which, under the wise and vigorous reign of his royal father, having been greatly prospered, and strengthened, and enlarged, and its enemies subdued, was left in the enjoyment of perfect peace.

The people appear to have been eminently contented and happy. We are told that "Judah and Israel were many as the sand which is by the sea in multitude, eating, and drinking, and making merry." 1 Kings iv. 20. The young monarch was popular ; the people expressed their joy by feasting and merriment. He immediately applied himself to those great works which afforded lucrative employment to large numbers, and tended to enhance the general prosperity. He erected the temple. He built, and repaired, and fortified a great number of cities. "He raised a large navy, and enriched himself and his people, by an extensive foreign commerce. He made silver as plenty in his days in Jerusalem as stones in the street. Never did the children of Israel enjoy so much peace and prosperity, as during his reign. "He had peace on all sides round about him. And Judah and Israel dwelt safely, every man under his vine, and under his fig-tree, from Dan even to Beersheba, all the days of Solomon." 1 Kings iv. 24, 25. The people had no excuse for being discontented or dissatisfied under his administration of the government. He employed all the resources of his noble and capacious mind for the benefit of his kingdom ; and probably retained his popularity with as little diminution as commonly falls to the lot of a monarch who reigned so long. Yet he lived to hear the rising murmur of discontent, and to know that he was beginning to be regarded as an old and foolish king, who was blindly and irrecoverably devoted to a chosen policy, and that the people were quite ready to have him out of the way, and to see a young man in his place. Reproaches which were uttered, however secretly, in closets and bed-chambers, in some manner came to his ears ; a bird of the air carried the voice, and that which had wings reported the matter. (Ch. x. 20.)

A young man, the son of one of his own servants, whom he had raised to an office of profit and honour, secretly aspiring to the throne, with consummate art and address, propagated the spirit of disaffection among the people. His office brought him in contact with the people ; he was a sort of receiver-general of taxes, in one of the most important tribes, and could easily employ his office to gain himself popularity ; he could tamper with the people, and instill into their minds the idea that the taxes were too burdensome, and were laid to carry out some indiscreet measures of a superannuated, and now weak-minded monarch. He particularly made the building of Millo, and the repairing of the breaches of the city of David, an occasion of persuading the unthinking multitude that they were unreasonably loaded with taxes, and thus of diffusing a disloyal and rebellious spirit. To stimulate still further the ambition of Jeroboam, the prophet Ahijah, just at this time, revealed to him that God would take ten tribes out of the hand of Solomon's son and successor, and give them for a kingdom to him ; and that he should "reign according to all that his soul desired." (1 Kings xi. 26–37). Indeed, it was probably God's threatening on account of

Solomon's idolatry, "I will surely rend the kingdom from thee, and will give it to thy servant," 1 Kings xi. 11, which first aroused the infatuated monarch to a sense of his sin, and led to that repentance of which the book of Ecclesiastes is the proof and monument. Jeroboam, however, could not wait for the death of the old king ; he commenced a conspiracy against him ; "he lifted up his hand against him ;" and it was on this account, and not because of the prophecy of Ahijah, that Solomon sought to bring him to punishment ; and to save his life it was necessary for him to flee to the court of Sesonchis. "Tell me not," Solomon might well say, "that a prosperous reign, over a confiding and admiring people, is sure to yield undisturbed happiness. Tell me not that palace walls can always exclude misery, or that the heart never beats with anguish beneath the royal purple. I am a king : I have been young and now I am old ; and I am ready to inscribe upon all my magnificence and honour as a king, YEA, THIS IS ALSO VANITY ?" What a change had taken place since the queen of Sheba surveyed his palace, "and the meat of his table, and the sitting of his servants, and the attendance of his ministers, and their apparel, and his cup-bearers, and his ascent by which he went up into the house of the Lord," and exclaimed, "Happy are thy men, happy are these thy servants, which stand continually before thee, and that hear thy wisdom. Blessed be the Lord thy God, which delighteth in thee, to set thee on the throne of Israel : because the Lord loved Israel forever, therefore made he thee king, to do judgment and justice !" The aged monarch bowed his head, upon the discovery that there were traitors and conspirators, who were laying snares, and opening pitfalls for his trembling steps; and that the ingrates who were thus engaged, were the very men on whom he had bestowed favours and honours; he trembled when he considered the character and talents of the true heir-apparent, Rehoboam, and how incompetent he was likely to prove for the troubles that were gathering. What availed all his vast treasures, and the incomparable "royal majesty" which had been bestowed on him? what availed his renown, and the society of learned philosophers, and gay courtiers? what availed his gardens and groves, and the delicious coolness of his fountains? Could we have followed him, as, rising up at the voice of the bird, he wandered forth in the stillness of the morning, we should have marked the dejection which sat on his countenance, and heard the sigh which heaved his bosom; could we have followed him to the pillow where he nightly sought repose, we should have heard wailed out from beneath the gorgeous canopy, "Vanity of vanities, vanity of vanities; all is vanity."

Nor was the experience of King David dissimilar to that of his successor; indeed it must have been more painful, inasmuch as the conspirator was a beloved son, and real heir to the crown. David had been a great benefactor to the nation; by his courage and skill in war, and his wise statesmanship, he had raised the nation to a degree of prosperity and power it had not known before. His influence had known no bounds; his very word was law. It is true that his reputation had been sadly impaired by his base treatment of a brave and gallant soldier of his army, Uriah; but the infirmities of age were now beginning to come upon him; and there were many restless persons who had nothing to lose by a revolution, who hoped that any change would better their condition, and who were ready to pay their homage to the rising, rather than to the setting, sun. As the heir-apparent, Absalom had begun to assume a regal state and airs, he prepared horses, and chariots, and fifty men, to run before him. In personal appearance he was remarkably captivating and commanding. "In all Israel there was none to be so much praised for his beauty as Absalom. From the sole of his foot even to the crown of his head, there was no blemish in him." He appeared in public most gorgeously arrayed. He possessed just those accomplishments which fit a man to gain popularity with the multitude. He took his station by the gate of the king's palace, in his splendid attire, surrounded by his bodyguard, and was all affability and attention to the humblest of the people, who had come from distant provinces, with various causes and complaints, to obtain judgment from the king. He inquired of each one the nature of his cause, and never failed to express a favourable opinion to the complainant, and to find fault with the delay to grant justice in such plain cases. He would exclaim, in the hearing of all, " Oh, that I were made a judge in the land, that every man which hath any suit or cause might come unto me, and I would do him justice ! And it was so, that when any man came nigh to him to do him obeisance, he put forth his hand, and took him, and kissed him." 2 Sam. xv. 4, 5. It was in this manner Absalom stole the hearts of the people. The standard of rebellion was raised at Hebron ; multitudes flocked around it ; Ahithophel, a counsellor of David, supported the claims of Absalom, and became his chief adviser and minister. David fled with a few hundred armed men toward the wilderness. He "went up by the ascent of Mount Olivet, and wept as he went up, and had his head covered, and he went barefoot; and all the people that were with him covered every man his head; and they went up, weeping as they went." 2 Sam. xv. 30. But it is not necessary to follow in detail all the events connected with Absalom's rebellion. A battle at length took place between his adherents and those who remained faithful to David. The scene of this battle was the wood of Ephraim; twenty thousand of the combatants fell. The beautiful, the indulged, the ambitious, unfilial Absalom was slain. On the evening of the day of battle, the anxious monarch stood before the gate of Mahanaim waiting for some tidings from the field; and no sooner did the breathless messenger appear, than there burst from the father's quivering lips the question, "Is the young man Absalom safe?" When he had learned his melancholy, yet richly-deserved fate, he hurried as fast as age and trouble would permit, to the chamber or lodge over the gate of the city, and there was heard that grief-cry which could only burst from a mourning parent's lips—"O, my son Absalom, my son, my son Absalom! would God I had died for thee, O, Absalom, my son, my son!" When the victorious army arrived, anticipating a warm greeting from the city, and especially from the king, whose throne had been saved by their valour, instead of shouts of triumph, and notes of rejoicing, all was gloom and sadness. As they stole through the gates into the city, rather as vanquished men, fleeing from battle, than as conquerors, they could hear the loud and bitter cry of the king, from the watchman's lodge above, " O my son Absalom ! O Absalom, my son, my son !" His faults were all forgotten by the fond father—were buried in the grave. He thought of him now as he was in childhood, " when a blooming, sprightly youth; when a fine, promising, beautiful young man, that had not his equal in all Israel. And now to keep the crown a few years longer on his aged head, that was trembling over the grave, Absalom must die. ' Ah, dearly recovered crown, how worthless now ! my poor, beloved Absalom, has it cost your life ? has it cost your life ?' "

Nor was this the only attempt at rebellion during the reign of David. Adonijah, the brother of Absalom, who regarded himself as being next in the succession, when the infirmities of age had still further increased on his father, exalted himself, saying, " I will be king." The warrior Joab, and the priest Abiathar, who had been faithful in their allegiance to David, at the time of Absalom's rebellion, and had done so much to defeat it, and reinstate the rightful monarch, favoured the claims of this new aspirant for the crown. The wisdom and promptitude of Nathan the prophet were probably all that saved the crown from being torn from the brow of the feeble old king, at this time, and placed on an unworthy son. Even such loyal subjects as Abiathar and Joab had been, were ready to say, " Better is a young man like Adonijah, than a superannuated, weak-minded old king like David ; the public interest, the welfare of the nation is at stake ; why should we scruple, why hesitate to make the change on account of his past services." Such is the inconstancy which the greatest

12

rulers are destined to feel among their most devoted, attached, and indebted subjects. Truly the greatest power of the most famous kings is vanity, and a mere striving after wind. A man in a conspicuous station is often like a lofty tree, which is swayed and broken by the wind which disturbs not the humble flower that blooms at its base, or the thrush's nest in its lowly bush.

"Ambition," says Jeremy Taylor, "is full of distractions, it teems with stratagems, as Rebecca with struggling twins, and is swelled with expectation as with a tympany, and sleeps sometimes as the wind in a storm, still and quiet for a minute, that it may burst out into an impetuous blast till the cordage of his heart-strings crack; fears when none is nigh, and prevents things which never had intention, and falls under the inevitability which either could not be foreseen, or not prevented." Jeroboam finds himself upon the throne of Israel; but no sooner is he established upon it, than he begins to fear lest the kingdom should return to the house of David. He knew that his power was ill-gotten, that he was a mere usurper; he had reason to fear that the people who were so faithless toward Rehoboam, might be no more faithful to him, that they might kill him, and return to the rightful sovereign from whom they had revolted. To alienate them more perfectly, he sought to alienate them from their religion, and confirm them in idolatry. How his heart must have sunk within him when the nameless prophet came out of Judah, and cried against the idolatrous altar which he had erected in Bethel, "O altar, altar, thus saith the Lord," and the altar was rent, and the ashes poured out, and his own hand, which he had stretched out to seize the prophet, was withered ! How he must have trembled at the message from Ahijah, the same prophet who had foretold to him that he should be king, " Go tell Jeroboam, Thus saith the Lord God of Israel, Forasmuch as thou hast done evil above all that were before thee, and hast cast me behind thy back, I will bring evil upon the house of Jeroboam, and will take away the remnant from the house of Jeroboam, as a man taketh away dung, till it be all gone." " They that come afterward shall not rejoice in him."

The lesson of uninspired and of modern history is the same ; vain is royalty, empty are the pleasures of the palace with its music, its feasts, its pictures, its terraces, its gardens, its fountains. On the first page of the history of one of the mightiest of modern monarchs,* who reigned more than threescore years and ten, we read, " He was viewed as a sun of glory and power, in the light of which all other lights were dim. Philosophers, poets, prelates, generals, and statesmen, during his reign were regarded only as his satellites. He was the central orb around which every other light revolved, and to contribute to his glory all were supposed to be born. He was most emphatically the state." On the last page it is written, " His power was broken. He was no longer the autocrat of Europe, but a miserable old man, who had lived to see irreparable calamities inflicted on his nation, and calamities in consequence of his ambition. He survived his son, and his grandson. He saw himself an object of reproach, of ridicule, and of compassion. His last days were embittered by disappointments and

* Louis XIV.

mortifications, disasters in war and domestic afflictions.   No man ever, for a while, enjoyed a prouder
pre-eminence.   No man ever drank deeper of the cup
of disappointed ambition and alienated affections.
No man ever more fully realized the vanity of this
world."

In 1774, a young man not far from twenty years of
age ascended the throne of one of the most powerful
kingdoms of Europe.   I refer to Louis XVI. of
France.   In natural disposition he was amiable and
virtuous ; he at once put a stop to the scandalous im-
morality which had marked the court, under the preceding reign.   He appears to have been sincerely
anxious to promote the happiness of the people.   He
committed the management of the finances, which had
become exceedingly disordered, to an enlightened,
able minister, and one of his first acts was to restore
the parliament, which had been taken away under his
predecessor.   He granted liberty of trade in corn between one province and another, abolished various
feudal exactions, and the practice of torture, granted
freedom of worship to Protestants, and established
some degree of economy and order, of which he set a
conspicuous example in the management of his own
household.   " His reign," says Alison, " from his ac-
cession to the throne to the meeting of the states-
general, was nothing but a series of ameliorations."
But the very reforms of this amiable and virtuous
monarch hastened the fearful calamities of his reign
and his own melancholy fate.   The assembling of the
states-general resulted in the formation of the national assembly.   This was in 1789.   The Bastile was
stormed ; on the 20th September the king was com-

pelled to sanction a decree, by which the entire royal authority was swept away. On the 6th October a mob attacked the palace of Versailles, massacred the guards, and compelled the king and royal family to remove to Paris. During the year 1790 they remained in the Tuilleries, in a condition hardly different from that of prisoners. In June, 1791, he made an abortive attempt to escape. In January, 1793, after a mock trial by the convention, the king was led out to execution, an act of atrocity which at once arrayed against France the moral sympathies of mankind.

We have sought in vain in earthly palaces, for the boon of real happiness. He alone will obtain it who seeks to become rich toward God, and to be made a priest and a king to him in his heavenly kingdom.

§ IX. Chap. V. 1–9.

(1.) *Keep thy foot when thou goest to the house of God; and it is better to draw nigh to hear than to offer the sacrifice of fools; for they know not that they do evil.*

Keep thy foot, i. e., look well to thy ways; take heed to thyself; go not in a thoughtless, careless, or formal manner to worship God. Solomon fully recognizes the spiritual nature of acceptable worship. If he had been ignorant of the doctrine of future rewards and punishments, or if this doctrine had been purposely concealed from the ancient Hebrews, he would not have addressed them in this manner. If this doctrine, according to Warburton and others, made no part of their religion, then what could their religion have been but a mere external observance, a set of national customs, an appendage of the State? If all the reward to which they looked forward, was reward in this life, was temporal, and carnal, then the obedience on which it was bestowed, must have been merely outward and visible. It would seem unnatural, if not absurd, to attempt to enforce spiritual obedience, that is, a right state of the heart, by the promise of only temporal good, and the threatening of only temporal evil. Human governments can not make laws, or if they make, can not enforce them, requiring men to embrace certain opinions, or to cultivate certain feelings and dispositions, but wisely confine themselves to imposing restrictions upon the actions of men so far as they relate to the rights of others, and the peace and good order of the State. Their penalties must be confined to depriving men of their civil rights, their personal liberty, their property, or their lives. If, then, the ancient Hebrews were ignorant of a future state of rewards and punishments, when Solomon attempted to enforce on them a spiritual system of religion, he must have been listened to as one speaking in an unknown tongue. Merely to offer sacrifices was not enough ; they must *hear*, that is, obey the law, which is heard or read. "Hath the Lord as great delight in burnt-offerings and sacrifices, as in obeying the voice of the Lord ? Behold, to obey is better than sacrifice, and to hearken than the fat of rams." 1 Sam. xv. 22. "And the Lord thy God will circumcise thine heart, and the heart of thy seed, to love the Lord thy God with all thine heart, and with all thy soul, that thou mayest live." Deut. xxx. 6. Comp. x. 16. "The sacrifices of God are a broken spirit : a broken and a contrite heart, O, God, thou wilt not despise." Ps. li. 17. This religion of the heart, known to Moses, to Samuel, and to David, was known to Solomon ; and such a religion could not have been enforced by the promise of mere temporal rewards, or the threatening of temporal evil ; and therefore we infer that if there had been no distinct mention of a future state of retribution in the Hebrew Scriptures, such a state must have been well known, and even a familiar truth to the ancient Hebrews. For how could they have known that they were doing evil when they offered sacrifices, without contrite and obedient, that is to say, with uncircumcised hearts, if they were altogether ignorant of the doctrines and motives which require us to serve God in spirit and in truth. There could have been no such thing as spiritual worship; but they all, without exception, must have been "fools."

(2.) *Be not rash with thy mouth, and let not thy heart be swift to utter a thing before God: for God is in heaven, and thou upon earth; therefore let thy words be few.*

The exhortation has reference to prayer. Reverence and humility therein are enforced from the consideration of the infinite majesty of the Being addressed in prayer. Solomon had the same spiritual views of prayer which are enforced in our Lord's sermon on the mount: "When ye pray, use not vain repetitions as the heathen do; for they think that they shall be heard for their much speaking. Be not ye therefore like unto them; for your Father knoweth what things ye have need of, before ye ask him." Matt. vi. 7, 8.

(3.) *For a dream cometh through much business; and a fool's voice is known by a multitude of words.*

Here the prayer, which is composed of a multitude of unmeaning words, is compared to the dreamy visions of the night, after a day of perplexing cares. How could the inspired writer have more impressively set forth the worthlessness of such a prayer!

(4.) *When thou vowest a vow to God, defer not to pay it; for he hath no pleasure in fools: that which thou hast vowed pay.*

Defer not or delay not to pay it ; that is, perform it while the sense of obligation which prompted it is fresh and strong, or before thou repent of thy promises. The fools here spoken of are such as make promises when in danger or distress, but as soon as the occasion which led to the making of them is over, think no more of the promises. They discover the highest folly in thinking thus to mock and deceive the omniscient God. In the laws of Moses there are several for the regulation and due execution of vows. See Lev. xxvii. The words of Solomon above are almost a repetition of the words of Moses, " When thou shalt vow a vow unto the Lord, thou shalt not slack to pay it ; for the Lord thy God will surely require it of thee ; and it would be sin in thee." Deut. xxiii. 21.

(5.) *It is better not to vow, than to vow and not to perform.*

The sincerity of the man who makes a vow can be tested only by his fulfillment of his promise. It is true that a man may perform a vow in an unwilling spirit, and therefore not acceptably. But the caution here is against making those sudden and rash promises, which, when the excitement of the mind under which they were made is past, we shall feel no disposition to fulfill. It is sincerity of heart, as well as fidelity in the performance of outward duty, which Solomon makes indispensable in our service of God.

(6.) *Let not thy mouth expose thy flesh to punishment ; neither say before the angel, that it was a mistake ; wherefore should God be angry on account of thy utterance, and destroy the work of thy hands ?*

Thoughtless or inconsiderate vowing is still the subject of the writer. *Thy flesh* is put for the man, *thee;* let not such vowing expose thee to punishment. And when the time to pay comes, do not say before the messenger, or the ambassador of God, that is, the priest, The vow was made inconsiderately, or by mistake. Why displease God with false promises, and provoke him to punish thee for insincerity ? It was the office of the priest, who is called the messenger, or angel of the Lord, (Mal. ii. 7,) to judge respecting vows, and to see them faithfully fulfilled.

(7.) *For in a multitude of dreams, there are indeed vanities ; so also in a multitude of words ; but fear thou God.*

Here the multitude of words refer both to the unmeaning, wordy prayers, and the rash and hasty vows described in the preceding verses. Such prayers and vows are likened to the dreams of the night ; they have no meaning, no value ; therefore avoid them.

Fear God. All who truly fear God will be preserved from such folly; for the fear of the Lord is the beginning of wisdom. Solomon does not here enforce the duty of fearing God, as he does at the close of the book, by declaring, in so many words, that he will bring every work into judgment in the great day. This, however, he substantially does in the next verse, wherein he carries the mind back to this subject, or the doctrine of a future judgment, as it was presented in connection with oppression and injustice in ch. iii. 16, 17, and iv. 1, etc.

(8.) *If thou seest the oppression of the poor, and perversion of judgment and justice in a province, be not disturbed on account of this; for over the high officer, a higher one watches, and over both of them, the Highest One.*

Solomon, having so clearly announced the doctrine of a future judgment, in iii. 16, 17, and iv. 1, etc., in connection with the oppressions and injustice which are permitted to exist among men, reasserts it here by an evident allusion to what he had said there. There is a Higher One in heaven to whom the highest earthly rulers are accountable. And if he takes cognizance of the oppressions and robberies which exist among men—and on this account we are not to permit our minds to be ruffled or distressed, as if there were no remedy—will he not also take cognizance of those acts by which men think to rob him? " Will a man rob God? Yet ye have robbed me. But ye say, Wherein have we robbed thee? In tithes and offerings." " Fear God, and pay unto him thy vows, for not to pay is robbery, and the High and Lofty One, who in the last great day will judge those who have been guilty of robbery of judgment and justice in a province, will surely bring robbery of himself into judgment."

(9.) *Moreover, the profit of the land is for all ; the kiny is served by the field.*

In the preceding verse he speaks of the accountability of earthly rulers to him who is King of kings, and Lord of lords, both to restrain their misrule and to check impatience under oppression from their hand. But, they are not only accountable in the same manner as other men are, they are on the same level with the humblest of their subjects, in another respect : they are served by the field, or, as Herzfeld translates, are *subject to the field*, that is, they are dependent on the products of the earth for food. They do not belong to a different race of beings ; they must eat and drink, must sleep, have garments and dwellings, must die and find a grave in the same dust at last. Let this restrain them from oppression, and afford a consoling lesson to the oppressed.

SCOPE OF ARGUMENT IN § IX.

Even the miserable systems of Pagan religion owe their influence over the popular mind to the doctrine of rewards and punishments in another life. As the heathen do not perceive that goodness receives its reward, or evil its punishment in this world, unless they expected that some difference would be made hereafter between the good and the bad, there would be no ground left on which to found an appeal to them to reverence the Deity, or perform any moral duty whatever. They would be left entirely to the guidance of mere natural instincts, and would be governed by no higher law, considered in a moral point of view, than that which governs the lower animals. Society could not exist, or it could exist only in the rudest state, and only while bound together by the might and cruelty of some head-man, who had made himself master, as the lion makes himself the king of the forest. All the philosophers, historians, and legislators of heathen antiquity, whether they favoured arbitrary power, or vindicated civil liberty, agreed in maintaining that the doctrine of future rewards and punishments was essential to the good order of society. As specimens of what may everywhere be found in their writings, take the following : Timæus, an early Pythagorean, who in Plato's judgment was skilled in the knowledge of philosophy, in discoursing on the remedies for moral evil, after speaking of the uses of philosophy, says: " But if we meet with a perverse ungovernable disposition, then punishments should be applied ; both those which civil laws inflict, and those which the terrors of religion denounce against the wicked from above and below," etc. In like manner the historian Polybius, who was employed by the Romans to frame laws for Greece, after it had become a province of their republic, speaks : " Since the multitude is ever fickle and capricious, full of irregular passions, and irrational and violent resentments, there is no way

left to keep them in order, but by the terrors of future punishment, and the pompous circumstance that
belongs to such kind of fictions."* The great geographer Strabo says : "The multitude in society are
allured to virtue by those enticing fables, which the
poets tell of the illustrious achievements of ancient
heroes, and the rewards conferred by the gods for
well doing. So again, they are restrained from vice
by the punishments these are said to inflict upon
offenders."† And Pliny the elder, though an Epicurean, acknowledged that it was necessary to society
that men should believe the gods concerned themselves in human affairs, and that the punishments
they inflict on offenders, though sometimes delayed,
yet are never to be evaded.‡ It affects not the argument in the least, to prove that these ancient philosophers did not themselves believe the doctrine of a
future state of rewards and punishments ; it is sufficient to show that they regarded the propagation of
such a belief among the people at large as essential
to the support of religion, or as a restraint upon
moral evil.

It seems also almost superfluous to call attention to
the fact that the religion of the New Testament, or
the religion of Christ, would be annihilated, if we
were to take away, or ignore the doctrine of an endless life. Christ is therein revealed not as a great philosopher, or as the Confucius of a religious system, but
as a Saviour to men, a Saviour from their sins, from a
sense of guilt here, and from the punishment of them
hereafter. Moral duties are enforced from the great

---

* E, Polyb., Hist. lib. vi., c. 54, 55.   † Strabo, Geog., I, i.
‡ Hist. Nat., I., ii., c. 7.

doctrine which stands out everywhere on the pages of the Gospel, that they are accountable to God not only for their actions and their words, but for the secret feelings which they cherish in their hearts. Christ appeared that he might bring to light—illuminate—life and immortality. Men are made to feel the reality of things invisible and eternal. How vain it would be—such is the depravity of human nature, so thoroughly weakened is every virtuous principle in fallen man—to attempt to enforce upon him, without the doctrine of retribution, the duty of submission and love to God, or of kindness and charity toward his fellow-creatures ! Why should men repent of sin, or seek to avoid it, if the law of which it is a violation, is not of sufficient consequence to be vindicated ? Why should they believe in Christ, if faith has no connection with their escape from destruction, and their eternal salvation ? Open the New Testament at almost any page, and how are we to feel the importance of its precepts, unless we keep in view the doctrine of future accountability and retribution : " Seek not ye what ye shall eat, or what ye shall drink ; but rather seek ye the kingdom of God. Sell that ye have, and give alms. Let your loins be girded about, and your lights burning. Seek those things which are above. Set your affection on things above." It needs only to be further remarked, that as men lose sight of the spiritual nature of the requirements of Christianity, enjoining the cultivation of the affections and a holy life, and of the doctrine of future retribution, their religion becomes a mere outward form, a decent observance ; and while, in respect to the public welfare, it may, in an imposing ex-

ternal form, still be of value, it is of value rather
as a part of a great system of police, than because it
reaches their hearts, and improves their characters.
It would be vain to tell men, who have lost the image
of God by their apostacy from him, that they must
content themselves to act in simple obedience to their
Maker ; that virtue and goodness are reward enough in
themselves in this life, though they were sure to have
no existence beyond it. " Religion," says the acute
Howe, " terminates upon God ; and upon him under
a double notion, either as we design service and honour
to him, or as from him we design satisfaction and blessedness to ourselves. Now if a man's thoughts be carried toward God under the former notion, how great
an abatement must it needs be to the vigour and zeal
of his affection, who shall with the most sincere de-
votedness apply himself to serve his interest and glory,
to reflect upon the universal mortality of himself and
mankind, without any hope of compensation to it by
a future immortality ! It is agreed on all hands, that
the utmost contributions of creatures can add nothing
to him ; and that our glorifying him doth only consist,
either in our acknowledging him glorious ourselves, or
representing him so to others. But how little doth it
signify, and how flat and low a thing it would seem,
that I should only turn mine eye upward, and think a
few admiring thoughts of God this hour, while I ap-
prehend myself liable to lose my very thinking power
and my whole being the next ! Or if we could spread
his vast renown, and gain all the sons of men to a
concurrence with us, in the adoring of his sovereign
excellences, how would it damp and stifle such loyal
and dutiful affection, to consider that the universal

homage so deservedly given to him, shall shortly cease forever, and that infinitely blessed Being be, ere long (again as he was from eternity before) the only witness of his own glory ! And if the propension of a man's soul be toward God under the latter notion also, in order to a satisfaction that shall thence accrue to himself, it can not be but an unspeakable diminution and check to the highest delights of this kind to think how soon they shall have an end ; that the darkness and dust of the grave shall shortly obscure and extinguish the glory of this lightsome scene."*

But while all this will no doubt be readily admitted, in respect to the religion of the New Testament ; it is well known that some have confidently asserted and have laboured to prove that the ancient Hebrews were ignorant of the doctrine of future rewards and punishments ; in other words, that their religion did not depend for its influence on the revelation of such rewards and punishments, but on the dispensation of immediate or present reward and punishment. This theory, it will be readily seen, reduces their religious institutions and moral duties, so far as the gronnd of obligation to them is concerned, to the same level with the institutions of the state, and the duties which men owe to the state. It converts the church into a mere appendage to the Jewish commonwealth —a contrivance to secure public order, and make the Hebrews better citizens. Why then was not Solomon content when men, in a decent manner, attended to sacrifices, when they made long and solemn prayers, and were ready on all occasions to enter into solemn vows ? Why was it necessary to look

* Vanity of Man as Mortal.

further than to an orderly and grave observance of those external rites and duties, essential to the good order of the civil society ? God could not reward a truly pious disposition in men, with exuberant harvests, with children, with long life ; nor punish an evil heart, concealed under a fair exterior, with famine, with war, with poverty ; neither the reward nor the punishment, in this case, would be suitable or proper. We must either deny altogether the spiritual character of the Jewish religion, or admit that it had some higher motives to enforce it than temporal rewards and punishments. If it deserves the name of religion at all, it must be contemplated as altogether distinct from the civil polity of the nation. And what candid reader of the most ancient books of the Hebrew Scriptures can deny that they reveal a spiritual system of religion, that they require a heart right, that is, renewed in the sight of God ?

It becomes important then that we should here glance at the moral inculcations of the Hebrew religion, as they may be gathered from these ancient books. At the very outset we are met with the fact that the Most High treated His creature man, from the moment of his creation, as a moral and accountable being ; He placed him under a law, promising him life on obedience, and threatening disobedience with death. He made him capable of knowing, loving, and enjoying Him. And after his fall, He instituted an economy of grace to recover him from his estate of sin and misery. But it is everywhere made evident that this economy did not exert a saving efficacy upon all. What a vast difference we observe in the characters of Cain and Abel ! One worships

God in sincerity and truth, offers a sacrifice in which he acknowledges that without shedding of blood there is no remission of sins ; the other withholds such worship, fails to recognize his dependence on atoning blood, and crowns his impiety by staining his hands with the blood of his unoffending brother. Next we read of men calling on the name of the Lord ; and the piety of one is described as *a walk with God.* Again, we are told that " God saw the wickedness of man was great in the earth, and that every imagination of the thoughts of his heart was only evil continually," but that there was one in this age of impiety, who walked with God, and found grace in the eyes of the Lord. But it is unnecessary to pursue the history, and show the distinction which it everywhere recognizes between pious and wicked men, in proof that God, at the beginning, had revealed to men a religion which required in them righteousness and true holiness ; that is, a religion of the heart. The books of Moses, and the entire Old Testament is nothing more nor less than a history of the conflicts—its triumphs and defeats—of this true and spiritual religion among men. This was the religion of Abraham. He was justified by faith. He believed God and it was accounted to him for righteousness. It was the religion of David, " who describeth the blessedness of the man unto whom God imputeth righteousness without works, saying, Blessed are they whose iniquities are forgiven, and whose sins are covered ; blessed is the man to whom the Lord will not impute sin." See Rom. iv. 3–8 ; Gal. iii. 6–9. It was the religion of all the pious patriarchs and holy men, who embraced the promises which they saw afar off.

Again, in the law which was given on Mount Sinai, we have the clearest evidence that the religion revealed to the Jews was something more than a set of rules, interwoven with their political regulations, to make them good citizens, or merely to preserve among men the doctrine of the Divine unity. It is strictly a moral law ; every precept contained in it is a moral precept. The purport of the whole has been comprehensively given by him, who spake as never man spake, as enjoining supreme love to God, and the love of our neighbour as we love ourselves. It could not be obeyed by a mere external decency of life. A man might scrupulously obey the law respecting burnt-offerings and sacrifices, might offer many and long prayers, and make many vows, and make no approach to that spiritual service which Solomon enjoined, when he said, " Keep thy foot when thou goest to the house of God ; it is better to draw nigh to hear than to offer the sacrifice of fools. Be not rash with thy mouth, and let not thy heart be swift to utter a thing before God ; for God is in heaven and thou upon earth ; therefore let thy words be few. It is better not to vow, than to vow and not to perform." There were many among the ancient Hebrews who, like the Scribe whom our Lord pronounced to be not far from the kingdom of God, were enlightened to see that " to love God with all the heart, and with all the understanding, and with all the soul, and with all the strength, and to love his neighbour as himself, is more than whole burnt-offerings and sacrifices." Mark xii. 33. Their inspired teachers expounded and enforced the law in this spiritual sense : " For I desired mercy and not sacrifice ; and

the knowledge of God more than burnt-offerings."
" Therefore turn thou to thy God ; keep mercy and
judgment, and wait on thy God continually." Hos.
vi. 6, xii. 6. "Wherewith shall I come before the
Lord, and bow myself before the high God ? Shall I
come before him with burnt-offerings, with calves of
a year old ? Will the Lord be pleased with thousands
of rams, or with ten thousands of rivers of oil ? Shall
I give my first-born for my transgression, the fruit
of my body for the sin of my soul ? He hath showed
thee, O man, what is good ; and what doth the Lord
require of thee, but to do justly, and to love mercy,
and to walk humbly with thy God ?" Micah, vi.
6–8. " Wash ye, make you clean ; put away the
evil of your doings from before mine eyes; cease to
do evil ; learn to do well ; seek judgment, relieve the
oppressed, judge the fatherless, plead for the widow.
Come now and let us reason together, saith the Lord :
Though your sins be as scarlet, they shall be as white
as snow ; though they be red like crimson they shall
be as wool." Is. i. 16–18. The early prophet Samuel
had the same spiritual views of the nature of religon, as
appears from his address to the disobedient Saul, when
he pleaded that it was for the honour of God in sacrifices he had spared the best of the sheep and the oxen
of the Amalekites : " Hath the Lord as great delight
in burnt-offerings and sacrifices as in obeying the
voice of the Lord. Behold, to obey is better than
sacrifice, and to hearken than the fat of rams." 1
Sam. xv. 22.

In like manner, Moses, and David, and Solomon,
inculcated a religion of the heart. They taught substantially the same doctrine which Paul taught, that

circumcision profited those only who kept the law, but
to breakers of the law, circumcision became uncircum-
cision,—that he is a Jew who is one inwardly, and circumcision is that of the heart, in the spirit, and not
in the letter ; whose praise is not of men, but of God.
(Rom. ii. 25–29.)   " The Lord thy God will circumcise thine heart, and the heart of thy seed, to love the
Lord thy God with all thine heart, and with all thy
soul, that thou mayest live."   " This commandment
which I command thee this day, it is not hidden from
thee, neither is it far off. It is not in heaven that thou
shouldest say, Who shall go up for us to heaven, and
bring it unto us that we may hear it and do it ?
Neither is it beyond the sea, that thou shouldest say,
Who shall go over the sea for us, and bring it unto us,
that we may hear it and do it ?   But the word is
very nigh unto thee, in thy mouth, and in thy heart,
that thou mayest do it." [Comp. Rom. x. 5–10.]   " I
call heaven and earth to record this day against you,
that I have set before you life and death, blessing and
cursing ; therefore choose life, that both thou and thy
seed may live : that thou mayest love the Lord thy
God, and that thou mayest obey his voice, and that
thou mayest cleave unto him ; for he is thy life."
Deut. xxx. 6, 11–14, 19, 20.   " And now Israel, what
doth the Lord thy God require of thee, but to fear
the Lord thy God, to walk in all his ways, and to love
him, and to serve the Lord thy God with all thy heart,
and with all thy soul, to keep the commandments of
the Lord and his statutes, which I command thee this
day for thy good." " Circumcise therefore the foreskin
of your heart, and be no more stiffnecked. For the
Lord your God is God of gods, and Lord of lords, a

great God, a mighty and a terrible, which regardeth not persons, nor taketh a reward." (Deut. x. 12, 13, 16, 17.) But when we turn to the Psalms of David for proof that the distinction of spiritual life from natural everywhere pervades the theology of the Jews, we know hardly where to begin or where to end. These songs of Zion contain the words of God's spirit, taught to his servant, when exercised with most intense experiences of conviction, penitence, and sorrow, on account of sin, or of faith, love, and joy, and are fit to express "the same most vital moods of every renewed soul." The humble, earnest Christian finds in them "full declaration of the deepest secrets of his faith, expression for his inmost knowledge of the truth, and forms for his most profound feelings upon the peculiar, and appropriate, and never-failing love of a covenant God toward his own peculiar people." "Behold I was shapen in iniquity, and in sin did my mother conceive me." "I acknowledge my transgression, and my sin is ever before me." "Have mercy upon me, O Lord, for I am weak ; O Lord, heal me for my bones are vexed." "Wash me thoroughly from mine iniquity and cleanse me from my sin." "Cast me not away from thy presence, and take not thy holy Spirit from me." "Create in me a clean heart, O God, and renew a right spirit within me." "Thou desirest not sacrifice ; else would I give it ; thou delightest not in burnt-offering. The sacrifices of God are a broken spirit : a broken and a contrite heart, O God, thou wilt not despise." "The Lord is my shepherd ; I shall not want. He maketh me to lie down in green pastures ; he leadeth me beside the still waters. He restoreth my soul ; he leadeth me in the paths of righteousness for his name's sake."

David was the religious instructor of Solomon, and sought, as Solomon himself testifies, to impress his mind with the nature of true religion. He gives us the substance of his instruction, which was, with all his getting to get wisdom, that wisdom which is the principal thing, which has its beginning in the fear of the Lord. (Prov. iv. 3, *seq.*) In the book of Proverbs, as well as in the book of Ecclesiastes, it is the religion of the heart which he inculcates. " The sacrifice of the wicked is an abomination : how much more, when he bringeth it with a wicked mind." "The thoughts of the wicked are an abomination to the Lord." " He that turneth away from hearing the law, even his prayer shall be abomination." " The fear of the Lord is the beginning of wisdom." "The fear of the Lord is a fountain of life, to depart from the snares of death." " By the fear of the Lord men depart from evil." " Better is it to be of an humble spirit with the lowly, than to divide the spoil with the proud." " I love them that love me, and they that seek me early shall find me." " Keep thy heart with all diligence, for out of it are the issues of life." " Trust in the Lord with all thine heart." " Whoso trusteth in the Lord, happy is he." " The hope of the righteous shall be gladness : but the expectation of the wicked shall perish."

Thus does it appear that the religious teachers of the Jews gave the most careful attention to inculcations designed to show that true religion is a vital, spiritual principle in the heart of man, and did not consist alone in the observance of external rites and ceremonies. Such a religion could not be enforced by earthly promises of good, and earthly threatenings of evil. Bountiful harvests, wealth, long life, might be held out as incentives to industry, frugality, temperance, justice, and an observance of those laws which seem to have been given to secure the agricultural prosperity of the land, and those sumptuary regulations which were intended to promote the good order of civil society ; but it would be an impeachment of the wisdom of the lawgiver, to maintain that such rewards were held out to encourage men to be penitent for their sins, or to seek to have new hearts created within them. It follows, then, that such a religion as Solomon inculcates, a religion of the heart, would be vain, because without any suitable and adequate motives to enforce it, if the doctrine of a future state of rewards and punishments had been unknown. His words, chap. v. 1–8, and in all the latter portion of Ecclesiastes, would be without meaning, if there were no motives to be drawn from a future state, to enforce them.

It is by no means denied that there was a special providence exerted over the Hebrews as a nation, by which they were separated from, and exalted above, all other nations of the earth ; nor that temporal rewards were offered to the good and obedient, and temporal judgments visited upon the idolatrous, disobedient, and profane. But it is denied that they were placed under an " equal providence," by which good and bad men were, in all cases, to be treated according to their deserts in this life ; and that this was the grand feature of the theocracy under which they were placed, which distinguished them from all other people in the world. There is no evidedce whatever that such an equal providence was established in their case ; there is evidence to the contrary. Did Abel receive the reward of his piety in this life ? It cost him his life, by the hand of an enraged brother. But

13

this was an event, perhaps it will be said, prior to the
establishment of the Jewish theocracy. Was "righteous" Lot receiving his reward in this life, when overwhelmed with shame and sorrow, in his mountain re-
treat ? Had the patriarch Jacob received his reward
here, when he exclaimed, "I will go down into the
grave unto my son mourning," or when at a later
period, he summed up his history, in the memorable
words, "Few and evil have the days of the years of
my life been ?" "Was Job, who was a Jew certainly
in his religion, receiving his reward, when he uttered
the words recorded in the third and the nineteenth
chapters of the book which bears his name ? Was
Moses receiving his reward in this life, when his soul
was so often vexed with the stiffnecked and rebellious
people over whom he was a leader—when he offered
that prayer so full of anguish, "Oh, this people have
sinned a great sin, and have made them gods of gold.
Yet now, if thou wilt forgive their sin—and if not,
blot me, I pray thee, out of thy book which thou hast
written"—or when he was denied the earnest longing
of his heart to " go over and see the good land which is
beyond Jordan, that goodly mountain and Lebanon ?"
It is in vain then to say that obedience to the moral
law was secured by an equal providence, under which
the Jews were placed ; for there is an utter absence
of evidence that any such providence was established
over them. We are driven back to the point from
which we started, viz., that a moral law, requiring
men to love God supremely, and worship him in spirit
and in truth, and to love their neighbours as themselves, can be enforced only by motives drawn from a
revealed state of retributions following death.

§ X. Chap. V. 10–20.

THE VANITY OF GREAT RICHES.

(10.) *He that loveth silver shall not be satis-fied with silver ; nor he that loveth abundance with increase.   This is also vanity.*

In the second chapter, Solomon had spoken of his great possessions and costly, gigantic works, as a king ; he here takes up the subject of wealth in general, as it may be obtained by men who are not kings, with the same great object in view, *viz.* : to show its utter vanity when men seek to find their whole happiness in its attainment and enjoyment.   The love of money, he declares, is a passion which money can not gratify ; that is to say, gratify in full.   The passion is increased in strength, and made more clamorous by that on which it feeds.   It is like the vicious thirst of the intemperate man, which is not allayed by a moderate draught, nor by a surfeit, but becomes more uncontrollable the oftener and longer it is indulged. Well then might he pronounce the attempt of a man to obtain substantial happiness in this way, *Vanity !*

(11.) *When property is increased, they are increased who consume it; and what profit is there to the owners thereof, save the beholding of it with their eyes ?*

" The more men have," says Henry, " the better house they must keep ; the more servants employ, the more guests entertain, the more give to the poor, and the more will they have hanging on them ; for where the carcase is, the eagles will be. What we have more than food and raiment we have for others ; and then what good is there to the owners themselves, but the pleasure of beholding them with their eyes ?" The common saying that all that the man, who has the care of the largest estate, receives for his labour and trouble, is barely his support, is nearly true. The only difference which Solomon recognizes between him and those who share with him in deriving their living from the same estate, is *the beholding of it with his eyes;* he looks upon that as his own from which others, as his servants, derive their daily bread, and, if a benevolent man, he can have the satisfaction of giving to the needy ; and in this he might find a real pleasure, were it not for the unreasonable demands and complaints of those to whom he furnishes employment, and the ingratitude of those on whom he bestows his charity.

(12.) *The sleep of the labouring man is sweet, whether he eat little or much; but the superabundance of the rich will not suffer him to sleep.*

Sleep is as necessary to the comfort and health of the body, and to a tranquil, well ordered mind, as food and houses to protect us from the cold and heat.

The labouring man enjoys refreshing sleep at night, because he is weary. If he has eaten much, the exercise to which daily toil subjects him, prevents his food from being an occasion of discomfort ; if little, his fatigue, nevertheless, makes his sleep sweet and undisturbed. But wealth tempts to that indulgence in the use of luxuries, which tends to disturb the nerves, and impair digestion, and thus render the nights sleepless. Its possessors, for the luxuries which gratify appetite, part with that luxury of sweet sleep which the humblest cottager enjoys, and which mere money can never buy. Or the meaning may be that the apprehensions and perplexities to which great estates give rise, rob their possessors of sleep. They may lose their wealth, or thousands thereof, if not all ; they are dependant on the assistance and fidelity of others, who may be false to their trust ; or storms, or frosts, or mildew, or fire, or wars, may cause serious disaster and loss.

(13.) *There is a sore evil which I have seen under the sun, riches kept to the hurt of the owner thereof.*

Another striking proof is here presented of the vanity of wealth, as the means of real, substantial happiness. It may become a positive evil. It may be accumulated to the harm of its possessors. Disasters, which a poor man entirely escapes in a time of disorder and revolution, are apt to fall with peculiar severity on the man who has large possessions. " The powers that be" may have a peculiar interest in causing them to escheat to the exchequer of the State ; and they may consequently be all which shall prevent their unfortunate owner from sharing in the benefits of a general amnesty. Or the *hurt* to which Solomon alludes may be of a different kind—that which is experienced in his own character, making him proud and oppressive, or dissolute ; or which is inflicted on his own family, particularly his children, encouraging them to habits of idleness and prodigality. But the injurious effects of riches upon the children of the wealthy are more distinctly brought out in the next verse.

(14.) *And those riches perish in fruitless speculations, and he hath begotten a son, and there is nothing in his hand.*

How often are vast estates soon frittered away ! The heirs of some man who, by rigid economy, industry, sagacious plans, has amassed great riches, enter upon extravagant expenditures, or into foolish speculations, and their inheritance is speedily wasted. There is nothing left in their hand. Some explain the passage thus, that a rich man, while he is rich, having begotten a son, loses his wealth by some calamity or reverse, and there is nothing left in his (the father's) hand to bestow on his son and heir. Either interpretation shows the uncertainty of wealth, and the folly of making it the portion of the soul.

(15.) *As he came forth from his mother's womb, naked shall he return, so that he may depart as he came, and shall take nothing of his labour which he may carry away in his hand.*

But should a man retain all his wealth, and go on adding thereto up to the very hour of his death, he must then leave it all. He can carry nothing away with him, when he dies. As he came into the world, so he must leave it. " As his friends," says Henry, "when he came naked into the world helped him with swaddling-clothes, so when he goes out they help him with grave-clothes, and that is all."

(16.) *And this also is a sore evil, that in all points as he came, so shall he go ; and what profit is there to him that hath toiled for the wind?*

At first view, this might seem to be a mere repetition of what is said in the preceding verse ; but it contains a further idea, that the man who makes riches his trust, not only loses them at death, but loses the labour of his life. He might have spent life in securing the true riches, and then, although he must part with all earthly riches at death, he would not lose the labour of his life, and be constrained bitterly to lament, *Oleum et operam perdidi.* He who lays up treasures where moth and rust do not corrupt, although he too must depart naked out of the world as he came into it, does not toil for the wind, or unsubstantial nothingness.

(17.) *All his days also he consumes in darkness, and in much vexation, infirmity, and irritation.*

The authorized version is more literal than the version here given, *all his days he eateth in darkness ;* that is, he partakes of his food in a gloomy, dissatisfied state of mind. But eating in darkness here is figurative of the manner in which he receives, and is affected by, all the bounties with which Providence crowns his life. He spends his days on the earth in gloom, in vexation, in disappointment, and repining. This is said in confirmation of the idea introduced in the preceding verse, that, in making gold his god, life has proved with him one grand miscarriage. He has missed of its great object ; he must leave his gold behind him at the grave, and as this was all he loved and sought, life's great labour is lost. His money could not so much as purchase for him exemption from melancholy, and vexatious, irritating cares ; it was, on the contrary, a constant source of perplexity, and turned life into one long, sad, and bitter trouble.

(18.) *Behold what I have seen which is good and comely! to eat and drink, and enjoy the good of all one's labour, which he takes under the sun all the days of his life, which God giveth him; for it is his portion.*

In pronouncing great wealth, as the means of securing solid and lasting happiness, to be vain, and especially in speaking so strongly of the wretchedness of the rich man, who depends exclusively on his riches for happiness, as he does in the preceding verse, Solomon did not wish to be understood as declaring that there is no real good in the things of this life, or that there is no rational manner in which wealth can be used, and be made to contribute to the happiness of its possessors. He turns the other side of the picture, and invites men to mark what he had seen which is good, that is, really good ; viz., the use of the gifts of Providence in a becoming manner for the glory of the Giver, and for our own good, and the good of our fellow-men—" not to starve ourselves through covetousness, but eat and drink what is fit for us ; not kill ourselves with labour, but take the comfort of what our hands have laboured for, and that not now and then, but all the days of our life which God gives us, not do the business of our calling as a drudgery, and make ourselves slaves to it, but rejoice in our labour." (Henry.) It was not the gratification of sensual appetites which he saw to be good and comely ; it was not Epicureanism which he sought to recommend, but a rational, cheerful use of the blessings of Divine Providence, consistent with purity and piety, and which gratitude demands.

(19.) *Moreover, if to any man God hath given riches and wealth, he hath given him also to enjoy them and take his portion, and to rejoice in his labour ; this is the gift of God.*

These words are expository of what the author had said in the preceding verse, that it is good to eat, and drink, and enjoy the good of all one's labour ; and they prove that he was speaking, not in an Epicurean sense, but religiously. Wealth is the gift of God, and is to be received as from him, and used for the creature's good, and for His glory. When received thus, men will not spend it upon their lusts, or employ it for their own injury, but will regard it as a sacred trust, a talent, in the proper use of which they are to secure to themselves " everlasting habitations." If taken from them, they recognize the right of the great Giver to reclaim what is his own, and are not made miserable, but are able to say, " the Lord gave, and

the Lord hath taken away ; blessed be the name of
the Lord."

(20.) *For he will not much remember the days
of his life, when God answereth to the joy of his
heart.*

This is a deeply pious sentiment, and thoroughly redeems Ecclesiastes from the charge of sanctioning indulgence in sensual pleasures, by what is said in v. 18 ;
ii. 24 ; iii. 12, 13, 22. The purport of it is that the
man who receives, and enjoys his wealth as the gift of
God, will be a truly happy man. Life to him will
not be like the life described in v. 17, one continued
scene of darkness, dejection, infirmity, and irritation ;
he will not look perpetually on the dark side ; he will
not dwell upon the days of darkness, which are many in
every man's life. He has learned to honour the doctrine of a Divine Providence, and is filled with a deep
reverential feeling toward God ; he commits his way
unto the Lord, and is at peace. (Hab. iii. 17, 18.)

Professor Stuart translates the last clause, *when
God shall cause* (*things*) *to correspond with the joy of
his heart,* and makes the beautiful suggestion that
God will cause every thing around such a right feeling man to chime in with his feelings, " *will cause a
response,* viz., in the things around him, to the tone
of the man's mind who is enjoying." And it is undoubtedly a correct and very important sentiment,
that a cheerful, pious spirit will reflect its own light
upon surrounding objects, will illuminate a scene
which would otherwise be one of unmitigated darkness. But the version above has been preferred as
more nearly expressing the writer's meaning, which is,

that when God answers a man's prayer, and makes his riches (or his poverty even, as he just as easily can do) a real blessing, he has not much occasion to remember the disappointments, the sorrows, or the shortness of life. God answers the prayer of such a man's life, as well as the specific, formal petitions of his lips, with blessings, if not in the exact form which he desired, yet to the joy of his heart. The deep spirit of piety of the penitent Solomon shines out here as much as in any other portion of this book.

SCOPE OF ARGUMENT IN § 10.

The bearing of this particular part upon the general subject of the entire book, is perhaps apparent enough without any further exposition. That subject is, the vanity of this world as man's portion, if there be nothing beyond. Solomon had shown the vanity of such great possessions as belong more appropriately to monarchs ; but it might be said that if a man was not perplexed with the cares of office, and if he could be more the master of his own actions than kings are permitted to be, the verdict might be altogether different. He therefore takes up the subject of wealth in general, as it may be possessed and enjoyed by men at large, and presents us with a series of weighty and most impressive reasons in proof that great riches can not make men truly happy.

1. Avarice is strengthened by that which it feeds upon, and is a most disquieting passion. It is disquieting, because it becomes stronger the more it is indulged ; and that which is the object of desire be-

comes less and less capable of satisfying it. The bodily appetites may be satisfied ; bread will appease for a time at least the cravings of hunger, water will quench thirst, but silver will not satisfy the love for silver. This is evident enough in respect to that monstrous form of covetousness which appears in the miser. And in the case of all those who love money for its own sake, as its own end, and not for its appli- cation to useful purposes, 'but still have not acquired the reputation and name of *miser,*' it is equally true. They are no better satisfied with a hundred thousand than they were with fifty, or ten ; and it matters not to what extent their revenues may be increased, they are never satisfied, but are longing and striving after more. They are in the condition of a man labouring under a fever, who persists in taking that which is sure to aggravate his febrile symptoms. Every ad- dition to their golden stores, instead of curing " the vile fever of their minds," adds new fuel to the fires which are consuming them. What a wretched con- dition would a man be in, if, when parched with thirst, water, instead of cooling and allaying it, should serve like sea-water, only to render it more in- tolerable ; or if, when fainting with hunger, whole- some food should increase his craving and his misery ! It has been well said that such men can not be said to possess wealth ; it rather possesses them, or else they possess it like a fever which burns and consumes them as if molten gold were circulating in their veins. The last hundred or the last thousand which they add to their possessions no more satisfies their love of gold than did the first. After running a long and weary race they are no nearer the goal than when they started ; the rich old man is just as far from it as the toiling, thriving young man ; as age advances, the restless, insatiable passion exerts a still mightier sway. Silver can not—it never did, and never can—satisfy the love of silver. What emphasis truly is there in the words of Solomon, " This is also vanity !"

2. Increase of wealth increases care and perplexity by increasing the number of those whom Providence makes dependent on the rich man, and who derive as much real good from it as the owner himself. For what is the amount of real good which a rich man receives from his wealth ? Wholesome food, suitable clothing, and a comfortable dwelling. This is the inventory, brief, but full. I have not included the means of gratifying virtuous and refined tastes ; for these do not necessarily belong to the inventory ; riches do not certainly imply the possession of such tastes to be gratified. Many a man possesses the one, who is an entire stranger to the other. Nor have I included the means of influence, for money is not always power ; something more is necessary to the possession of influence in its highest sense ; men must possess character, and the disposition to use their property in a right manner. And the ability to leave to one's children an independent fortune is of very questionable utility ; therefore it was not included. The history of men most distinguished in the world of letters and science proves how little the world is indebted to the possession of great estates in producing individuals, who have made the greatest progress in the highest species of culture. It is evident, then, in speaking of the real benefits which the merely rich man derives from his money, that we express all when

we say *food, garments, and a home.* He can procure no purer air or water, or more cheerful light, or refreshing breeze, or sweeter sleep, than the tenants of his farms, the sailors in his ships, or the operatives in his mills. They derive a comfortable livelihood for their services, in the care and improvement of his estate. Their wages are their own, and " better is little, with the fear of the Lord, than great treasure and trouble therewith." Prov. xv. 16. " A little that a righteous man hath is better than the riches of many wicked." Ps. xxxvii. 16. His proprietorship is more extensive than that of his dependents, but his anxiety is only the greater ; so that to have any real advantage over them he must possess religious principles and pious motives for the disposition and right use of his property. Without such principles and motives the little that a righteous man has is better than all that he beholds with his eyes, and calls his own. To suppose him to be a benevolent man, that his great object is to furnish employment, and provide ways of living for others, or that he may have to give to the needy, is supposing what Solomon did not, *viz.,* that he is a really good man, and is not looking to his money as a good in itself, but rather as a means of doing good. Solomon is considering whether wealth without religion is sufficient to make men truly happy.

3. Enjoyment of food and sleep must be essential to the happiness of one who looks to this world alone for his happiness. It is true that in this we consider men as mainly creatures of sense ; and it was as such creatures precisely that the writer of the book of Ecclesiastes considered them, when he inquired whether wealth, or the most ample means of procuring sensual

gratification, was sufficient to render them truly happy. In respect to the enjoyment of food and sleep, he compares the rich man, with whom the necessity for active labour does not exist, with the labouring man ; and does not hesitate to assign to the latter the advantage. "Sweet is the sleep of the labouring man, whether he eat little or much ; but the superabundance of the rich will not suffer him to sleep." The labouring man can not afford to indulge in hurtful luxuries ; he toils through the livelong day, and when evening comes, his bed, though it be but a pallet of straw, is welcome. Not so with the rich ; their superabundance betrays them into indulgences which impair health, and rob them of rest at night. Or the weary, overtasked mind does not court sleep, as the weary body does, but rather repels it. What avail sumptuous apartments, and beds of down to him whose body has been made restless by intemperate indulgence, and whose mind is made equally restless by the revulsions of commerce, the fluctuations of trade, or by startling tidings which put a new aspect upon all public affairs !

4. Great riches often expose their possessors to dangers and positive evil, from which the poor, or men in moderate circumstances, entirely escape. Their greatest danger is doubtless one to character ; they are tempted to be haughty, overbearing, and oppressive toward their fellow-men. No amount of property can be a sufficient remuneration to a man for so great a hurt to his moral nature, as the fostering and strengthening of that pride which is so natural, and at the same time, so degrading to it. Or the injury may be one to his reputation in another respect ; his riches are

"kept," *i. e.*, parsimoniously hoarded, and he is despised among his fellow-men as mean and penurious. He may be rich in houses and lands, in stocks and ships, but he has no *wealth of soul*. Just as he has increased in silver and gold, just as rapidly, and in the same proportion, he has impoverished his soul. "There is that withholdeth more than is meet, and it tendeth to poverty"—a poverty more to be dreaded than that which reduces a man to hunger and rags. Of, alas! too many has this been seen to be deplorably true ; instead of multiplying their charities as their means increase, they adopt a descending scale, and reduce them in almost the precise ratio of their increase. Then, again, what perils surround men, possessed of overgrown estates in disturbed and revolutionary times ! They are singled out as the objects of popular fury, or to gratify the vindictive hate of some revolutionary leader. Condemned for treason, their sequestered wealth will furnish the sinews of war ; while the storm passes over the poorer man at his side, as the whirlwind which prostrates the oak leaves unharmed the lowly bramble.

5. Great wealth often proves most disastrous to the children of its possessors. It begets dispositions and habits which unfit them to meet the reverses, and the rebuffs of life. The expectation of a large inheritance prevents their cultivation of those self-reliant feelings, and those habits of application to some useful employment, which are of greater advantage to a young man, than the most extensive patrimony. How helpless does a family become, that has grown up under the influence of such expectation, when, even before the act of God makes them heirs, the estate to which

they had been looking is scattered to the winds! Or suppose no such disaster befalls them ; suppose that they enter upon the inheritance unimpaired, how often does their new possession of liberty and power, of wealth now held in their own right, and at their own disposal for the first time, seem to intoxicate the brain, and lead them to plunge into expenditures and extravagances, and indiscreet speculations, sufficient to waste away, in a brief period, the most princely estate ! With the very grand ideas in which they have grown up, they disdain labour. These pampered children, their riches having perished, know not how to reinstate themselves in affluence, or even in competency. They see others who have been trained up to habits of industry and economy, rising to respectability and influence, while they, at every step, are taking a lower place. But penury is the least of the disasters which are liable to befall the children of the rich. The vices which they contract, and which serve to squander their estates, pollute their souls, and expose them to the wrath of heaven. Verily, poverty, or disease even in its most dreadful form, is an evil not to be mentioned in comparison with corruption of the heart.

6. Death at last robs him who has put his trust in uncertain riches, of all, his labour as well as his riches. He can carry nothing away with him at his departure from this world. As he came empty-handed so he must go. We have a good comment on verses 15 and 16, in the words of our Saviour : " The ground of a certain rich man brought forth plentifully ; and he thought within himself, saying, What shall I do, because I have no room where to bestow my fruits ?

And he said, This will I do ; I will pull down my barns, and build greater ; and there will I bestow all my fruits, and my goods. And I will say to my soul, Soul, thou hast much goods laid up for many years ; take thine ease, eat, drink, and be merry. But God said unto him, Thou fool, this night thy soul shall be required of thee ; then whose shall those things be which thou hast provided ? So is he that layeth up treasure for himself, and is not rich toward God." Luke xii. 16–21. Just as a man has accomplished the chosen object of his life, has amassed a great property, and thinks he will enter on its enjoyment, death comes ; his soul is summoned away ; and those things which he had provided go to enrich others. But the most melancholy circumstance is not that he must leave his earthly riches behind, but that he has missed the great object of his earthly probation ; he is not rich toward God ; he has no treasure laid up in heaven. That which is true of the greatest lover of filthy lucre, the most devoted disciple of Momus, that he must leave his money behind him at death, is true of the rich man, who may also be eminent for his righteousness. There is no difference between them in this respect ; but there is a mighty difference in the other, for the righteous man has not made his money an end in itself, and therefore he has not missed of the great object of life ; at death he does not leave all his good things behind, but goes to enter upon an inheritance incorruptible, undefiled, and that fadeth not away.

Such is the estimate, the true estimate, which Solomon puts on riches alone as the great end of a man's earthly existence, or as the means of making him truly happy. " This is also vanity." If this was all man was made for, then it might well be asked, " Wherefore hast thou made him in vain ?" It is in this way that he necessitates the conclusion that there must be another life. Nay, he goes on directly to show how gratitude, reverence, and submission to God, in other words, true religion, can redeem even wealth from its vanity ; how, with the blessing of God, wealth received and used as his gift, in answer to prayer, may contribute to preserve joy of heart and future blessedness. He did not mean to disparage riches, but to teach that while, as the great end of life, they may be ranked among the vainest of vanities, used rationally and piously, as from God, and in his fear, they may be made the means of great good to ourselves and others, and even of promoting the glory of the Giver.

THE VANITY OF THE LONGEST AND MOST PROSPEROUS LIFE.

(1.) *There is an evil which I have seen under the sun, which presses heavily upon men.*

(2.) *A man to whom God hath given riches, wealth, and honour : neither doth he lack any thing which he desireth ; yet God giveth him not power to eat thereof, but another eateth it. This is vanity, and a sore evil.*

There is a transition here to a new phase of the same general subject, suggested by the premature death of a man who has come into the possession of great wealth, and the splendour which attends wealth. God gives him not power, or allows him not opportunity, by reason of premature death (this is the sense, as may be gathered from the succeeding context), to enjoy his possessions. This was the sore evil which Solomon had seen pressing heavily upon the sons of men ; and it suggested a new phase of the subject, presented in the following verses.

(3.) *If a man beget a hundred children, and live many years, so that the days of his years be many, and moreover, there be no burial to him, and his soul be not satisfied with good ; I say that an untimely birth is better than he.*

He tarries not to consider the vanity of the most princely inheritance, when a man is prevented by premature death from enjoying it ; but in contrast with such an event, he selects the strongest imaginable case ; he employs hyperbole ; he supposes the law ("the days of our years are threescore years and ten"), in respect to the length of human life to be suspended, and that the man lives on, the days of the years of his life being multiplied ; he does not indeed suppose the man to live on forever : but he postpones the day of his death so far, as not to predicate any burial in his case. In supposing him to be the parent of a hundred children, during this protracted existence on the earth, he is carrying out the same hyperbolical method of speech. A numerous family and long life, were regarded among the Jews as the most signal blessings. Solomon supposes that this man can count his children by the hundred, and that his life is prolonged indefinitely, or that his death is put off to so great a distance that his burial need not be spoken of ; yet he declares that if it be impossible for him to satisfy his soul with good—as it is certainly impossible for men to satisfy their souls with mere temporal good —a stillborn child is better than he, *i. e.*, it would be better to perish at the threshold of existence than to drag through this long life, with a soul never satisfied with good, and perish at last. " Better the fruit that drops from the tree ere it is ripe, than that left to hang till it is rotten."

The expression *there be no burial to him* has been supposed by others to refer to the denial of the rites of sepulture to this long-lived, prosperous man, as an additional circumstance in his misery, to that of his soul not being satisfied with his portion. But this lacks verisimilitude ; indeed it is wholly unnatural to suppose that a man possessed of riches and honour, the father of a numerous progeny, who had come down as the remnant of a generation long since passed away, should fail at last of a respectful and honourable burial.

(4.) *For this cometh in vanity, and departeth in darkness, and its name is concealed in darkness.*

(5.) *Moreover, it hath not seen the sun, nor known ; this hath rest rather than the other.*

The *he* in the authorized version, refers to the untimely birth (ver. 3), and should have been translated *this* or *it*, as above. It cometh in vanity or nothingness ; it really has no existence in this world ; it never sees the light ; it is never numbered in the family, or in the census of the people ; it receives no name, no mention is made of it, and there is no remembrance of it on earth. He had said before that an untimely birth is better than the man who should live a protracted life on the earth, and never be satisfied with good ; and he is here assigning the reason for a declaration which might sound so strangely in the ears of men ; that reason is, that *this hath rest rather than the other.* *He* spends a long existence in this world, and never finds rest to his soul ; but *it* lies still and is quiet ; it sleeps and is at rest. (Job iii. 13.)

(6.) *Yea, though he live a thousand years twice told, and see no good: do not all go to one place?*

This verse is nearly identical in meaning with the third, preceding. There he supposes that a man's life is so prolonged, that his death and burial are placed at an indefinite remove in the future ; here he specifies two thousand years as its supposed length. This verse is really expository, and helps us to understand the difficult expressions in the former. The meaning of the entire passage is, that, if the man to whom God hath given riches, wealth, and honour, instead of dying prematurely, should live thousands of years, and never be satisfied with good, it would be better not to have existed at all, or rather to have perished like an untimely birth ; for after this prolonged, troubled existence, he must go to the same place, the grave. His fate at last is the same, while he has the vexation which the infant that breathed but once, and died, escaped. How is it possible to conceive of a stronger representation of the folly of seeking real happiness out of God, or of the fruitless striving of men, when they leave eternity out of view ?

SCOPE OF ARGUMENT IN § XI.

Here again the meaning is so plain, and its appositeness to the design of the writer so patent, as hardly to require any additional explanation, or attempt at clearer statement. But there can be no disadvantage following the plan hitherto pursued, in re-stating the matter, free from the trammels which a strict exegesis imposes.

"It is because life is so short," some men will say, "and not because of the nature of worldly good—its own insufficiency to make men truly happy—that we must admit your estimate of it to be correct ; could a man live longer to enjoy the world, it would not be altogether vain." "But no," says Solomon, "let a man live to twice the age of Methusaleh, and have riches, and wealth, and honour, and be surrounded by a numerous and prosperous family, he is still mortal, and must die at last ; it is only a postponement, it is not an escape. His protracted life only strengthens his attachment to the world, and imparts intensity to the sickening sensation which he can not always avoid, that death awaits him, and that he must sooner or later say to 'corruption, thou art my father ; to the worm, thou art my mother and my sister.'" The fact has often been noticed that the longer men, whose hopes are all below, live in this world, the stronger is their attachment to it, and the more unwilling are they to leave it. Youth have been seen to bid adieu to the world with composure, with joy and triumph even, while old men have clung to it with a grasp which death only could sever. Now suppose this man, who has lived in all the splendour which wealth can furnish, is drawing near the end of his protracted existence on earth, his bi-millenial period, what has he gained by the long postponement of death ? Here is death at last, not stripped of a single one of its terrors ; here is that "one place," the grave, to which all come, yawning to receive him ; yea, those terrors are enhanced in proportion to his increased love for a world which he has sought and served so long ; just so much as he may be supposed to gain by delay, he loses by the greater dread, with which he regards death, when it finally comes. The longevity of the antediluvians no doubt contributed to that fearful state of wickedness which brought the judgment of God on the old world ; and it may be presumed that a man living in affluence and luxury for two thousand years, and seeking all his good things here, would experience a similar demoralizing influence on his character, which would be very far from preparing him to meet death with cheerfulness and submission. But this is the less important view of the subject.

Solomon may well pronounce it something more than a " vanity," it would be " a sore evil" for a man to spend a twice-told antediluvian life on the earth in a fruitless striving after good, ever trying, but never successful in satisfying his soul, and constrained to close all with a confession similar to that which Goethe, the celebrated German, made in advanced age : " They have called me the child of fortune, nor have I any wish to complain of the course of my life. Yet it has been nothing but labour and sorrow ; and I may truly say that in seventy-five years, I have not had four weeks of true comfort. It was the constant rolling of a stone that was always to be lifted anew." This eminent man might well, by the generality of men, be called the child of fortune, loaded as he was from early life to old age with public honours, with lucrative offices, and regarded as the Coryphaeus of polite literature, by his learned countrymen. But in speaking of his life, he falls into almost the exact phraseology of Ecclesiastes ; he calls it *labour and*

14

sorrow. Some twenty-five or thirty days, out of seventy-five years, would cover the whole period during which he made any approximation to happiness. And how affecting is the comparison of his life to the doom of Sisyphus in the lower world—"the constant rolling of a stone that was always to be lifted anew !" And now suppose that instead of living eighty years, the number of his years had been multiplied by itself, and during this period, he was doomed to roll a huge marble block to the top of a hill, which as soon as it reached the top always rolled down again, we should have almost exactly the case supposed by Solomon— that of a man to whom God gives riches, wealth, and honour, yet who sees no good, can not satisfy himself with good. Taking Goethe's description of what was deemed the happy life of a child of fortune, the representation of Solomon is strictly true, that an untimely birth is better than he. The man, however prosperous and favoured his lot, whose hopes of happiness are all limited to this world, must experience an amount of disappointment and heart-sickness, of labour and sorrow, which may well lead a reflecting man to regard a very long existence in this world as a punishment, rather than as a reward.

And why must this be so ? The answer is implied in what Solomon says about the soul of such a man not being satisfied with good, *i. e.*, with temporal good. He supposes him to have abundant wealth, honour, a numerous family, a long life ; he exhausts the catalogue of earthly blessings, which a man would select who is intent on making himself as happy as possible, and still he is not satisfied ; and thus indirectly avers that it is impossible for him to satisfy his soul with these things. The soul makes other and higher demands, and it would be as impossible thus to satisfy its cravings as it would be to satiate thirst with an empty silver cup, or the appetite of a hungry man, by sitting him down at a table, groaning under the weight of golden dishes, which contained not a single morsel of food. The silver cup and golden dishes delude the man's imagination, only the more cruelly to mock his hunger and thirst.

> "Affections are too costly to bestow
> Upon the fair-faced nothings here below."

It is an abuse, a degradation of them to spend them on the vanities of the world ; they resent the affront, the mockery ; and it is the revulsion which is thus caused in the heart of man, which will not suffer him to be happy. It is true that neither Solomon nor Goethe were centenarians, nor millenarians ; but they had lived long enough, and in such circumstances as to make a fair experiment ; and the former was constrained to say, "vanity of vanities, all is vanity," and the latter that his life was like " the constant rolling of a stone that had always to be lifted anew." If eighty years (which was the age of the latter) did not furnish time enough fairly to test the experiment whether the greatest worldly prosperity could render a man truly happy, what hope was there that in eighty twice told, or in eighty multiplied by itself, the result would have been any different ? If in a long life a man has never discovered that his appetite for food could be satisfied with husks and stones, why should he wish more years to be added that he may continue the experiment ? Long life, riches, and children were esteemed great blessings by the ancient Hebrews, but their own experience must have taught them that they were to be considered as merely temporal rewards, and that—even if there had been no direct revelation to them of a future life—there must have been some better things reserved for those who feared the Lord.

That God is the author of our moral constitution, can not be questioned for a single moment : that he should have exercised his skill in fashioning our bodies, and neglected the nobler part of our nature, is an opinion unworthy of any attempt at refutation. As the soul of man is the glory of his being, so it is to be regarded as the chief of the works of God. The body is of the earth, earthy; but the soul is spiritual, is that which bears the impress and image (now alas! faded) of its glorious Maker. He endowed it with the power of thought, and with affections. He made it capable of believing, hoping, fearing, loving, of experiencing the noblest and purest bliss, and of enduring the keenest anguish. Nor will it be questioned that a system of revealed truth should be adapted to the nature, that is to say, to the moral wants of man. Both the wisdom and the benevolence of God dictate that the conduct required, and the temper enjoined, by his revealed law, should be consistent with the highest good—nay, promotive of the highest good and happiness, of his creatures. Now it is susceptible of demonstration, because it may become a matter of consciousness in the experience of men, that there is a correspondence between the moral constitution of man and the duties enjoined on him by his Maker, which renders obedience indispensable to his happiness and peace of mind. The books of Moses, as well as the Gospels and Epistles of the New Testament, point out the only path of peace, the prescribed sphere in which the subjects of the Divine moral government are to move; and it defines and fixes its limits with the utmost precision. They encourage goodness by promises of the richest reward; warn us of a righteous retribution hereafter, and open up scenes of glory and immortal blessedness, as the inheritance of those who walk with God. Revealed religion co-operates with natural—co-operates with the great frame of the visible world—co-operates with every pulse and feeling of our own hearts "in establishing the delightful truth that God is love; and, in calling upon us to love him, not from any cold and lifeless picture of the abstract beauty of holiness, beautiful as it unquestionably is in itself, but from the touching and all-subduing motive—BECAUSE HE FIRST LOVED US." But these views may, perhaps, be rendered clearer, and their application be better seen, if somewhat further expanded.

Man is possessed of affections which demand suitable objects for their exercise, and revelation alone— revelation as it is found both in the Old and the New Testaments—presents those which are worthy of engaging them. Search where we will, we shall find something in human nature which leads the less, as well as the more cultivated, of the race, to approve virtue and condemn vice, even where their own conduct is involved in the condemnation; man will love, and will seek his happiness in loving some object or another; and he is a monster, and not a man—perhaps I should have said a fiend—who can not love. Now God created the human soul for himself, and imparted to it affections, and capacities, which can be satisfied with nothing short of himself. It pants for something more pure and spiritual than can be found on earth. It asks, "where is God, my Maker?" and, when it finds him, its craving desires are appeased. Nothing else can fill the soul with good; but the love of God satisfies it. He who hath *it* can say, "Whom have I in heaven but thee? and there is none on the earth that I desire beside thee." The law of the ten commandments, requiring us to love God supremely, and our neighbours as ourselves, is not an arbitrary command, but has reference to our very nature, to the affections implanted within us. Man was created thus to love his Maker, and his kind; and before his fall, did thus love. When, therefore, men bestow, or attempt to bestow, their supreme regard upon mere earthly good, the soul, as if conscious of its noble spiritual extraction, loathes and rejects, and will not be satisfied with the poor bauble; and it is the contest which arises in consequence of the effort to make it take up with what is beneath its own dignity, and is so insufficient to satisfy its wants, which is so hostile to human happiness. Moreover, it is the fickle, uncertain tenure of sublunary things, which creates in the human breast a longing for some more fixed and established good—something of a more permanent and enduring nature, that will not vanish before we have fairly grasped it. How evanescent are the objects on which worldly men rely for happiness! They fix their gaze upon them, devote their life to the attainment of them, submit to toil and privation, to irritating, vexing cares, while distance spreads over them its hazy, deceptive colouring, and when, at last, they reach the goal at which they have long been aiming, they discover that they have been pursuing a shadow, or grasping at a bubble; or even before they have reached that goal, they may reach that "one place" to which all go—THE GRAVE.

§ XII. Chap. VI. 7–12.

(7.) *All the labour of man is for his mouth,
and yet the appetite is not satisfied.*

As bread or meat is sometimes put for all food, so
food, or that which men seek, by their toil, to provide
for the mouth, is put for all which can gratify the appetites of the body. But let men toil however much,
they can never satisfy these desires so that they shall
not return, and be just as pressing in their demands
as they were before. Take the craving for food ; men
have never yet discovered an article which is capable
of appeasing it once and forever. They eat and their
hunger is satisfied ; but the same craving returns, and
they must eat again. To gratify insatiable appetites
is like the constant rolling of a stone, which always
has to be lifted anew.

(8.) *What advantage, then, is there to the wise
man over the fool ? What hath the poor, who
knoweth how to walk, before the living ?*

How little advantage has a man who is sagacious
in his worldly plans, and accumulates a large store,

over him who is less successful ! The abundance of his store, or the means which he can command for gratifying his appetites, will not prevent their return. A man of little wit, or one who depends on his daily labour, can find out ways of satisfying his oft returning hunger. Or, what advantage has a poor man, who knows how to manage his affairs in the living busy world, with discretion, and to provide for his daily wants, over his fellow, who does not know how thus to walk before the living ! His ingenuity and industry in procuring a livelihood do not supersede those corporeal desires which demand to be gratified, and to which he is as much a slave as his simple-minded neighbour, or the poor savage of the forest. All men, the rich, the industrious, the acute, the poor, the ignorant, and the half-witted, stand on the same level in their subjection to the demands of fleshly appetites.

(9.) *Better is the sight of the eyes than the wandering of desire. This is also vanity and striving after wind.*

Restless, never satisfied desires or lusts of the flesh are here more generically pointed out. He had spoken particularly of the appetite for food, and of the vanity of man's making his chief happiness consist in an attempt to satisfy that which is insatiable. He now predicates the same vanity of all fleshly desires, or of all attempts to find real good or happiness in yielding the soul up to their wild, irregular impulses. To provide for our hunger is essential to the continuance of life ; but other appetites and passions are not so necessary to its continuance ; *i. e.*, may be restrained, or denied, without shortening our days, or seriously affecting the health. Imagination, and the association of ideas may lend their aid, and stimulate them into more vigorous activity, until a man is so enslaved as to exhibit humanity in one of its most degraded forms. Instead of enjoyment, they fill him with insupportable misery. " Better," says Solomon, " restrain these wandering desires." This is the import of the words, " Better is the sight of the eyes than the wandering of desire," " Set a limit to those passions, which may become irregular and imperious, and sweep the soul away on their turbid, tumultuous waters."

(10.) *That which hath been,—his name already hath been pronounced,—and it is known that he is a man, and that he can not contend with him who is mightier than he.*

That which hath been is man, considered with all his powers and endowments, whether he be wise or foolish, rich or poor ; a mere creature, a poor mortal, of the earth (Adam), earthy, and destined to return to the dust out of which he was taken. Let not such a creature think to contend with him who is mightier than he, his Creator ; let him not murmur and complain on account of the vanity and misery to which the race is subjected, brought upon them by their own rebellion and sins against that mighty One. Solomon is about to finish his account of the experiments which it is possible for men to make in their search after happiness in this world. Of each and all of them he has been constrained to say, " Vanity, vanity, all is vanity ;" but let not the poor, dependent, sinful, mortal man, reply against God and say, " Why hast thou made us thus?" There is a remedy, and he is about more clearly or directly to point it out; he is about to answer the question, "Who knoweth, and who can tell what is good for man in this vain life!"

(11.) *Seeing there are many things which increase vanity, what advantage hath man?*

This is the conclusion of the discussion which occupies all the foregoing portion of the book, respecting the vanity of seeking one's happiness exclusively from this world, together with a question as to what, or where is the real advantage or good, to the attainment of which a man should earnestly apply himself. Seeing he can not obtain that "good" which his soul desires in any of the ways, or by any of the methods, which have been named, and tried over and over again, only to increase vanity, what good is there for him? and how can it be found?

Some prefer to render, *as many words tend to increase vanity, what advantage is there to man? i. e.,* why say more? to multiply words to make more plain what has been already proved, would be only to add another vanity to those already named: *cui bono?* This, while I think the former interpretation is to be preferred, shows equally well that we are brought to the turning-point in the discussion, and that the author is about to turn it to some practical purpose.

(12.) *For who knoweth what is good for man all the days of his vain life, which he spendeth as a shadow? for who can tell man what shall be after him under the sun?*

These are the questions which come back and demand an answer, which are pressed home, by man's

fruitless striving to find happiness in the world.
" What is the great end of this vain life, which passes
away like a shadow ; what real good is attainable from
it ? and who can tell or promise that the future experience of men will be any different from that of those
before them ?" The author has taken the stand-
points successively of the mere man of learning, the
gay, frivolous man, the busy man, the monarch, the
rich man, the long-lived prosperous man, the sensualist—he has contemplated worldly good by itself, in
every conceivable form, and has reached no satisfactory result ; the questions still remain unanswered.
The verses 10, 11, 12, have been included, for the sake of
convenience in this division, although it properly closes
with verse 9, and these verses are really the transition
to the SECOND PART of the book, and must be re-
curred to, when we have concluded what remains to be
said on this final division of the FIRST PART.

SCOPE OF ARGUMENT IN § 12.

Multitudes, in seeking their happiness from forbid-
den sources, have violated the laws of morality and of
their own natures, in the fruitless search, and rashly
conclude that there is nothing within the reach of
man, deserving this name. What tears have moistened
the path of life, from those who have sought, only to
be disappointed, to quaff enjoyment from mere earthly
fountains ! How many votaries of the world have at
length been compelled to write upon all their most
cherished pursuits, plans, and hopes, " vanity and

vexation of spirit !" The world exhibits a delusive picture. It contains far more unhappiness than meets the view. How many wear the exterior of gayety, while the heart is corroded with anxiety, or disappointment ! Alas ! with how many is happiness

> " The gay to-morrow of the mind
> That never comes !"

Not that they are without their fitful, short-lived enjoyments ; but these do not constitute happiness in any proper sense of the term. Many of them are of that artificial, high-wrought nature, that they soon pall upon the appetite, or exhaust themselves by their own excess and violence. He who is a candidate for happiness, must not take into account the present moment only, but the whole of life—or of existence, rather. If, on the contrary, he adopt the maxim of the epicure, " Live while you live," and say, " Let us eat and drink, for to-morrow we die," let him not boast that he has found out the specific for making life happy ; for all that he has found out is only a specific for throwing both life and happiness away at the same moment. " He may have had a few, fitful bursts of enjoyment ; but the price has been enormous—a costly birthright for a mess of pottage. He alone can fairly boast of happiness, place it in whatsoever way you please, who on casting up the account, can honestly say that it has accompanied him through the long run."

Appetites, in themselves considered, or so far as they are directed only to their respective objects, for the preservation of the species, before they come under the control of the will, possess no moral character, either good or bad. In our physical economy they have, however, most wise and benevolent ends. The appetite for food, for example, directs to those articles which are agreeable to it, and to the seasons when the animal economy demands this sustenance, as well as the quantity which it demands. The same is true of the bodily appetites in general ; when directed to their only legitimate ends, and confined within proper limits, they are not only harmless, but indispensable to the continuance and preservation of the race. But they may be sadly abused ; men may attempt to extract a greater amount of enjoyment from them than they were designed to yield ; they may stimulate and provoke them, and at length nurse them into fierce avengers, to turn the palace of the human heart into a pandemonium—to become fiends who, for every forced drop of bliss, shall press "bitter bowls" to the lips of those who dared to pervert and degrade them. And was it ever known that a man proposed to gain his happiness in the gratification of sensual appetites, who did not pervert and abuse them ?

But we may first suppose that he confines the indulgence of them within proper limits. It is the doctrine of Solomon that experience will show, even then, the utter vanity of a man's seeking his happiness, his whole happiness, in such indulgence. He can not satisfy these appetites ; he may appease them momentarily, but they re-assert their demands with every returning day. The abundance of wealth can effect no more than the leanness of poverty ; for it serves but to pamper them, and render them more fastidious ; and when it has accomplished this, may take to itself wings and fly away, leaving the poor mortal in a condition more forlorn than that of his neighbour, who never possessed the means of stimulating his desires into unnatural activity. Wisdom and art can here confer no advantage on their possessors ; for wisdom can discover no fruit which shall minister perpetual and unfailing sustenance to a wasting body ; and art can compound no viands or condiments to put the appetite into a profound and final repose. Is this the great end of existence, to wait on appetites, which are not content with an occasional, but demand a constant service ? " Who can think," says John Howe, " the satisfying of these lusts the commensurate end of man ? Who would not, upon the supposition of no higher, say with the Psalmist, ' Wherefore hast thou made all men in vain ?' To what purpose was it for him to live in the world for a few years upon this account only, and so go down to the place of silence. * * * If the question were put, Wherefore did God make man ? who would not be ashamed to answer, He made him to eat, and drink, and take his pleasure, to gather up wealth for he knows not who ; to use his inventions, that each one may become a talk and wonder to the rest ; and then when he hath fetched a few turns upon the theatre, and entertained the eyes of beholders with a short scene of impertinences, descend, and never be heard of more ? What, that he should come into the world furnished with such powers and endowments, for this ! It were a like case, as if one should be clad in scarlet to go to plough, or curiously instructed in arts and sciences to tend swine."*

But when a man proposes to find his happiness in

---

* Vanity of Man as Mortal.

the gratification of sensual appetites, he does not stop with the food and drink which are merely necessary, or best fitted, to satisfy his hunger and thirst; the inevitable tendency is for him to pamper and stimulate them, by excessive indulgence, and artificial appliances. They become "wandering desires," licentious, wild cravings, which can not be satisfied with that measure of indulgence which may be allowed to the passions in their normal state, and which is indispensable to the health and welfare of our bodies. It becomes necessary, therefore, in order to have a complete view of the meaning of that portion of Ecclesiastes now under consideration, to inquire what relation there possibly can be between the excessive indulgence of the animal passions and real happiness. When Solomon said, " Better is the sight of the eyes than the wandering of desire," he spoke from experience. He knew the insupportable misery which is consequent on excessive indulgence of appetite and lust. He had sought to stimulate his flesh with wine (ii. 3), and at the same time to retain his discretion; the humiliating narrative in 1 Kings xi. 1–3 acquaints us with the extensive scale on which he made trial of licentious pleasures; and in the book of Ecclesiastes we have the result, from his own lips, of the terrible experiment; " vanity, and vexation of spirit;" "I find more bitter than death the woman whose heart is snares and nets, and her hands as bands; whoso pleaseth God shall escape from, but the sinner shall be taken by her" (vii. 26). It seems indeed almost superfluous to ask the question whether the excessive indulgence of the corporeal appetites can possibly ever promote the real happiness of men ; and it might be dismissed with its bare statement, as containing its own sufficient answer, were it not for the manner in which multitudes consent to debase and enslave themselves to tyrants that are permitted to give them laws, and enforce them as with a lash of scorpions.

1. There are the pleasures of the table, the gratification which the epicure seeks in a great variety of delicious, highly-seasoned food. The air, the sea, and the forest must be ransacked ; the most distant climes must bring their tribute, to help furnish this variety ; cooks and confectioners ply all their skill and art ; but the rarest articles soon pall on the capricious, pampered taste ; the craving for some new combination, or freshly invented ragout, whose delicate flavours shall excite the languid palate, becomes a troublesome passion, so that when he hears of some new product of culinary art, he is wretched, and can not enjoy his abundant luxuries, until it has been provided for his own table. What a degradation for a man to live with no higher object in view than to minister, with so much devotion, to masters so fickle and so clamorous ! What a wrong he does to the nobler faculties of his soul ! Why should he have been endowed with these nobler faculties to serve such ignoble masters ? The appetites should be the ministers of the soul ; but he has reversed this proper subordination, and subjected the soul, the spiritual part, to the corruptible body.

And when a love for the pleasures of the table leads to gluttony, it is even more debasing ; it may well be said to be beastly, for it tends to reduce man to the level of the sloth, or the brutes of the stye, who gorge themselves, to sleep and wake, to gorge and sleep again. What a miserable existence ! when he who was created a little lower than the angels, sinks himself to where he is but a little above the brutes ! When he does not eat that he may live, but lives only that he may eat ! The demoralizing effects may not be equal to those of an appetite for intoxicating liquors and drugs, but such over-stimulus of the body can not be otherwise than externally unfavourable to the cultivation of those affections and finer sensibilities, and that purity, on which the happiness of such a being as man must mainly depend. It develops and fosters the coarser, and more cruel parts of his nature ; it makes him so thoroughly sensual as to predispose to the whole tribe of kindred vices ; it awakens into more vigorous action the worst and most tormenting passions of the mind, anger, hatred, malice. And then again, instead of health, it fills the body with diseases. Rich feeding, it has been well said, is slow poison. High sauces, rich and artificial dishes, are the least adapted for being assimilated into chyle and blood, and serve but to convey into the body the germs of disease. A host of unwelcome dieases make him their victim, and declare his body their lawful prize. And this is the happy life which the epicure and glutton secures to himself ! Surely man was not created for pleasures so low, and which are more than outweighed by the pains with which they are sure to be accompanied.

2. Nor do those who betake themselves to intoxicating beverages and drugs meet with any better success in their search for happiness. They may thus stimulate their nervous systems, and produce a temporary exhilaration of the spirits ; but the pleasurable

excitement soon subsides, and is followed by a languor
which another resort to artificial stimulants must relieve ; and thus the infatuated man goes on, brutal-
izing his nature, and plunging himself, at every step,
into deeper misery. Strong drink may, for a moment,
allay an acquired, unnatural craving ; diffuse an unnatural energy through the frame ; cause gay visions
to float before the mind ; and drown, in a brief forgetfulness, the miseries and disappointments of the
hour. But it can not in reality lighten life of one of
its burdens, or soften down one of its rugged features.
On the contrary, it aggravates the very miseries to
which it may produce a temporary insensibility, and
introduces new forms of suffering. What is the state
of the system after a season of debauch ? To say
that it is devoid of happiness would be to give a better account of it than it deserves. It is full—full of
bitterness, self-reproach, and sickness at heart.

Intemperance is a wasteful, extravagant vice. It is
related of an ancient queen,* that at at the close of
a feast which she gave at Tarsus in honour of a Roman
general, she broke a pearl of immense value from one
of her ear-rings, and dissolving it in an acid, mingled
it with wine and drank it. Many a rich estate has
been dissolved in the wine-cup, and swallowed with
that which, at the same time, robbed its owner of
wit, reputation, and virtue. And the love of wine
has made many a poor man poorer. It is the parent
of idleness. He is drawn into other expensive and
wasteful vices ; he makes foolish bargains ; he indulges
in extravagant expenditures ; he pursues diligently no
honest avocation to add to his diminishing property ;

* Cleopatra.

and ere long he finds himself in the condition of the prodigal son, when he had wasted his substance in riotous living. Intemperance, under all circumstances, is a foe to domestic happiness ; but a home that was wretched before will be no happier when haggard want has entered and taken his place by the hearth-stone to extinguish the last embers there, and at the table to consume the scanty loaf. The temper that was sour before will be no sweeter now ; the disposition that was cruel or disobliging will be no kinder ; the fireside that was before a scene of contention and wrangling will not become peaceful and calm. But more than all, this vice demoralizes and debauches the character, weakens the moral principles, strengthens the corrupt propensities, and excites the wicked passions. It opens new avenues to temptation, exposes its victims to the worst influences, and counteracts those which are good. And will a man persist in " looking upon the wine when it is red, when it giveth its colour in the cup, when it moveth itself aright," and fancy that he has a vision of bliss ? Can a man take fire into his bosom and his clothes not be burned ? Can one walk on burning coals and his feet not be burned ? To seek happiness in the immoderate use of wine is as if one should build huge fires in his dwelling on a hot, sultry day in midsummer ; or rather as if he should set fire to his house in the dead of winter, and think to find a comfortable protection for himself and children beneath the leafless hedge. He kindles the fires of passion which must consume his comforts, and sooner or later, unless extinguished, consume both his body and his soul.

3. There is one other form of sensual indulgence in

which deluded men think to find enjoyment, which can not be overlooked in an attempt to explain a book which must be regarded as a monument of the repentance of Solomon—the licentious commerce of the two sexes, a life of lewd debauchery. The man who leads such a life, drinks wormwood and gall ; he takes fire into his bosom. The fruit, so fair and tempting to the sight, like the fabled apples of Sodom, fills his mouth with bitter dust, and his flesh upon him hath pain, and his soul within him doth mourn. The wise King of Israel himself uttered the most earnest warnings on this subject : " The lips of a strange woman drop as a honey-comb, and her mouth is smoother than oil ; but her end is bitter as wormwood, sharp as a two-edged sword. Her feet go down to death ; her steps take hold on hell. Her house inclineth unto death, and her paths unto the dead. None that go unto her return again, neither take they hold of the paths of life. Remove thy way far from her, and come not nigh the door of her house ; lest thou give thine honour unto others, and thy years unto the cruel : lest strangers be filled with thy wealth, and thy labours be in the house of a stranger ; and thou mourn at the last, when thy flesh and thy body are consumed, and say, How have I hated instruction, and my heart despised reproof !" (Prov. iii. and v.) Strange that the giver of such warnings and counsel should have at length disregarded them ; but he lived to escape from the fearful snare (Ecc. vii. 26) ; and his bitter experience serves to give weight to his solemn words, and greater force to the result of that hazardous experiment which it is one object of the book of Ecclesiastes to record. " None that go unto her return again, neither take they hold of the paths of life." Escape is almost hopeless ; the language, however, is not to be taken in its most absolute, literal sense, for then Solomon himself could not have escaped. Of all the vices, licentiousness seems to hold men in the strongest bonds, and affords the least prospect of reformation. The fetters which it weaves around them, while they serve to bind, serve also, the longer they are worn, to weaken the strength of the captive, and diminish the hope that he will ever cast them asunder. He loves to wear the chain which makes him the most miserable of slaves. No vice makes such havoc in the soul ; it is a concentration of impurity, cruelty, and contempt of both God and man ; it produces a self-loathing and abhorence, which, instead of working reformation in the man, renders him more desperate and abandoned. It kindles a fire which scorches and sears the whole surface of the soul, but not like the flames which sweep through the forest or over the prairie—they burn until there is nothing left to be consumed ; or rather they burn to the lowest hell. At length he awakes, when he feels the dart striking through his liver ; the enchantment is dispelled ; abused nature will have its revenge, will make a road of every nerve and vein, " for the scorching feet of pain to travel on ;" and the poor wretch finds himself in the purlieus of perdition, even before his spirit leaves its tenement.

This vice, however it may seek to conceal its deformity, or perfume itself " with myrrh, aloes, and cinnamon," and deck itself with gay tapestry—whether practiced in high life, or in low, is essentially the same, in the misery it inflicts on men. It shows no more

mercy to the mighty ruler than to the humblest
of his subjects, and the obscurest of his slaves.
Mark Antony was a man of commanding talents, indomitable courage, aspiring ambition, and possessed
of certain noble traits which made him the idol of
his army. But in the midst of his career, we find him
suddenly becoming timid and inefficient, all the fires
of his ambition, and all that was noble and generous
in his heart extinguished, and his soul subjected to
the vilest and most ignoble pleasures. He disowns a
most devoted wife, betrays every public trust, alienates
the affections of his countrymen, and ends his career by
becoming a fugitive and a suicide. His bleeding,
dying body dangling from the ropes, by which the
woman, to whose fascinations he had yielded himself,
with her maids, was straining to draw it up to the top
of the sepulchre in which she had taken refuge, was
truly a piteous, yet instructive spectacle. When their
strength failed, there he, the once mighty warrior,
and proud ruler hung, like a slaughtered ox in the
shambles. This was the end of a life of guilty pleasure ; this was the end of a brave soldier, of a man
who had been at the head of the mightiest nation on
earth. "She hath cast down many wounded : yea,
many strong men have been slain by her. Her house
is the way to hell, going down to the chambers of
death !"

Thus end, and here may well end, those experiments
which men can make to find their happiness in any
of the possessions, pursuits, and pleasures of this life.
"VANITY UPON VANITIES, VANITY UPON VANITIES, ALL
IS VANITY." Solomon has shown the *vanity* of seeking happiness in sensuality—the *vanity* of the most

protracted and prosperous life—the *vanity* of great riches—the *vanity* of a formal religion—the *vanity* of office and exalted station—the *vanity* of society, by reason of the imperfections of those who compose it— the *vanity* of government and laws—the *impossibility* of understanding the mysteries of Providence, by the mere light of this world—the *vanity* of an enterprising, busy life—the *vanity* of mirth and worldly splendour—the *vanity* of learning, and the *vanity* of the material universe, and the continued existence of the human race, if man be not immortal, if there be no future existence in which the mysteries of the present, and man's chief end, shall be unfolded. It is thus he proves that man was created for something nobler, better, higher, and more enduring, than " this vain life which he spendeth as a shadow."

He now advances, as will be seen in the SECOND PART, to higher ground, asserts the doctrine of a future life with the greatest distinctness, and, in describing wisdom as true religion, helps us to see in the very particulars in which the reproach of vanity had engaged his attention and perplexed his mind, how it is removed by the disclosures and hopes of this divine religion.

ANALYSIS OF PART SECOND.

I.—THE FEAR OF GOD REDEEMS LIFE FROM ITS VANITY, BY TURNING TO ADVANTAGE EVEN ITS MOST SORROWFUL SCENES, AND EXPERIENCES; Chap. vii. 1—6.

II.—RELIGION REDEEMS THE WORLD FROM VANITY, BY FORTIFYING THE SOUL AGAINST BOTH ITS SMILES AND ITS FROWNS; Chap. vii. 7—10.

III.—HEAVENLY WISDOM IS BETTER THAN RICHES ALONE; IT MAKES THEM A REAL BLESSING, AND PRESERVES ITS POSSESSORS FROM THE WORST EVILS; Chap. vii. 11—19.

IV.—TRUE PIETY, ALTHOUGH IT DOES NOT MAKE MEN PERFECT, NOR PRESERVE THEM FROM GREAT SINS, IS AN ENDURING PRINCIPLE, AND WILL FINALLY PREVAIL, BY RESTORING THE BACKSLIDER; OR, THE CONFESSION OF SOLOMON; Chap. vii. 20—29.

V.—RELIGION ENJOINS OBEDIENCE AND SUBMISSION TO MAGISTRATES AND RULERS—WARNS THEM AGAINST MISRULE AND OPPRESSION, AND THUS PROMOTES THE WELFARE OF SOCIETY; Chap. viii. 1—13.

VI.—Revelation discloses the only ground of Submission and Cheerfulness, in respect to the seeming Inequalities of Divine Providence in the Present Life; Chap. viii. 14—17; ch. ix. 1—6.

VII.—God's Favour toward a man spreads a Cheerful Light over the whole Scene of Human Affairs, Furnishes the Great Motive to an Active, Useful Life, and Prepares him for a Happy Death; Chap. ix. 7—12.

VIII.—Wisdom and Folly, or Religion and Irreligion Contrasted, and, notwithstanding the False Judgments of men in regard to them, the Former shown to be Immeasurably Superior to the Latter; Chap. ix. 13—18; ch. x. 1—20.

IX.—The Religious Life one of Active Benevolence; or the Excellence of Religion as seen from its Inculcation of Beneficence; Chap. xi. 1—6.

[Hence, Piety makes Life truly Happy; Chap. xi. 7.]

X.—The Subject Applied to the Aged; Chap. xi. 8.

XI.—To the Young; Chap. xi. 9, 10; ch. xii. 1—7.

XII.—Conclusion; Chap. xii. 8—14.

§ I. Chap. VII. 1–6.

(1.) *A [good] name is better than precious ointment, and the day of one's death than the day of his birth.*

Here commences the answer to the question in vs. 11 and 12 of the preceding chapter, which is continued to the end of the book, and constitutes what may be designated as its Second Part : "If such be the vanity of all worldly things, who knoweth what is good for man ?"

A name, i. e., a name for goodness, is put for that virtue or piety from which alone it can be derived ; it is a reputation for whatsoever things are true, becoming, honest, pure, lovely, and of good report. It is not a reputation for merely supposed, but for real excellences, known to Him who seeth the heart, and approved by him. The estimation which the Hebrews put upon oil or ointment, which this name is said to excel, may be seen from Deut. xxxiii. 24 ; Ps. xcii. 10 ; cxxxiii. 2 ; Is. xxxix. 2. This article which was so useful and valuable among them is made here, by synecdoche, to represent all those worldly blessings which men most prize. True virtue or piety is worth more than all these blessings. Its chief excellence is that it can make the day of a man's death better than the day of his birth. When death overtakes the truly good man, it settles the matter in respect to him, that he has not run in vain, neither laboured in vain ; but at his birth no one could foresee how it would result with him. Unless the passage means that the day of his death, who leaves a good name behind him, is better than his birth, there seems to be no agreement whatever between the former and the latter clause. The former must be viewed as stating the reason why his death is to be considered in so favourable a light ; viz., that he has lived to good purpose. A birth in a family is considered a joyful event ; but the death of a good man may be considered a more joyful one ; for then the battle is fought and the victory won, and it is said to him, " Well done, good and faithful servant."

(2.) *It is better to go to the house of mourning, than to go to the house of feasting ; for that is the end of all men ; and the living will lay it to heart.*

There is a close connection between this and the preceding verse. Birth-days were made feast-days. Pharaoh and Herod celebrated theirs by splendid banquets, Gen. xl. 20 ; Mark vi. 21. Men are tempted in such scenes, to immoralities, to gluttony, and drunkenness ; but in the house of mourning they are reminded of the end which awaits all men, which awaits them, and will be restrained from those follies and vices which pollute the soul, and destroy "a good name." However others may be affected, the truly good man, who keeps his "soul embalmed and pure in living virtue," will lay the solemn lesson, which is addressed to him, when he looks upon the coffin of a fellow-creature, and the stiffened clay within, to his heart. He is not tempted to withdraw his mind, or banish death from his thoughts as an unwelcome intruder. He can derive profit from thinking of the time when men shall be gathered to his own funeral, and the mourners shall go about the streets.

(3.) *Sorrow is better than laughter; for by the sadness of the countenance the heart is made better.*

We have the same thought still further expanded. *The sadness of the countenance* is put for those serious reflections, which the scenes of death are fitted to awaken, because the face is the mirror where our feelings will show themselves. Such reflections improve the heart, or make it *sound*. And this expression helps us to understand what Solomon intended by "a good name" (v. 1) as something more than a fair report among men, even that upon which such a name must always rest for a secure foundation, a good heart. To have our hearts made good, and to make them better, is what we need in order to meet death in peace, and give up our account with joy.

(4.) *The heart of the wise is in the house of mourning; but the heart of fools is in the house of mirth.*

Here the righteous are denominated *wise*, and the wicked *fools*, after the manner so common in the book

of Proverbs. The thoughts of a good man are frequently upon the most serious things, the vanity of
this life, death, and judgment, while the thoughts of
the wicked are devoted to the vanities and follies of
life. In describing the nature and influence of true
piety, he carries along in contrast with it, a description of irreligion.

(5.) *It is better for a man to hear the rebuke
of the wise than to hear the song of fools.*

The rebuke, the admonition, or the instruction
which a good man receives in the house of mourning,
or when his heart is there, and he is solemnly medi-
tating on death and eternity, is better than to be exposed to the influences to which the thoughtless sinner is exposed in the house of mirth. The reason has
been already given.

(6.) *For as the crackling of thorns under a
pot, so is the laughter of the fool. This, also, is
vanity.*

The comparison points not only to the empty, unmeaning nature of the fool's laugh, but to the short
continuance of his hilarity, which is " quenched as the
fire of thorns" (Ps. cxviii. 12), or goes out quick, like
the fire which rages fiercely among stubble. He may
persist in turning life into a caper and a merry song ;
but like dry twigs or grass, or a handful of shavings,
burning under a pot, his frantic joys will soon come to
an end. This truly, is vanity.

§ II. Chap. VII. 7–10.

RELIGION REDEEMS THE WORLD FROM VANITY BY FOR-
TIFYING THE SOUL AGAINST BOTH ITS SMILES AND ITS
FROWNS.

(7.) *Surely oppression maketh a wise man
mad; and a bribe corrupteth the heart.*

Solomon is speaking of the tendency of oppression
and bribery. The wise or good man finds the former
very hard to endure. He is tempted to anger and
revenge, or to restlessness and impatience ; he may
suffer so much as almost to forget the meekness which
should govern his words and actions, and that there is
a God in the heavens who will avenge the cause of
the oppressed. He contrasts with this, gifts, favours,
by which the powerful sometimes seek to bribe the
good to wink at their wicked deeds. There is great
danger in receiving such gifts from such men, lest the
purity of the heart should be destroyed. But he suggests the remedy in the following verses.

(8.) *Better is the end of a thing than the beginning thereof: better is the patient in spirit
than the proud in spirit.*

Look to the end. Judge not from present appear-
ances alone. The oppressor may now be powerful,

and your external condition be very unhappy. But, be patient ; there is One in heaven who seeth and knoweth all, and is over all. Or, if the powerful smile instead of frown, and offer gifts instead of insults and wrongs, yet look to the end, and be not tempted to flatter him in his pride, or to become proud thyself. Sacrifice not your purity of soul, by being provoked to madness and indiscretion by his oppression, or to connive at sin, by his favours.

(9.) *Be not hasty in thy spirit to be angry ; for anger resteth in the bosom of fools.*

Here is a further caution against indulging in anger, to which we have so many temptations in an unjust and wicked world ; it is a temper which characterizes the wicked ; it finds its proper abode in their hearts. The religion which Solomon inculcated was a religion of the heart ; and it is such a religion alone which is fitted to be our safeguard, exposed as we are to vexations and provocations on all sides.

(10.) *Say not, Why is it that the former days were better than these? for thou dost not inquire wisely concerning this.*

Thus true religion teaches, we are not, under those oppressions and evils which are so severe a trial to good men, to imagine that we have fallen on peculiarly distressing times, and indulge in a fault-finding, repining spirit. How little we know of the former times, and of the great troubles which others have experienced ! How prone is every one, when in deep affliction, to cry out, " Behold and see, if there be any sorrow like unto my sorrow?" [Lam. i. 12.] We are not to forget that God is upon the throne, and that he can make the wrath of man to praise Him, and afflictions in whatever form they come, "which are but for a moment, to work out for us a far more exceeding and eternal weight of glory."

15*

§ III. Chap. VII. 11–19.

HEAVENLY WISDOM IS BETTER THAN RICHES ALONE; IT
MAKES THEM A REAL BLESSING, AND PRESERVES ITS
POSSESSORS FROM THE WORST EVILS.

(11.) *Wisdom is good as well as an inheritance ; yea it is better to them that see the sun.*

As in this portion of Ecclesiastes the terms the *wise*
and the *foolish* are used, as in the book of Proverbs, to
designate the good, and the wicked, so *wisdom* is for
the most part used for godliness or the fear of the
Lord, and *folly* or its cognates, for wickedness. While
the text would be true if understood of ordinary prudence, it is more eminently true of that wisdom
which consists in the fear of the Lord. The words of
the apostle furnish an excellent commentary, "Godliness is profitable unto all things, having promise of
the life that now is, and of that which is to come ;"
"Godliness with contentment is great gain," 1 Tim.
iv. 8. vi. 6. True piety makes wealth a great blessing
to its possessor and the world.

(12.) *For wisdom is a defence, and money is
a defence ; but the excellence of wisdom is, that
it giveth life to them that hath it.*

We have here the reason assigned for what had
been stated before, that wisdom is better than an in-

heritance. Its pre-eminence consists in this, that it giveth life to them that possess it. Praise like this could hardly be given to human knowledge or prudence. The foresight of the wisest, while it may sometimes serve to protect them against dangers, can not preserve or prolong their lives ; neither can religion ; therefore we infer that life here is to be taken in its highest sense, and refers to spiritual and eternal life. Heavenly wisdom quickens the soul to life, and makes it a partaker of immortal felicity in heaven ; and those that have it may, at the same time, possess all the advantage which is to be derived from riches as a defence against the ills of life.

(13.) *Consider the work of God; for who can make that straight which he hath made crooked ?*

It is not the work of creation, but the work of Providence which we are commanded to consider. God is over all ; we can not, by our wishes and strivings, alter the course of things which he ordains. The man who is under the influence of this doctrine of religion has a better protection against disappointment and misery, than if he had an inheritance alone, or had to contend with the ills of life, by the aid which can be derived from a cold and speculative philosophy.

(14.) *In the day of prosperity be joyful, but look for the day of adversity ; for God hath set one over against the other, in order that man should not discover any thing which shall be after him.*

If God sends prosperity, be grateful. It is not inconsistent with the dictates of religion for a man, thus blessed, to rejoice and with gladness eat the fruit of his labour. There will be little danger of his running into excess, if while he rejoices, he remembers the days of adversity, and looks for their coming. Solomon recurs again to that wonderful Providence which is over the good man, by which days of adversity are made to alternate with days of prosperity, so that the future is always to him uncertain. So long as he remembers this uncertainty, and expects change, his wealth will be a real blessing, and not a snare.

(15.) *All this have I considered in the days of my vanity ; there is a righteous man that perisheth in his righteousness, and there is a wicked man who liveth long in his wickedness.*

Solomon here acquaints us with subjects to which his mind was specially directed during the period when he was making his vain efforts, or trying his vain experiments. It particularly attracted his attention, and excited his amazement that a righteous man should be permitted to perish on account of his righteousness ; and a wicked man prolong his life by wickedness. It may have shaken his faith, and led him to ask, " Can there be a righteous God?" and thus emboldened him to sin. His consideration of this apparently unequal allotment, in the case of the righteous and the wicked, led him, in the days of his vanity, to such thoughts as are contained in the following verses.

(16.) *Be not righteous overmuch, neither make thyself overwise ; why shouldest thou make thyself desolate ?*

If there be no righteous God in heaven, who makes a difference between good men and bad, and religion be vain, why be so scrupulous in respect to conduct? Why be so attentive to religion, to the rules of a strict life, and separate thyself from the lovers of pleasures and vanities, and lose their good opinion? Why keep thyself apart, and make thyself desolate?

(17.) *Be not wicked overmuch; neither be thou a fool ; why shouldest thou die before thy time ?*

But be not tempted into those excesses which are inconsistent with the dignity of a rational creature, which tend not only to impair the reason, but destroy the health and the life. When Solomon gave himself up to mirth and gay pleasures, and resolved to stimulate his flesh with wine, and surround himself with unexampled splendour, it was, as he declares, his purpose that his mind should be still guided by discretion, and that his wisdom should remain with him (ii. 3, 9). He would not be tempted, because all the difference which was made between the righteous and the wicked seemed to be in favour of the latter, to plunge madly into those sensual indulgences which tend to cut men off, in the midst of their days.

(18.) *It is good that thou shouldest take hold of this ; yea, also from that withdraw not thine hand : for he that feareth God shall come forth of them all.*

The *this* which he exhorts us to *take hold of*, is the caution in the preceding verse, not to be overmuch wicked ; and the *that* from which, also, we are not to *withdraw*, is the prudent caution implied in the sixteenth verse, to wit, the affectation or ostentation of righteousness. The only safety of a man is in the fear of God ; that fear, when he would avoid ostentation and formality in religion, will preserve him from renouncing it altogether. While he would first rebuke the thought or temptation respecting being righteous overmuch, which visited him in the days of his vanity, he admits that there may be such a thing as too great scrupulousness in respect to unessentials. But he that feareth God shall escape this as well as the other danger.

(19.) *Wisdom strengthens the wise more than ten mighty men who are in the city.*

Wisdom here again is true wisdom, a term convertible with the fear of the Lord. It strengthens, by preserving a man from turning to the right hand or the left, either to great wickedness, or to an empty, ostentatious piety. " Thrice is he armed," who always adheres closely to the rule of his duty ; he is safer than the wicked man who is guarded by mighty warriors. The " defence" or protection which true piety affords its possessors is the subject of the preceding verses (11–19). He first compares it with riches, and then shows how it preserves from the opposite extremes referred to in verses 16 and 17, to wit abuse of religion, and the temptation to extreme wickedness, to which the possessors of great wealth, without restraining principle, are peculiarly exposed.

§ IV. Chap. VII. 20–29.

TRUE PIETY, ALTHOUGH IT DOES NOT MAKE MEN PER-
FECT, NOR PRESERVE THEM FROM GREAT SINS, IS AN EN-
DURING PRINCIPLE, AND WILL FINALLY PREVAIL, BY
RESTORING THE BACKSLIDER. THE CONFESSION OF SOL-
OMON.

(20.) *Truly there is not a just man upon
earth who doeth good and sinneth not.*

The particle, which the authorized version translates
by *for*, sometimes marks a transition, or stands at the
beginning of a new discourse, as in Job xxviii. 1, and
may then be translated *surely*, or *truly*. The doctrine
of the passage, to wit, that all men are sinners, is one
that was perfectly familiar to the mind of Solomon.
Thus he says in Prov. xx. 9, " Who can say, I have
made my heart clean, I am pure from my sin ?" and
in his prayer at the dedication of the temple, " There
is no man that sinneth not." 1 Kings viii. 46. The
relevancy of the subject here introduced will be seen
if we bear in mind that he had just spoken of the
"days of his vanity," *i. e.*, the days of his backsliding,
and notice that he goes on to attribute his reclamation
to the grace of God. This religion, the excellency of
which he is setting forth, does not make men perfect,
or insure them against falling into great sins. He

does not say that there is not a man upon earth that sinneth not, but "there is not a just man on earth who doeth good and sinneth not." The best of men, described as just or righteous, those who do good, have many imperfections ; defect cleaves even to their good deeds ; their sanctification is but partial, so long as they remain in this world.

(21.) *Moreover, give no heed unto all the words that are spoken ; lest thou hear thy servant cursing thee.*

Such is our imperfection that we can not expect—the best of men can not expect—that all that is said of them will be in their praise. Their dependants, members of their own families, who might be supposed to be partial, will discover faults that will call forth their reprehension. We are not to listen to all the words they utter, and be disappointed if they are not always in our praise ; for our own servants do but discover that in us which we discover and reprobate in others, as stated in the next verse.

(22.) *For thine own heart also knoweth that oftentimes thou thyself hast cursed others.*

We should no more expect that others will approve of all that they see in us, and done by us, than we can approve of all the conduct of others, even the best of men. *Cursed* is not to be taken in the sense of wishing or imprecating evil, but rather in that of reprobation, or unqualified disapproval. We may detest and disapprove of the evil we see in a man, without cursing the sinner. And it is as much our duty to disapprove of the faults and sins of good men, as of the impiety and vices of the most abandoned transgressors. Indeed, sin, in one who has been enlightened, and made the subject of saving grace, especially the sin of backsliding, is only the more aggravated by reason of the favour from which he falls.

(23.) *All this have I tried by wisdom : I said, Let me become wise ; but it was far from me.*

Solomon, having spoken of the sins of good men, feelingly and penitently alludes to his own case—to his vain and rash attempts to find out some other wisdom than that which begins in the fear of the Lord. He refers to these attempts before spoken of (i. 13 *seq.* ii. 12, 13), and uses wisdom in the same sense as in the former part of the book, where he describes his resort to mere worldly wisdom to ascertain, if possible, how to redeem this world from its vanity. We have in this, and the remaining verses of the chapter, what may well be styled the confession of the royal penitent.

(24.) *That which is far off, and very deep, who can find it out ?*

True wisdom is here meant. Who by his own unaided faculties can find this out ? It is far off from man ; it is very deep. It is knowledge which is too wonderful for him ; it is so high he can not attain unto it ; " it is high as heaven, what canst thou do ? deeper than hell, what canst thou know ?" (Job xi. 8. Comp. Ps. cxxxix. 6-9.) God himself must reveal it to his creature. It was a vain effort for Solomon, having ignored revelation, to attempt to find out what God alone could teach him. And it is equally vain for any man to attempt to discover, by his own reason, the truth which it is the exclusive province of revelation to declare.

(25.) *I applied my heart to know, and to explore, and to seek out wisdom and intelligence, and to know wickedness and folly, even foolishness and madness.*

He here manifestly refers to the singular experiment detailed in the former part of the book ; " And I gave my heart to know wisdom, and to know madness and folly :" (i. 17) " And I turned myself to behold wisdom, and madness, and folly" (ii. 12). It was not sacred, divine wisdom which he sought out ; but he strove, as a philosopher, to find out what happiness could be derived from an unrestrained indulgence of the strongest and lowest animal passions. It was a most strange attempt to keep his heart acquainted with wisdom, while he stimulated his flesh with wine, and went to the extreme limit in concupiscence. He tells us with what miserable success he met.

(26.) *And I found more bitter than death the woman whose heart is nets and snares, and her hands bands ! whoso pleaseth God shall be delivered from her ; but the sinner shall be taken by her.*

" The mouth of strange women is a deep pit : he that is abhorred of the Lord shall fall therein." Prov. xxii. 14. Who can doubt that we have the same speaker in both these instances ? The imagery is the

same, and the leading thought the same ; only in Ecclesiastes there is greater intensity of expression, as
from one who now spake from experience. He had
found the strange woman " more bitter than death,"
her heart " snares and nets," and her hands chains,
which bind her victim fast. This was the result of
his attempt to seek out wisdom, by knowing wickedness and folly. What bitter self-reproaches, what a
sense of pollution, what an agony of feeling, were
wrought within him, by his madness and foolishness !
He ascribes his escape entirely to the favour and interposition of God ; neither learning, nor a good disposition, nor a good resolution, nor any thing except
God's grace, is sufficient to deliver from the power of
lewd passions, long and freely indulged. There hardly
seems to be the least shadow of hope for the sinner,
who seeks and receives no help from the Lord. Such
help was granted to Solomon. The Lord had loved
him in infancy, and in early life, and had caused him
to be named Jedidiah, *i. e.*, beloved of the Lord.
"Did not Solomon, king of Israel, sin by these things ?
yet among many nations was there no king like him,
who was beloved of his God, and God made him king
over all Israel : nevertheless, even him did outlandish
women cause to sin," Neh. xiii. 26. It was because
he was beloved of God that he escaped. He bitterly
lamented, and forsook his folly.

(27.) *Behold, this I have found, saith the
Preacher, adding one thing to another, to find out
knowledge.*

The *this* refers to what he describes himself as having discovered in the preceding verse. *Adding one*

thing to another means that it was no hurried, careless experiment, but most deliberately, and minutely prosecuted, as he resolved it should be, as a philosopher, to find out, if possible in this way, the knowledge of true happiness.

(28.) *That which my soul perseveringly sought, I have not found. One man among a thousand have I found, but a woman among all these have I not found.*

There is no comparison here as to the relative worth of the two sexes ; but he means to say that he had sought in vain for a single one among all the strange women he had known, who was worthy of his esteem. He had not found many worthy of the name of a man —not more than one in a thousand ; but among the thousand women who belonged to his harem, he had not found one who did not bear the character given of the strange women in ver. 26, " whose heart is snares and nets, and her hands bands."

(29.) *Lo, this only have I found, that God made man upright; but they have sought out many devices.*

But if he did not find what he especially sought, he discovered something he was most deeply impressed with, to wit, that God created man holy that he might be holy and happy in life, but that by his own perverseness, by sinful indulgences, he had created many sorrows and sufferings for himself. Or the allusion may be to his own early piety, which he means to acknowledge was the work of God, but from which he sadly declined in seeking to find out wisdom, and to know madness and folly. These attempts he denominates "inventions," or *devices.* The passage supports an important doctrine whichever interpretation be adopted ; if the former—that God's work, as it proceeded from his hands, was perfect, he did not create man a sinner ; if the latter, that God is the author of true piety in the heart of man, but that even such piety does not prevent him from falling into great sins. The latter, it seems to me, should be preferred, as it accords better with ver. 20, and the entire scope of the passage.

§ V. Chap. VIII. 1–13.

RELIGION ENJOINS OBEDIENCE AND SUBMISSION TO MAGIS-
TRATES AND RULERS, WARNS THEM AGAINST MISRULE
AND OPPRESSION, AND THUS PROMOTES THE WELFARE OF
SOCIETY.

(1.) *Who is as the wise man who knoweth the
explanation of a thing? A man's wisdom maketh
his face to shine, but haughty arrogance disfigureth his countenance.*

Or, what is there like the wisdom which cometh
from above to make us truly wise? Who is equal to,
or can be compared with, the man who has been enlightened by this wisdom, in respect to understanding
the secret of true happiness? The countenance of a
good man will reflect the purity, benevolence, and
peace within; his piety will soften the harsh expression which his countenance wore, when he nourished
malignant passions in his heart.

(2.) *I counsel thee to keep the king's commandment, and that on account of the oath of God.*

The teaching of the New Testament is similar:
"Let every soul be subject unto the higher powers. For

there is no power but of God ; the powers that be are ordained of God. Whosoever therefore resisteth the power, resisteth the ordinance of God." Rom. xiii. 1, 2. " Submit yourselves to every ordinance of man for the Lord's sake ; whether it be to the king as supreme, or unto governors ; as unto them that are sent by him for the punishment of evil-doers, and for the praise of them that do well." 1 Pet. ii. 13, 14. *The oath of God* here is the oath of allegiance to the king. See 1 Chron. xxix. 24. Revealed religion enjoins obedience to the civil magistrate. Such obedience it recognizes as a duty of the highest obligation. Civil government has not its origin in a mere social compact entered into by men, but in the will and authority of God. Hence its authority. Consequently religion is the grand conservator of public order. But as the oath in question recognizes the supremacy of God, it does not, and can not bind subjects to do any thing contrary to his laws.

(3.) *Do not hastily go out of his sight; do not persist in an evil thing; for he doeth whatsoever pleaseth him.*

Be not in haste to cast off his authority, and quit his service or obedience. It is an exhortation against rebellion or opposition to the lawful civil authority of the land. This is the *evil thing* in which men are not to persist, unless they wish to incur the punishment, which the king, under such circumstances, will feel bound to inflict. Stuart translates the second clause, *do not make delay in regard to a command which is grievous ;* i. e., that men are not to hesitate to obey any command of the king forthwith, let it be what it may. But this does not appear to be well supported, and would be inconsistent with what follows. Solomon is clearly advocating simply subjection to the magistrate, in the exercise of his lawful authority.

(4.) *Where the word of a king is, there is power; and who may say unto him, What doest thou?*

There is a lawful power which resides in civil government, whether it be an absolute or limited monarchy, or republic, to punish rebels and evil-doers. It is armed with majesty because it is lawful; its punishment is not retaliation or revenge; when it takes away the life of a murderer, it does not commit murder, but performs a humane and beneficent act. " Wilt thou not then be afraid of the power ?" Men may well be afraid to stand up against a power which they can not resist as evil-doers, without incurring guilt, and forfeiting their liberty,. or perhaps their lives. The question, *who may say unto him, What doest thou ?* does not contain an implied approval of arbitrary or tyrannical power. Men may ask this question where civil rulers abuse their authority; but it is difficult and dangerous, to oppose one's self to the lawfully constituted authorities of the state, when they confine themselves to their proper functions.

(5). *Whoso obeyeth the command shall feel no evil thing; and the wise man's heart regardeth both time and judgment.*

These words state the benefits which accrue to the peaceful, obedient citizen. Good rulers are not a terror to the good, but to the evil. The heart of the wise man, or of the truly pious man, pays a proper regard to all the duties which grow out of his several relations, and performs them in their season. He has reference not merely to present time, but to future judgment. *Judgment* here is the same as that referred to in iii. 17, and xii. 14. He remembers his accountability to God, and this makes him a faithful citizen. There will be retribution. The connection, says Dr. Noyes of Cambridge, requires us to understand a time of judgment, which denotes retribution.

(6.) *For to every thing there is a time and judgment; for injustice toward man presseth heavily upon him.*

Substantially the same truth is here repeated which we have in Chap. iii. 1, 11, 17. Solomon had given counsel respecting obedience to kings ; but kings are often oppressive ; they make their yoke heavy on the necks of men. The evil of men is not only that which they do, but that which they suffer from the cruelty of others ; and this latter is here specially referred to, and the sufferers are directed to look forward to a season of retribution.

(7.) *For no one knoweth that which shall be ; for who can tell when it shall take place?*

Men know not the full severity of that retribution which awaits them for their sins ; and they know not the time of judgment. This uncertainty as to the time of judgment, and the severity of the punishment, should awaken them to fear, and stir them up to watchfulness. Our Saviour made use of the ignorance of men respecting the time of their Lord's coming, to excite them to vigilance and preparation, "Watch, therefore ; for ye know not what hour your Lord doth come. But know this, that if the good man of the house had known in what hour the thief would come, he would have watched, and would not have suffered his house to be broken up." Matth. xxiv. 42, 43. Thus distinctly does the book of Ecclesiastes reveal a coming retribution ; and as we see not this retribution in the present life, it must take place in the world to come.

(8.) *No man hath power over the wind to restrain the wind, nor hath power in the day of death ; neither is there any discharge in that war ; neither shall wickedness deliver those that are given to it.*

The same word which means spirit means wind. The meaning is that if man has not control over the wind to "hold it in his fist" (Prov. xxx. 4), neither has he power to retain the breath of life, or keep back his soul in the day of death. If he can not do the less, how can he do the greater ? When the hour of death, which is unknown to him, arrives, he can not hinder his immortal spirit from taking its departure from the body and entering into the presence of the Judge. It is a war in which there can be no discharge, a conflict from which none can escape. By wicked, deceitful art, men may elude justice, and punishment in this world—and this may be especially true of powerful rulers—but the time will come when all their power and expedients will avail no longer.

(9.) *All this have I seen, and I gave heed to every work that is done under the sun ; there is a time when a man ruleth over another to his own hurt.*

He had been an attentive observer of the course of human affairs ; and, although a king himself, he was not blind to the faults of kings. He well knew that they could abuse their authority, and instead of being a terror to evil-doers, become a scourge and a terror to the just. But the victims of their cruelty are not the only ones who suffer injury ; they rule to their own hurt ; they are guilty of a great sin of which the Ruler of the universe takes cognizance, and must give an account thereof in the day of judgment. Let tyrants then take warning, and their subjects who are groaning under an iron sway, be consoled. There is a day of reckoning approaching.

(10.) *And so I saw the wicked buried who had gone to and from the place of the holy, and they were forgotten in the city where they had so done. This also is vanity.*

Wicked rulers, especially in their character as judges, are here meant. *The place of the holy* is the throne or the judgment-seat,—called so because on it they sit, as it were, in the place of the Deity to men,—to which he had seen them go, entirely heedless of the solemn, responsible nature of their office and functions. Kings are regarded as sacred persons, anointed of the Lord for their office ; hence the palace or judgment-hall is denominated a holy place. He had seen them buried, yet all the splendour which

surrounded them while living, and the parade which
attended them to their tombs, did not save their
names from oblivion. They left this world to be
judged by God, and to be forgotten and despised by
men.

I see no reason for confining *the place of the holy* to
Palestine or to Jerusalem ; it may apply to the palace
of any king ; nor any reason for regarding the phrase
gone from the place, etc., a euphemism to denote
death. The expression *coming in and going out before
the people* is frequently applied to the administration
of public justice, or government, see Numb. xxvii. 17,
and Deut. xxxi. 2.

(11.) *Because sentence against an evil work
is not executed speedily, therefore the heart of the
sons of men is fully set in them to do evil*.

The Divine forbearance and long-suffering toward
unjust and oppressive rulers, instead of leading them
to repentance, often seems to embolden them to
greater wickedness. They interpret delay of judgment
to mean that judgment will never come, and therefore
their heart is fully set in them to do evil.

And this that is true of wicked rulers, is true of
sinners in general. They do wrong ; and because
punishment does not immediately follow the sinful
act, they go on in wrong-doing, as if there were no
God who takes notice of the conduct of men, and will
visit them according as their sins deserve. But it is
a signal mistake into which they fall, as we learn from
the succeeding verses.

(12.) *Though a sinner do evil a hundred times
and prolong his days, yet surely I know that it*

*shall be well with them that fear God, that fear
before him.*

(13.) *But it shall not be well with the wicked,
neither shall he prolong his days: as a shadow
is he that feareth not God.*

The wicked ruler may go on and repeat his wicked
acts, without number, and live to old age, without being overtaken by retribution, but let not our confidence in the Divine rectitude and justice be shaken ;
it shall be well with them that fear God, however
much they may be oppressed now ; they shall obtain
their reward. *He* says this who elsewhere says " all
things come alike to all," " as the wise man dieth, so
dieth the fool." Where, and when are they to receive
their reward ? Of course, in a future state. Neither
shall the oppressor, or any wicked man prolong his
days, so as to escape retribution ; the longest life is
but a shadow that passes quick away. But if retribution does not overtake him in this life, where will it
overtake him ? In another world. It is in this plain
manner that a future life and future retribution are
taught in Ecclesiastes.

It is thus that revealed religion supports and pro-
tects civil society, checks that disposition in great
rulers, which otherwise might turn the institution of
government into an engine of oppression.

§ VI. Chap. VIII. 14–17.   Ch. IX. 1–6.

(14.) *There is a vanity which is done on the
earth: there are righteous men to whom it happeneth according to the work of the wicked, and
there are wicked men to whom it happeneth according to the work of the righteous; I said that
this surely is vanity.*

He had just declared, in the preceding verses, that
men do not meet with the due reward of their deeds
in this life, and yet they shall meet with a just retribution; of course necessitating us to suppose that it
awaits them in a state subsequent to the present.
This leads him to recur to a topic, already more than
once brought to view in this book, and which was very
familiar to the minds of the ancient Hebrews, forced
upon their attention by the facts of every-day life and
experience, to wit, that in this life, the wicked often
seem to enjoy the highest prosperity, while the righteous endure painful afflictions.   Just that state of
things which we might be led to anticipate, under the

government of a wise and righteous God, seems often reversed. This he styles *a vanity;* it would be an inexplicable mystery, if it were not for the doctrine of another life ; or rather if it did not presage to men, even irrespective of a divine revelation, a future judgment, it would stamp this world as the most consummate of all vanities, by proving it to be so sadly misgoverned.

(15.) *Then I commended joy, because it is good for a man under the sun to eat, and to drink, and be joyful; for this shall abide with him in his toil, all the days of his life which God giveth him under the sun.*

This is founded on the truth contained in v. 12, that it shall, whatever be the aspect of the passing moment, certainly be well with them that fear God. They are not, on account of present annoyances and afflictions, to allow themselves to be deprived of the good which may be derived from the present. The doctrine of future retribution should not only reconcile them to passing troubles, but dispose them to make the most of current blessings—to partake of the bounties of Divine providence, with gladness of heart. A grateful, cheerful spirit will go with a man through his toil, all the days of his life, and enable him to sustain the burden, however heavy and painful it may be the will of God he should bear.

(16.) *When I applied my heart to know wisdom, and to consider the business which is done on the earth, for neither day nor night does one see sleep with his eyes,*

(17.) *Then I saw the whole work of God, that a man can not find out the work that is done under the sun; how much soever he may labour to search it out, yet shall he not comprehend it; yea, though a wise man resolve to know it, yet shall he not be able to find it out.*

The idea here is, that when men ignore a future state of retribution, which God has revealed, in their own hearts, and in his word, and attempt, by reason, to search out the mysteries of Divine Providence, especially the mysteries which appear in permitting the wicked to prosper and the righteous to suffer, the attempt must prove abortive. The wisest philosopher can not make his way here, by the light alone of his own reason. Providence is to him, as it is to other men, a vast abyss, " too deep to sound with mortal lines." Solomon tells us how earnestly, and how vainly, he applied his own mind to comprehend this *work of God.* He describes himself as giving no sleep to his eyes, nor slumber to his eyelids ; it so perplexed his mind that he found no rest at night. The *one* of whom he speaks, who, neither day nor night, saw sleep, is unquestionably himself. " It is a modest designation of himself," says Poole, like that of Paul, 2 Cor. xii. 2, " *I knew a man in Christ,*" etc. He went over the subject again and again, from beginning to end, and came to the conclusion that, leaving the doctrine of retribution out of view, the wisest of men, whatever may be his strength of purpose, and his perseverance, will labour in vain and spend his strength for naught.

(CHAP. IX. 1.) *For all this I considered in my heart, and searched out all this, that the righteous and the wise, and their works, are in the hand of God; also love and hatred; neither do men know all that is before them.*

He goes on, and lets us see how his mind operated while he was prosecuting the painful inquiry. He felt assured that *the righteous and the wise*, however they might seem, in the course of Divine Providence, to be neglected by God, were under his paternal care and direction, were in his hand, or at his disposal; and that the love, or the disfavour of God toward them was not to be judged of by their external condition in this life, because they do not receive their reward here. The excellence of a man's character does not, and can not, determine whether prosperity or adversity awaits him in his future days on earth.

(2.) *All things happen alike to all; there is one event to the righteous, and to the wicked; to the good, to the clean, and the unclean; to him that sacrificeth, and to him that sacrificeth not; as is the good so is the sinner; he that sweareth as he that feareth an oath.*

This is a faithful description of what strikes the mind of every man who surveys the world. The course of nature is without respect of persons; we see no laws suspended to favour the good or to punish the bad. Miracles of mercy have sometimes been wrought, and special judgments have sometimes been sent upon men, but these are exceptions, and do not

give character to the general course of human affairs.
In the same hand where is the hiding of his power,
God hides both love and hatred ; he does not mark
out the good among men, by making them the immediate objects of his love, nor the wicked, by directing
instantly against them his judgments. Yet the inspired writer does not lose sight of the great distinction between the two classes of men, and he recognizes the eternal distinction between moral good and
evil, by the terms which he applies to them—the
righteous and the wicked, the clean and the unclean,
the worshiper and the despiser of God's worship.
And " there is a vast difference," Henry well remarks,
" between the original, the design, and the nature of
the same event to the one and to the other ; the
moral effects and issues of them are likewise vastly
different ; the same Providence to the one is a savor
of life unto life, to the other of death unto death,
though, to outward appearance, it is the same."

(3.) *This is an evil among all things which
are done under the sun, that there is one event
to all ; therefore also the heart of the sons of
men is full of evil, and madness is in their
heart while they live, and after that they go to
the dead.*

The sentiment of the passage is similar to that in
viii. 11. Because God does not at once make a difference between good and bad men, the bad are emboldened to greater sin ; their love and practice of
evil becomes a sort of madness, which bears them on
wildly to a fearful end—to the dead. The description

of the career of a wicked man, in this place, becomes fearful. He is like a maniac, who raves and laughs by turns, who rushes forward, and stops not when he reaches the verge of the precipice, but plunges into the abyss. He has no hope in his death ; he paid no regard to a hereafter while he lived, and he leaves the world as if none awaited him.

(4.) *For there is hope for him that is joined to all the living ; a living dog is better than a dead lion.*

There is no discrepancy between this and what is said in ch. vii. 1, respecting the day of death being better than the day of one's birth. Here the inspired writer is speaking of the death of the wicked ; there, as was shown, of the death of the righteous. The men whose hearts are fully set in them to do evil, because they do not see sentence against an evil work executed speedily, regard this life as if it were the whole of existence ; when therefore, it is ended, all is forever gone which they valued. Such sinners, when dead, may be compared with themselves, as they were when alive, or with others who are leading the same insane and desperately wicked courses. The *hope* here spoken of is not the hope of the righteous which living men may embrace, but the hope of worldly good which animates wicked men : death brings this to an end. A living sinner is better off than a dead one, though he be only worthy of being compared to a dog, while the dead one may be compared to the lion. The object is to state distinctly and strongly that the sinners who are described in the context have all their good things in this life.

(5.) *For the living know that they must die,*
but the dead know not any thing, neither is there
any more reward for them; for the memory of
them is forgotten.

Solomon contemplates the death of the wicked,
who are before described, viii. 11 ; ix. 3, as they themselves regarded it, as the end of their existence, and
compares them with the living in respect to their
knowledge, and their interest in the advantage or reward which men have in this life ; particularly he
notices how quickly they pass into utter oblivion.
He leaves out of view what he elsewhere so clearly
teaches, to wit, the immortality and the accountability
of the wicked as well as the righteous. Over the
grave of these wicked men he stands and compares
as a wicked man might do, life with death. Their
death is oblivion. But much more, as we have a right
to infer from other parts of the book, is meant than is
said. He takes these men to this awful position that
they may see precisely how the matter, according to
their principles, stands ; and may be led to ask, " Is
this all ? Is there no better hope than an earthly one ?
no better reward than that which we are now reaping ?
no other life than the present ?"

(6.) *Their love also, as well as their hatred,*
and their envy, is now perished; neither have they
a portion any more forever in any thing which
is done under the sun.

In this, Solomon follows out the contrast between
the living and the dead which he commenced in verse
4, and for the same purpose. They are not only for-

gotten, but their interest in the affairs and the inhabitants of this world ceases. There is an end to their friendships and their enmities, and to their interest in any of the affairs of this life. As he elsewhere clearly teaches that the spirit is entirely distinct from the body, and enters at death upon a conscious existence in another world, it is manifestly his only object here to let the sinner, who lives in utter disregard of the retributions of another life, and seeks to find the great end of his existence in this short life, see how insufficient an end can be found in this—or he is giving to the world the reflections and course of thought which passed through his mind, when he sought, by the mere light of human reason, through sleepless nights and days, to find out the work of God, in respect to the little difference which, for the present, seems to be made between good men and bad, in the disposal of events.

GOD'S FAVOUR TOWARD A MAN SPREADS LIGHT OVER THE
WHOLE SCENE OF HUMAN AFFAIRS, FURNISHES THE
GREAT MOTIVE TO AN ACTIVE, USEFUL LIFE, AND PRE-
PARES HIM FOR A HAPPY DEATH.

(7.) *Go thy way, eat thy bread with joy, and
drink thy wine with a cheerful heart ; for now
God is pleased with thy work.*

In the preceding verses, Solomon has been recording the severe struggle which his mind passed through
in relation to the course of Providence in this world,
toward good and bad men. He here returns to the
animating view of the final result he was constrained
to take in verse 15, of the preceding chapter, when
his mind had settled down upon the conviction, that
it shall be well with them that fear God (viii. 12).
The apostrophe, which extends to the end of verse
10, appears to be to himself. He rises up as from
deep waters in which he had been struggling, with a
countenance radiant with the smile of victory, a more
cheerful as well as a wiser man, and says to himself,
" Go thy way, pursue thy pilgrimage, eat and drink
with gladness ; thy God has heard thy mourning
voice, accepted thy repentance, and looks upon thee

with favourable regard." The expression, *for now God is pleased with thy work*, or favourably regards thy work, must refer to the restoration of his favour, when Solomon returned from his backslidings. He continues the apostrophe :

(8.) *At all times let thy garments be white : and let not thy head lack precious ointment.*

White garments and oil were signs among the ancients of rejoicing, as sackcloth and ashes were of mourning. They may also be taken for signs of inward peace and purity ; the words therefore may be regarded as including an exhortation, to avoid in future the things which tend to produce sorrow and remorse, and practice whatsoever things are pure. When the soul is made to experience that Divine love, it may well rejoice, " Bless the Lord, O my soul ; and all that is within me, bless his holy name. Bless the Lord, O my soul, and forget not all his benefits."

(9.) *Enjoy life with the wife whom thou lovest all the days of thy vain life, which he (God) hath given thee under the sun, all the days of thy vanity ; for that is thy portion in life, and in thy toil which thou takest under the sun.*

There is a peculiar fitness in these words when viewed as part of an apostrophe which Solomon addressed to himself, after his repentance, and restoration to Divine favour. They evidence a return to that early piety, which made their author the " beloved of the Lord." They strikingly agree with the language he employed in his earlier and better days ;

"Drink waters out of thine own cistern, and running waters out of thine own well. Let them be only thine own, and not strangers' with thee. Let thy fountains be blessed ; and rejoice with the wife of thy youth. Let her be as the loving hind and pleasant roe ; let her breasts satisfy thee at all times ; and be thou ravished always with her love," Prov. v. 15–19. The joys of virtuous wedlock are the portion which God gives to man to lighten his toil, and to augment, reduplicate his happiness. "Even in Paradise," says Henry, "it was not good for man to be alone." It is not the voluptuary that speaks here, but one who had been brought, by a painful experience, to know that the society of a virtuous wife is worth more than all the meretricious charms of hundreds of those whose hearts are snares and nets, and their hands bands. He proves that he still had the highest esteem for the female sex.

(10.) *Whatsoever thy hand findeth to do, do it with thy might ; for there is no work nor device, nor knowledge, nor wisdom in the grave (or, the world beyond) whither thou goest.*

Solomon still addresses himself : as if he had said, "Much of thy life has run to waste ; years have been lost, wasted in folly and sin ; now then, arise, bestir thyself ; the day is far spent, the night is at hand ; redeem the time by doing with thy might whatsoever thy hand finds to do ; for when life ends, the work of life ends, probation ends ; no work or wisdom after death can make amends for a mis-spent life." It is an exhortation to be diligent in the great work of life, while life lasts. It was very natural that Solomon should thus exhort himself to redeem the past, in the only way in which this was possible, by greater diligence during the residue of his days.

The word translated grave is *Sheol*, and here means the invisible, or eternal world. In speaking of the wicked dead (v. 5) he followed them no further than the grave as the end, according to their own expectations, of existence ; but here he says that in that invisible world to which the spirits of men depart at death, where separate from the body, they are still conscious and active, there is no work, device, nor knowledge, by means of which they can repair the failures and shortcomings of this life.

(11.) *I turned and saw under the sun, that the race is not to the swift, nor the battle to the strong, nor yet bread to the wise, nor riches to men of understanding, nor favour to men of knowledge ; but time and opportunity happen to all of them.*

This verse is closely connected with the preceding, and contains a deeply pious sentiment. In that, he had exhorted himself to the most earnest prosecution of the great business of life, for the glory of that God who had shown him favour ; but here, he cautions against too much reliance on one's own strength and wisdom. Lord Bacon remarks on the maxim, *Faber quisque fortunæ suæ*—Every man is the architect of his own fortune—that it is " an insolent and unlucky saying, except it be uttered as an hortative or spur to correct sloth. For otherwise, if it be believed as it sounds, and a man enters into a high imagination that he can compass all accidents, and ascribes all successes to his own drift and reaches, and the contrary to his errors and slippings, it is a profane speech, and it is commonly seen that the evening fortune of that man is not so prosperous, as of him that, without slacking his industry, attributeth much to felicity and providence above him." There are favourable seasons and opportunities granted to men for the accomplishment of the great business of life, especially for making their peace with God, and preparation for death, failure to improve which involves the loss of the blessing itself. There are acceptable times, years of the Lord's right hand, times of refreshing from the presence of the Lord.

(12.) *For man also knoweth not his time; as fishes which are caught in an evil net, and as birds which are caught in a snare, so are the sons of men snared in an evil time, when it falleth suddenly upon them.*

This is a solemn warning against delay or procrastination, in making preparation for death. *His time* which man knoweth not, is the time of his death. Thus Hitzig and Berger explain. The vulgate translates by *finem suum*, which, though the true sense, is an interpretation rather than a translation. It comes upon men unexpectedly ; they are taken by it as fishes in a net, or birds in a snare. Occur when it may, to most men death comes suddenly and unexpectedly. Hence the wisdom of being always in readiness for it. No voice will warn us of the ap-

proach of the grisly king, and cry to us that our hour
has come. The fire of ambition may still light the
eye, the rose of health bloom on the cheek, and physical vigour nerve us with strength for the battle, or
swiftness for the race of life. Worldly enterprises
may be in the full tide of success ; friends may caress ;
and the flowers of love bloom in our path ; and nothing
admonish us that our hour has come. " Be ye also
ready, for in such an hour as ye think not, the Son of
Man cometh."

WISDOM AND FOLLY, OR RELIGION AND IRRELIGION, CON-
TRASTED, AND NOTWITHSTANDING THE FALSE JUDG-
MENTS OF MEN IN REGARD TO THEM, THE FORMER SHOWN
TO BE IMMEASURABLY SUPERIOR TO THE LATTER.

(13.) *Even this wisdom have I seen under the sun, and it seemed great to me.*

What the *wisdom* was which *seemed great* to him, he is about to describe by an example, or in a parable. Some have imagined that the writer of Ecclesiastes in the following verses [14–16] alludes to certain actual events, *e. g.*, that the poor wise man may have been Archimedes who saved Syracuse by his burning-glasses and machines ; or that the little city was Athens, the great king, Xerxes, and the poor wise man Themistocles ; or again, that the allusion is to the besieging of the little town of Dora on the sea-shore, by Antiochus the Great. It is better, however, to understand Solomon here (for it is he, and not some later writer who is speaking), as speaking in a parable, to illustrate a great and important truth, viz., that *men are often ignorant of their real benefactors, and blind to their greatest advantages and benefits.* As we proceed we shall see how this truth develops itself, and its application to the subject of this book. The parable, as well as proverbs, was a method of conveying instruction, familiar to the ancient Hebrews. Thus we have the parable of Jotham, in which the trees are represented as having a mind to choose the bramble for their king [Judg. ix. 7, 8] ; the parable of Nathan, in which he reproved David [2 Sam. xii. 2, *seq.*] ; and of the woman of Tekoah, sent by Joab, to reconcile David to Absalom [2 Sam. xiv. *seq.*] In Solomon's parable, he selects that sagacity, which often proves more effectual, for the protection of a city or state, than armies and munitions of war, and may reside with the humble poor man, rather than with those who are at the head of affairs. As its possessor may be overlooked, and his wisdom despised, when the danger is passed, so men are often insensible to the blessings they should most value.

(14.) *There was a little city, and the men in it were few; and there came against it a great king, and beseiged it, and built over against it great bulwarks.*

(15.) *And there was found within it a poor wise man, and he by his wisdom delivered the city ; yet no one remembered that same poor man.*

(16.) *Then said I, Wisdom is better than strength, yet the poor man's wisdom is despised, and his words are not listened to.*

Nothing is to be judged of by the estimation which men in general put upon it ; for then the most valua-

ble things would be trifles, and trifles chief treasures
—the political or military sagacity, which saved the
beseiged city, would be of less account, than the boasting, pompous words of the man who is able to make
himself ruler over an ignorant, silly people. The simple lesson of this parable, as it strikes me, has been
already expressed ; it points to the folly and mistakes
of men, in respect to the blessings which are placed
within their reach. It illustrates the manner in which
that wisdom, which cometh down from above, is often
treated by men. Notwithstanding the undeniable
blessings which true religion confers on them, both in
their individual and associated capacity, it is often
overlooked and despised. It does not come with observation, with pompous words, with imposing display,
it does not condescend to employ the arts of deception
and intrigue.

The little city, with few defenders, may represent
the weakness of man, in comparison with the number
and power of his spiritual enemies. He needs a helper,
and will certainly be destroyed by the powerful king
who has come up against him, unless some deliverer
appear. The *poor wise man* may personify that same
wisdom, so beautifully described by Solomon, in the
allegory contained in Prov. viii. : " She crieth at the
gates, at the entry of the city, at the coming in at the
doors : Unto you, O men, I call ; and my voice is to
the sons of man. O ye simple, understand wisdom,
and ye fools, be ye of an understanding heart. All
the words of my mouth are in righteousness ; there is
nothing froward or perverse in them. Wisdom is better than rubies ; and all the things that may be desired are not to be compared to it. The fear of the

Lord is to hate evil : pride and arrogancy, and the
evil way, and the forward mouth do I hate. By me
kings reign, and princes decree justice. I lead in the
way of righteousness, in the midst of the paths of
judgment: that I may cause those that love me to
inherit substance ; and I will fill their treasures. The
Lord possessed me in the beginning of his way, before
his works of old. I was set up from everlasting, from
the beginning, or ever the earth was. He that sinneth
against me wrongeth his own soul : all they that hate
me, love death." In this beautiful allegory, the ancient fathers, and most modern expositors, have
found that WISDOM, the divine Logos, who gave himself to save a perishing race.

And why may we not, in the "poor wise man" of
Ecclesiastes, discover at least a type of Christ. He
was poor—despised and rejected of men—a root out
of dry ground—when he appeared to save Jerusalem,
men saw no beauty in him, but hid as it were their
faces from him. He did not strive nor cry, neither
did any man hear his voice in the streets. Yet what a
salvation he wrought ! He saved Jerusalem, not the
earthly city from the siege of the Romans, but the
spiritual city, the church of the living God. Yet the
infatuated people listened more to the scribes and
priests than to this same poor, wise man. But if it
be thought that there is no warrant for such an application of Solomon's parable, it will not be denied that
it strikingly illustrates the manner in which men manifest their disregard for that fear of the Lord which is
the beginning of wisdom, and that knowledge of the
Holy which is understanding. Solomon himself had
been guilty of overlooking this wisdom, and pre-

ferring to it, for a season, mere worldly wisdom and power.

(17.) *The words of the wise, heard in quiet, are better than the clamorous voice of a ruler among fools.*

The comparison is between the words of the " poor wise man" and the loud, senseless clamour of one who is ambitious of being popular with, and a ruler over, the unthinking multitude. Some will hear the quiet voice of wisdom, although the multitude continue to be more operated on by the noisy shouting of the leader among fools. So heavenly wisdom, although it may be scorned by the great multitude, loses not its value by their neglect—and it will be heeded by some, at least ; the still small voice will point them to the path of safety and peace.

(18.) *Wisdom is better than weapons of war ; but one sinner destroyeth much good.*

The wisdom of the poor man saved the city which weapons of war could not save, therefore it is better as a defence than such weapons. But the ruler among fools, the sinner, may do much to counteract or defeat that wisdom. Here again, what is said of political sagacity illustrates the superiority of true piety as a protection to men against the greatest evils or dangers—those which threaten their eternal welfare. The influence of one bold transgressor, in opposing such piety, and destroying its happy influence, may be very great.

(CHAP. X. 1.) *A dead fly causeth the oint-*
ment of the apothecary to ferment, and send
forth an offensive odour ; so a little folly is
often more weighty than wisdom and honour.

The singular number of the verbs in the first clause
requires the nominative to be singular, *a dead fly.*
Besides, it is the writer's object to notice how slight a
cause will corrupt the precious mixture. The presence of a dead insect in a composition valued for its
purity and fragrance, disposing it to decomposition
and putrescence, is a striking illustration of the manner in which only a little folly will spoil a reputation
for wisdom and uprightness. Notwithstanding the
excellence of wisdom, he had said that men often
prefer clamorous and empty words to it, and that one
sinner destroyeth much good. He adds, in confirmation of the same general truth, that such is the
deleterious nature of folly or wickedness, that one sinful act often weighs more against a man in the estimation of others, than much that is wise and excellent
does in his favour ; it shakes the confidence of men in
his integrity. It causes them to suspect that the
virtues which he professed, and the excellences which
once seemed to belong to him, were nothing more
than hypocritical pretences. The corrupt are too
ready and too willing to believe that all are as bad as
themselves, not to put the most unfavourable construction on conduct which may seem to favour this
belief.

(2.) *A wise man's heart is at his right hand ;*
but a fool's heart at his left.

17

As the Hebrews could not have been ignorant that the heart, the primary organ of the blood's motion, is situated on the left side of the body, this word in this place must signify the mind or the understanding, and the words *right hand* and *left* are used figuratively. The meaning is, that the wise man has a ready command of his faculties ; he knows how to adapt means to their proper end ; and as goodness is involved in the wisdom here referred to, he is ready to do good—his heart directs to the performance of deeds which are graceful and beautiful, morally considered ; but the fool does not employ his faculties wisely ; and, as this is but another name for sinner, neither does his heart lead him to perform benevolent actions, but rather those which are sinister and corrupt.

(3.) *And even when a fool walketh by the way, his understanding faileth him, and he saith to every one that he is a fool.*

Everywhere, and at all times, the folly of a fool, and the wickedness of a sinner, are apparent—by the way, as well as in the house. Wickedness, like folly, is conspicuous in him who is given to it. It is displayed on all occasions, in public as well as private ; he proclaims himself a sinner, a fool in the most melancholy sense. Men may make mistakes, may despise true wisdom, and prefer folly to it ; but their mistakes do not alter the nature of these things, or change their relative value. Solomon, in the comparison which he draws between them, takes a wide range ; but he does this that it may be made to appear only the more triumphantly that in wisdom, or true piety, man is to find his safety and peace. He proceeds to consider a conspicuous instance in which wickedness seems to be preferred to virtue, and for a time has the pre-eminence ; but we shall see how goodness triumphs at last. This whole chapter, although it reminds us very much of the book of Proverbs, and so far as similarity of style is concerned, points indubitably to the same author, is not a mere collection of wise, sententious, but disconnected sayings ; a careful examination will show one great subject underlying these apothegms, to wit, the one suggested above, the superiority of religion over irreligion, which the blindness of men often prevents them from seeing. It is the same subject, or truth, carried out and applied to a variety of matters, which the parable (ix. 14–16) was designed to illustrate.

(4.) *If the spirit of a ruler rise up against thee, leave not thy place ; for gentleness quieteth great offenses.*

The ruler in this place may be such a ruler as is described in ix. 17. If the wrath of such a one be awakened against thee, do not imitate his wickedness and folly. Be firm, wait for his anger to exhaust itself in words, and when an opportunity is given, speak not rashly and arrogantly as a foolish and wicked man, but with gentle, soothing words. Angry passions excite angry passions. The dignity and gentleness of the man who fears God will prove the best shield against that wrath of a king which is said to be as messengers of death, and which only the wise man can pacify. (Prov. xvi. 14.)

(5.) *There is an evil which I have seen under
the sun, as an error which proceedeth from the
ruler.*

(6.) *Folly is set in high places, and the rich
sit in obscurity.*

He specifies an error into which unjust rulers may
fall, that of preferring the incompetent and unworthy
to fill important places, while *the rich*, which expression
here undoubtedly means wise, worthy, and noble men,
as opposed to the foolish in the former clause, are suffered to remain in uninfluential and obscure stations.
This injustice must not provoke the good man to impatience and sin, to forget his forbearance. He must be
content to seek the public good in a more private way,
like " the poor wise man" who delivered the city, when
in extreme peril, and was so soon forgotten.

(7.) *I have seen servants upon horses, and
princes walking as servants upon the earth.*

He further states the error which proceeds from the
foolish ruler, by contrasting the elevation of servants,
or men of a servile, mean character, with the contempt
shown to princes, or men capable and worthy of filling
high stations.

(8.) *He that diggeth a ditch shall fall into it;
and whoso breaketh through a hedge a serpent
shall bite him.*

This, and the following proverbs, appear to refer to
the " ruler among fools," " the sinner that destroyeth
much good," and they teach a truth which may well

lead the virtuous and wise, not too soon to lay aside their gentleness, but to wait for Him who saith, "Vengeance is mine, I will recompense." Men who, to carry out their schemes of ambition and self-aggrandizement, dig pits for the feet of others, are almost sure to fall into them themselves ; and especially the rulers who are so short sighted as to break down the ancient landmarks and safeguards of society, may themselves receive a wound unto death. The allusion is to a species of serpents which made their dens in old hedges.

(9.) *Whoso removeth stones shall be hurt therewith ; and he that cleaveth wood shall be endangered thereby.*

The figures are very forcible and apt, to set forth the folly and danger of the man who ventures to disturb the foundations of society, or to sever those ligaments which should bind it together as firmly as the solid trunks of trees are held by their interwoven fibres. He that attempts to remove the stones which are imbedded in the foundation of the social fabric, by exalting weakness to the places which strength alone should fill, will find it rough and dangerous work ; and he that splits wood may, from the flying splinters, receive his death-wound.

(10.) *If the iron be blunt, and he do not whet the edge, then must he put forth more strength ; but wisdom is preferable to give success.*

The figurative language here is evidently continued from the last clause of the preceding verse. The ax is the instrument used in cleaving wood ; and if it be dull, the increased strength necessarily required, does but increase the danger to him that swings it. His desperate blows may recoil on himself. The king who attempts to rule by putting weak men in high places, is like one who labours to cleave solid wood with a dull ax. Wisdom is better ; it is like a keen-edged instrument. " The wicked is snared in the work of his own hands," Ps. ix. 16. " He made a pit and digged it, and is fallen into the ditch which he made. His mischief shall return upon his own head, and his violent dealing shall come down upon his own pate." Ps. vii. 15, 16.

(11.) *Surely a serpent, if not enchanted, will bite ; and a flatterer is no better.*

He has said that a prince who employs the unworthy in responsible stations, is like a man attempting to cleave wood with a dull ax ; the instrument may become a dangerous weapon to himself. He now speaks more plainly, and likens the flatterer—for the incompetent and unprincipled generally ingratiate themselves with foolish rulers by flattery—to a serpent who will surely bite his charmer, when he neglects to use his incantations. Flatterers, if their own vanity is not continually stimulated, will turn their hatred and spite against those from whom they have received favours. The foolish ruler can rely upon them only so long as he ministers to their selfishness. The allusion is to a curious and well-established fact in natural history that some kinds of serpents may be charmed so as to render them harmless. *A flatterer ;* the margin translates the Hebrew more literally, *the master of the tongue.* But this does not mean an eloquent man, or a man who knows how to speak, or to keep silence at the proper time, but one who may properly be compared to a snake-charmer, who is skilled in all the arts of soft, honeyed, and deceptive speeches. Such unprincipled men surround unprincipled rulers. Parasites can flourish only where there are persons who are willing to support them in return for their flattery; but like the plant from which they derive their name, which absorbs all the juices of other plants to which they cling, they are sure to injure or destroy those on whom they fawn.

(12.) *The words of a wise man's mouth are gracious; but the lips of a fool destroy him.*

The *wise man* here is the good man; his words are true, honest, and are therefore kind; even when they convey rebuke they are calculated to do good to those to whom they are addressed. *The fool* is the wicked fool, the babbler, the slanderer; his words are not only injurious to others, but they injure himself; the deception at length becomes too transparent to be tolerated, and his hypocrisy and malignity react upon himself.

(13.) *The beginning of the words of his mouth is folly; and the end of his talk is mischievous madness.*

This verse fully states the manner, as indicated above, in which a foolish talker and flatterer destroys himself. His deceitful arts constantly react on himself, in making him more and more unscrupulous, until his talk becomes *mischievous madness.*

(14.) *The fool also multiplieth words, when man knoweth not what shall be; and what shall be after him, who can tell?*

He talks when he should be silent; he is full of promises and brave speeches, and boasts of knowledge which is entirely beyond him. He is a rash adviser, because he presumes on knowledge, which no mere mortal ever possesses.

(15.) *The toil of fools wearieth him who knoweth not how to go to the city.*

The toil of fools, i. e., their talk, their incessant babbling, wearies, or confuses the simple-minded, honest man, not acquainted with the artifices of urbane life; who has yet to learn that language may be employed to conceal one's real meaning. Was ever flattery—unmeaning compliments, or invitations never intended to be regarded as sincere, and promises uttered for politeness' sake, only to be instantly forgotten—more admirably described? It wearies, it confounds the unsophisticated rustic.

(16.) *Woe to thee, O land, whose king is a child, and whose princes revel in the morning!*

A child; the reference is not so much to a child in years, as to one who is a child in knowledge, experience, and the love of follies and amusements, but especially, one who is easily imposed upon by flatterers and designing men. The principal meal in the East was not taken until evening; hence for princes to devote the morning to feasting was the same as to neglect the public business.

(17.) *Hail to thee, O land, whose king is the son of nobles, and whose princes feast in due season, for strength and not for reveling!*

This description presents an exact contrast to that in the preceding verse. If we may pity a nation under the government of a weak prince, who is devoted to sensual pleasures, and attracts around him swarms of sycophants and flatterers ; we may congratulate the land whose ruler is truly noble, and shows himself to be worthy of his station.

(18.) *By much slothfulness the building decayeth, and by the slackness of the hands the house leaketh.*

This proverb is uttered with reference to those rulers who neglect the affairs of the government. *The building* is a figure of the state, or nation ; its interests suffer ; it decays, until at length it becomes like an old house, which trembles in the wind, and affords but slight protection against the rains of heaven.

(19.) *For reveling, they make a feast; and wine maketh merry, and money provideth every pleasure.*

They ; the princes described in v. 16. The truly noble rulers eat for strength, but these feast out of season, for reveling ; they drink for intoxication ; and money is not spared for any kind of licentious gratification, which it can purchase. The public revenues which should be employed to strengthen the civil fabric, are wasted on unlawful, expensive pleasures.

(20.) *Curse not the king, no, not in thy thoughts; and curse not the rich in thy bed-*

chamber; for a bird of the air shall carry the voice, and that which hath wings shall tell the matter.

This is a caution, which grows out of what has been said, in the preceding verses, respecting the folly and misgovernment of incompetent or unprincipled rulers. Do not, on account of these things, be tempted to speak unadvisedly of the great and powerful, in a manner which can do no good, and will only expose thyself to vengeance. In the most private apartments of your own house, still be on your guard in this matter. "The king will hear of it by unknown and unsuspected hands, as if a bird had chanced to be at the window when thou didst speak the words, and did hear them, and carry the report of it unto the king. It is a proverbial expression, as when we say, *hedges have ears*, and *the walls will speak*. Hence kings are said to have long ears" [Matthew Poole]. Some have supposed that there is an allusion in this verse to those winged couriers, carrier pigeons. "The pigeon," says Paxton, "was employed in carrying messages, long before the coming of Christ, as we know from Anacreon's odes and other classics ; and the custom seems to have been very general and quite familiar."— The exact meaning of the passage, then, is this that instead of uttering maledictions against rulers or the abuses of government, when it can do no good but only evil, it is better to suffer in silence, and quietly to seek, like the poor unrewarded wise man, to promote the public good, assured that for our sufferings and labours we shall in the end, not fail of our reward. And here end the lessons which the parable of the poor wise man was intended to convey.

§ IX. Chap. XI. 1–10.

THE RELIGIOUS LIFE ONE OF ACTIVE BENEVOLENCE; OR THE EXCELLENCE OF RELIGION AS SEEN FROM ITS INCULCATION OF BENEFICENCE.

(1.) *Cast thy bread upon the waters; for thou shalt find it after many days.*

The figurative language is drawn from agriculture. As the husbandmen sow beside all waters, or in moist and fruitful places, and after many days reap a bountiful harvest, so good and charitable deeds will in due time bring a harvest of blessedness to those who perform them. Do good; seek to make others better and happier, is the purport of this exhortation.

(2.) *Divide a portion to seven, and also to eight; for thou knowest not what evil shall be upon the earth.*

In your charities be not confined to a single object, but have an interest in many; scatter abroad; the investments are safe; an evil day may come when you will need that mercy which you show to others.

(3.) *When the clouds are full of rain, they empty themselves upon the earth, and when a tree falleth toward the south, or toward the north, in the place where the tree falleth, there it shall be.*

The liberal man is compared to a cloud full of rain, which empties itself on the earth, upon the wilderness and desert, as well as upon the inhabited country, and the fruitful field. God gives wealth to some that they may, like those impartial almoners of the sky, the clouds, distribute it to their fellow-men. It is not so easy, at first sight, to see how the other part of the verse, *when a tree falleth toward the south, etc.*, illustrates, or bears upon the subject of liberality. But the suggestion made by Poole, Henry, and others, is satisfactory, to wit, that when a tree falls, either by the violence of the wind, or is cut down at the direction of the owner, it matters little, whether it fall to the north or to the south, there it lies ready for the owner's use; so our charity, if bestowed with an honest heart, even though it should be misapplied, and abused by the receiver, shall redound to the benefit of the giver; he shall not fail of his reward. Grotius explains the meaning in a slightly different manner, "that benefits should be bestowed without much consideration of the object upon which they are bestowed, as he who cuts down a tree does not care much which way it falls."

(4.) *He that observeth the wind shall not sow; and he that regardeth the clouds shall not reap.*

The husbandman, if he is afraid to sow until the wind blows exactly from the right quarter, may miss of the proper seed-time ; and if in harvest he is deterred from reaping by every sign of unfavourable weather, he may lose the fruits of his labour. So in the exercise of charity, and in the discharge of duty generally, if we wait until every real or imaginary obstacle is put out of the way, we shall lose the opportunity. We must attempt to do good, in the face of obstacles and discouragements.

(5.) *As thou knowest not what is the way of the spirit, nor how the bones are formed in the womb of her that is with child; so thou knowest not the works of God, who causeth all things.*

The spirit, many prefer to translate *wind*, but I have chosen to follow the authorized version here, as agreeing better with the following clause. We know not the origin of life in the human being, or how the mysterious principle of life and growth is imparted to an unborn infant. This is God's work. In like manner we are ignorant of the issue of our projected deeds of piety, and of all future events ; but we are not to be slack or weary in well-doing on account of this ignorance ; we are not to yield to distrustful fears. We are to commit ourselves, and our works to Him who alone can make us useful.

(6.) *In the morning sow thy seed, and in the evening withhold not thine hand ; for thou knowest not which shall prosper, whether this or that, or whether they both shall be alike good.*

Do not defer good deeds, do not desist from their performance, because you are ignorant of the issue ; but do good to all, at all times, in all places. One attempt may fail ; therefore repeat it constantly, that if the seed sown in the morning produce nothing, you may have something to reap from that sown in the evening, "I must work the works of him that sent me, while it is day ; the night cometh when no man can work," John ix. 4. Religious considerations tend to overcome those objections and excuses which self-ishness suggests against making a charitable use of our possessions.

Having thus shown how religion, or true wisdom, redeems life from its vanity (chap. vii. 1 to xi. 6), 1, by turning to advantage its sorrowful experiences ; 2, by fortifying the soul against its frowns and smiles ; 3, by making riches a real blessing ; 4, by reclaiming men from their backslidings ; 5, by its happy influence on civil society ; 6, by the motives it suggests to submission in view of the seeming inequalities of Providence ; 7, by preparing men for a happy death ; 8, by the test which it furnishes to aid our judgment in comparing good with evil ; 9, by the happy influence which that benificence it inculcates exerts on the world (in all which it will be observed that he meets those examples of human vanity, which engaged his attention in the former part of this book, in this work styled the FIRST PART), Solomon now prepares to draw to a close. The dejection and sadness which pervade some of his utterances near the beginning, are now gone. He has solved the problem which perplexed his mind, and we no more hear him say as in chap. ii. 17, "I hated life ;" but he speaks, with the cheerfulness and animation becoming a true friend of God, as in the next verse :

(7.) Truly the light is sweet, and a pleasant thing it is for the eye to behold the sun.

Light is a pleasing figure of life (Comp. Job iii. 16, and Ps. lvi. 13). Revelation dispels its darkness, puts another aspect upon life. It is like a sun, rising upon travelers benighted in a forest. When Solomon wrote such words as we find in ii. 15–17, he spake like one bewildered, he uttered bitter, complaining words ; but when he wrote those now before us, it was in view of the cheering hopes and consolations of religion. Religion can make life sweet, and a most pleasant thing for us to behold the sun. With gratitude we should receive its blessings, and rejoice in them all. It is not, however, of hilarity, or mere worldly joy of which he speaks, but that which is rational, and consistent with right views of life, and a sense of accountability to God. He seems to have felt it peculiarly important to guard the subject, either on account of the manner in which he had spent a large portion of his life, or on account of the character of the age in which he lived. He does this and points out its practical importance to two great classes.

1. To the Aged.

(8.) *For if a man live many years, let him rejoice in them all; but let him remember the days of darkness, for they shall be many.   All that cometh is vanity.*

Piety can make life to the aged sweet, can make them rejoice under all the infirmities of years.   The exhortation to remember the days of darkness proves that a happy old age can be secured only by taking that sober view of life which true piety dictates.   Religion does not alter the course of human affairs; it does not strike out of the calender of the good man's life dark days.   Life will continue to be vanity; therefore its happiness must depend upon those right views concerning it, and that right use made of it, which religion enjoins.   Some have understood the *days of darkness* to denote the long night of death, *dies quos homo in orco transigere debebit;** but this seems forced and unnatural, and is inconsistent with the true drift and scope of this part of Ecclesiastes.   How we venerate a good old man !   How true piety adorns him !   " The hoary head is a crown of glory if it be found in the way of righteousness," Prov. xvi. 31. But how melancholy a spectacle is an aged infidel and sensualist, who has wasted life in sinful pleasures !   If there are any in whom we contemplate piety with

* Burger.

greater satisfaction than in the aged, they are those who are still in the morning of life. To them Solomon next addresses himself.

2. To the Young.

(9.) *Rejoice, O young man, in thy youth; and let thy heart cheer thee in the days of thy youth, and walk in the ways of thy heart, and in the sight of thine eyes: but know thou that for all these things God will bring thee into judgment.*

(10.) *Therefore remove sorrow from thy heart, and put away evil from thy flesh; for childhood and youth are vanity.*

We have here an animated, moving appeal. Solomon had presented the most weighty arguments in support of religion, and had illustrated and enforced them from his own experience and observation; and now, with a pathos which is irresistible, he makes a direct address to some young man—perhaps to his unpromising son, Rehoboam, more ready to follow the sinful than the pious example of his father. The giddy youth says, or seems to say, " It may be all as you represent; religion may be a very good thing, and necessary to my happiness; and the world may be a very vain and unsatisfying portion without religion; but I choose to make trial of the pleasures of the world, and of the flesh for myself. You tried them for yourself, and have escaped; nay, have become wise and good. According to your own confession, you have run the whole round of worldly pleasure; I prefer to follow your example in this, and try the experiment for myself. Let me alone—let me try it for myself."

"Then try it for yourself," is the thrilling, terrible response ; "rejoice, O young man, in thy youth ; and let thy heart cheer thee in the days of thy youth, and walk in the ways of thy heart, and in the sight of thine eyes : but know thou that for all these things God will bring thee into judgment." Be a sensualist ; give the reins to every lust ; but be assured that the day of reckoning will come. Or perhaps we are rather to regard the youth who is so solemnly apostrophized as an avowed free-thinker. His mind has been poisoned with infidel sentiments ; he does not believe in religion ; he thinks, or tries to think, that death is the end of man ; and therefore he resolves to give himself up to the unrestrained indulgence of his appetites and passions. Solomon throws himself in the path of such a young man, and conjures him to pause and reflect, to think of the day when God shall bring every work into judgment, with every secret thing, whether it be good, or whether it be evil.

The exhortation in verse 10 is founded on the solemn declaration which goes before, that God will bring him who walks in the ways of his heart, and in the sight of his eyes, into judgment. *Therefore remove sorrow from thy heart*—put away that which is the chief cause of grief, sin, and those evil passions which lead to sin—put away the lusts of the flesh which plead so strongly for indulgence ; and thus be at peace with thy judge, and prepare for that day which is coming, when thou must give account of all the deeds done in the body. In childhood and youth we are peculiarly exposed to vanity and folly ; the imagination is active, the spirits volatile, and the passions require to be curbed by such considerations as can be drawn only from religion. Youth, moreover, is a fleeting season. But fleeting as it is, vain as it is, it is far more favourable to one becoming truly religious than a later period. Hence the considerations, drawn from the infelicities of old age, which Solomon proceeds to address to the young man (xii. 1–7), to persuade him to remember his Creator in the days of his youth.

(CHAP. XII. 1.) *Remember thy Creator in the days of thy youth, before the evil days come, and the years draw nigh when thou shalt say, I have no pleasure in them.*

This follows naturally the exhortation in the preceding verse to cease from evil. *Remember thy Creator* is a comprehensive precept, meaning that it was the duty of the youth addressed, to fear, love, and faithfully serve and worship God. Youth is a better time than old age to attend seriously to the duties of religion and the cultivation of pious affections. Old age will bring its infirmities, its evil days, obduracy, and sadness, if not despair. He proceeds, by way of enforcing his exhortation, to describe in highly tropical language, the infirmities of body and mind, which commonly overtake men in advanced life.

(2.) *Before the sun and the light, and the moon and the stars, grow dim, and the clouds return after the rain;*

The imagery is beautiful. Before the dejection of age, which is represented by the obscuration of light, overtake thee, remember thy Creator. This seems better than to suppose that the allusion here is to the decay of mental or bodily faculties. *The clouds return after the rain* ; *i. e.*, the sky does not clear after the storm, but the clouds immediately begin to gather again. " In Palestine, the summer showers are short and violent, and are succeeded by a blazing sun. But in winter, day after day, the clouds return, and rains are incessant during much of the time. This season then, is the image of old age, the winter of life.*

(3.) *In the day when the keepers of the house tremble, and the strong men bow themselves, and the grinders cease because they are few, and those that look out of the windows are darkened,*

The *house* is a figure of the earthly tabernacle, the body ; and *the keepers, the strong men, the grinders, and those that look out of the windows*, represent, as commentators have generally agreed, the hands or arms, the legs, the teeth, and the eyes. Accordingly, the verse is descriptive of those physical decays which come upon the body in old age.

(4.) *And the doors shall be shut in the streets ; and while the sound of the grinding is low, they rise up at the voice of the bird, and all the daughters of music are brought low.*

The first clause should have been joined to the preceding verse as a part of the description of those decays of the body, incident to age. *The doors* must be understood of the lips. The same figure is found in Job xli. 14, and Micah vii. 5.* The meaning here is that men in extreme age become dull and listless, and have but little appetite for food ; or the lips, because the teeth are gone, are caved in, and, even in eating, are kept in this compressed position. *While the sound, etc.* The orientals usually ground their corn every day, which was the first work of the morning ; the aged are described as restless, as rising from their beds, of which they have become weary, as soon as any body is stirring, as soon as the cock or the chirping of lesser birds welcomes the return of the dawn. It is not the sound of the grinding which disturbes them, nor the confused voices of an awakening world; for even the songs of the women grinding at the mill are scarcely heard, by reason of their impaired sense of hearing.

(5.) *When also they shall be afraid of that which is high, and fears shall be in the way, and the almond shall be refused, and the locust a burden, and the caper-berry shall be in vain; since man goeth to his everlasting home and the mourners go about the streets;*

Eminences are very wearisome to the aged. Through failure of sight, and loss of agility, they learn to be afraid of falling in the beaten path. The objection to the translation, *the almond tree shall flourish,* or blossom, as intended to be figurative of the hoary head, is that it is said the blossoms of these trees are not white, but rose-coloured. Gesenius renders, *et spernetur amygdala,* the almond shall be despised or rejected,

* Poole.

and explains it of the fruit, which, however greatly esteemed, can not be masticated and enjoyed by the toothless old man.—*The locust shall be a burden.* Both Noyes and Stuart explain this in harmony with what precedes respecting the almond—the locust as an article of food can not be eaten or digested by the old man. *The caper-berry shall be in vain.* This rendering is also on the authority of Gesenius, who refers to Plutarch and Pliny for proof that the ancients regarded the caper-berry as a stimulant to appetite and lust. His desire has failed beyond the reach of any artificial stimulant. This failure of the powers of nature, this decay of the bodily strength and faculties are sure indications that a man's earthly race is almost run, and he is about to go hence, and the mourners to go about the streets.—Such are the infirmities of age, such the "evil days" which await man, if his life is lengthened out ; and it is in view of them that Solomon counsels the young man to remember his Creator in the days of his youth. These infirmities will not be favourable to his giving proper heed to a duty which he has neglected all his life ; but early piety, or piety which has been cherished and cultivated from youth up, will enable its possessor to submit patiently to these infirmities, and all the trials of his earthly lot.

(6.) *Before the silver cord is loosed, or the golden bowl is broken, or the pitcher is shivered at the fountain, or the wheel broken at the cistern.*

Having spoken of man's going to his everlasting home at death, death is here described as a sundering of the silver cord of life, the breaking of its golden bowl, the shivering of a pitcher at the fountain, or the breaking of the wheel by which water was raised from a well. The words, "Remember thy Creator" must be supplied at the beginning of this verse, *i. e.*, attend to this great duty before death comes and cuts life short. "The mataphor, by which loss of life is denoted, is borrowed from a lamp suspended from a ceiling by a silver cord. The golden bowl is the bowl or reservoir of oil, from which it is distributed into the branches, in which the wicks are placed, from which the lights proceed, see Zech. iv. 2, and Job xxix. 3. The chord by which this golden bowl, or reservoir of oil is suspended, being decayed with age, giving away, and so suffering the bowl of oil to fall upon the floor and be broken, and thus extinguish the lamps, affords a striking image of the breaking up of the human machine, and the extinction of its life, which by a very common metaphor, is said to be suspended on a brittle thread. We need not inquire what internal part of the body is denoted by the silver cord, or the golden bowl; whether by the former is denoted the spinal marrow, the nerves, the veins, or arteries ; or whether by the golden bowl is denoted the heart, the brain, etc., since it is extremely doubtful whether the preacher refers to either." "By the images of the broken bucket and wheel, in consequence of which no water could be procured, is set forth the decay and dissolution of the human body through age, in consequence of which life can not be retained in it. Some have undertaken to point out what internal part of the body was denoted by the bucket, the fountain, the wheel and the cistern ; I do not think that the preacher intended such a particular application of the terms."*

* Noyes, *in loc.*

(7.) *And the dust shall return to the earth as it was, and the spirit shall return unto God who gave it.*

The dust is the body, "Dust thou art, and unto dust shalt thou return," Gen. iii. 19. We know what this means. The body being dead is committed to the grave, and there turns to dust. But Solomon declares that an entirely different destiny awaits another part of man—*the spirit.* Is it possible that this can mean no more than the vital spirit, or breath of life? If so, why should it be said to return to God? In what sense can a man's breath be said to return to God, when it leaves his body? It must mean the living, immortal soul; and the passage must teach that the soul is distinct from the body, and may, and will exist independently of it. The future existence of the soul is a doctrine, as has been shown, on which this entire book is predicated; and here that doctrine comes out in as simple and clear a statement as can well be framed in language. When the body dies, the soul will go into the immediate presence of God. Before this solemn hour of departure from the world, and entrance into the presence of your Judge comes, remember, O young man, thy Creator; walk not in the ways of thy heart, and in the sight of thine eyes, for know that for all these things God will bring thee into judgment; and know that if death finds thee unprepared for that judgment, then the evil days will indeed come, and the weary, unwasting years will draw nigh, in which thou shalt say, "I have no pleasure in them."

(8.) *Vanity of vanities, saith the Preacher (Convener); all is vanity.*

He returns to the point from which he started (i. 2), or states again what some have been pleased to denominate the text of the *preacher's* sermon. In the sense in which these words were explained at the beginning, they are here repeated, as containing that which Solomon has proved in this book, to wit : *That if there be no hereafter, no future day of righteous adjudication, then vanity must be predicated of the " all," the universe.* From the unbelieving worldling's stand-point he shows that "all" is one complex vanity. It is only when he takes the stand-point of the humble believer, that he breaks out in those delightful words, " Truly the light is sweet, and a pleasant thing it is for the eyes to behold the sun."

(9.) *And since the Preacher was wise, he moreover taught the people knowledge ; yea, he gave good heed, and searched out, and set in order many proverbs.*

Moreover, i. e., elsewhere, before, in other writings. There is an evident allusion here to that fountain of

18

wisdom, the book of Proverbs. In that he sought to instruct the people ; and he here refers to it as a proof of his wisdom, and as a commendation of this new production. It was no novice who claimed the attention of his fellow-men, but a man who had made the study of wisdom the great business of his life.

(10.) *The Preacher sought to find out acccepta-ble words, and to write down correctly words of truth.*

He studied carefully the meaning of words ; he did not use language at random. He made truth the touch-stone of all his utterances. Whoever reads the book of Proverbs must confess that he was a great "master of sentences." In this species of writing " what can a man do that cometh after the king?" Ecclesiastes is interspersed with similar wise and pithy apothegms. But the general style of the book is different : as its object was different, it required a different style. The proverbs it contains are introduced to illustrate the one great subject which runs through the whole. As an ethical or philosophical essay, if we judge of it, not by the rules of modern logic, but by those principles of composition which the times and genius of the Hebrew people admitted, it too must be pronounced a master-piece.

(11.) *The words of the wise are as goads, and as nails driven in are those who collect the sayings of the wise, which are given from one Shepherd.*

The words of the wise—such sayings as we have in Proverbs and Ecclesiastes make a lively impression on

the minds of men, and quicken them to activity and
the discharge of duty, as the goad excites the dull ox
to put forth more strength. And these sayings, collected and put into a permanent form, so that they shall
not be forgotten by men, are like nails driven in, or
infixed firmly into the wall of a house. These sayings,
whether in their oral or written form, *are given from
one shepherd.* This certainly can be no other than
God, from whom cometh every good and perfect gift.
In respect to inspired writings this is eminently true,
for all Scripture is given by inspiration of God ;
and the image of a shepherd in its application to the
Divine Being must have been perfectly familiar to the
mind of Solomon. Others prefer to interpret the
phrase *one shepherd* of Solomon himself, and to
translate it *one teacher,* who, having devoted himself
to explore, winnow out, and compile the best from
among the "many proverbs" of the wise, assures
learners that they can find all they need in him, or in
his writings.

(12.) *And further, by these, my son, be admonished : of making many books there is no
end, and much study is a weariness of the flesh.*

By these ; i. e., by the sayings of the wise, particularly he refers to those contained in his own writings ;
he commends them to the especial attention of
Reboboam, the heir-apparent, or makes him in the
address the representative of every reader. He then
adds, "Much more might be written ; the world
might be filled with books, but the multitude of
books will never make men truly wise ; and if you
heed not what I have written, neither would you be

convinced if I should write books without end."
(Comp. John xxi. 25, and Luke xvi. 31.)

(13.) *Let us hear the conclusion of the whole
matter : Fear God, and keep his commandments,
for this is the duty of every man.*

(14.) *For God will bring every work into
judgment, with every secret thing, whether it be
good, or whether it be evil.*

There can be no more comprehensive description
of true religion than we have in the words, *Fear God
and keep his commandments.* This is the duty of
every man ; and it is enforced by the great doctrine
which lies at the basis of this entire book, that there
is to be a judgment, which will extend to every secret
thing, in which our works will be estimated, not according to their outward appearance, but by those inward dispositions and motives which give character to
conduct. It is this doctrine which rescues this world
from the reproach of being the most consummate of
all vanities. "There is no book in the Old Testament," says Professor Stuart, "that has so many
references to the retribution and judgment at a future
period, as Ecclesiastes."* Its closing words have drawn
even from neologists the reluctant confession that a
future judgment is meant. "The author," says
Bruger, "while he does not seem to have taught the
doctrine of immortality, seems nevertheless to have
been inclined to adopt an argument which Kant used
many ages afterward, who placed immortality *inter pos-
tulata rationis,* among the postulates of the reason, or

* Comm. p. 49.

primitive judgments of the mind, because we do not
see in this world virtue and vice visited with righteous
retributions, which, however, would seem to be necessary for the vindication of divine justice."* But
Knobel speaks more decidedly as to the meaning, the
unmistakable meaning of these final words of Ecclesiastes. He says that "the particularity of the
assertion, viz., that every work and every secret thing
shall be brought into judgment, makes it certain that
a future judgment is meant." He states two reasons
for this conclusion ; first, because *every* work is said
to be brought into judgment ; and secondly, because
the expression *every secret thing*, according to the
usage of Scripture (he refers to Rom. ii. 16 ; 1 Cor.
iv. 5 ; 1 Tim. v. 24, 25), is employed with reference
to a judgment after death. But as, in his opinion,
the author of Ecclesiastes knew nothing of a future
judgment, he concludes that the passage is spurious,
and must have been added by a later writer than the
author. But the assertion that the writer of Ecclesiastes was ignorant of the doctrine of a future judgment is a bold assumption, entirely without proof,
or rather, as I am fain to believe all candid readers
of the preceding pages will agree, entirely against the
clearest, and most satisfactory proof to the contrary.
Let the meaning of Solomon in Eccles. i. 2, and xii.
8, be determined by the neological interpretation of
Eccles. xii. 14, and the theory, which the present
volume was designed to make out, is established.

WE MUST ADOPT SOLOMON'S CONCLUSION, THAT GOD
WILL BRING EVERY WORK INTO JUDGMENT, WITH EVERY

* Comm. p. 82.

35*

SECRET THING, WHETHER IT BE GOOD, OR WHETHER IT BE
EVIL, OR WE ARE SHUT UP TO THE OTHER ALTERNATIVE,
" VANITY OF VANITIES, VANITY OF VANITIES, ALL IS
VANITY,"

FINIS.

1981-82 TITLES